MICHAEL A. STUSSER IS a Seattle-based writer and game inventor. His "Accidental Parent" column (*ParentMap* magazine) recently won the prestigious Gold Award from the Parenting Publications of America. Stusser is a contributing writer for *mental_floss* and *Seattle Magazine*, and his work is frequently published by *Law & Politics, Yoga International Magazine*, and *Go World Travel Magazine*.

Stusser is also the cocreator of The Doonesbury Game with Garry Trudeau (winner for "Best Party Game of the Year," *GAMES* magazine, 1994); EARTHALERT, The Active Environmental Game; and Hear Me Out.

THE DEAD GUY INTERVIEWS

Conversations with
45 of the Most
Accomplished, Notorious,
and Deceased
Personalities in History

Michael A. Stusser

PENGUIN BOOKS

PENGUIN BOOKS
Published by the Penguin Group
Penguin Group (USA) Inc., 375 Hudson Street, New York, New York 10014, U.S.A.
Penguin Group (Canada), 90 Eglinton Avenue East, Suite 700, Toronto, Ontario, Canada M4P
2Y3 (a division of Pearson Penguin Canada Inc.)
Penguin Books Ltd 80 Strand, London WC2R 0RL, England
Penguin Ireland, 25 St Stephen's Green, Dublin 2, Ireland (a division of Penguin Books Ltd)
Penguin Group (Australia), 250 Camberwell Road, Camberwell, Victoria 3124, Australia
(a division of Pearson Penguin Australia Group Pty Ltd)
Penguin Books India Pvt Ltd, 11 Community Centre, Panchsheel Park,
New Delhi – 110017, India
Penguin Group (NZ), 67 Apollo Drive, Rosedale, North Shore 0632, New Zealand
(a division of Pearson New Zealand Ltd.)
Penguin Books (South Africa) (Pty) Ltd, 24 Sturdee Avenue, Rosebank,
Johannesburg 2196, South Africa

Penguin Books Ltd, Registered Offices:
80 Strand, London WC2R 0RL, England

First published in Penguin Books 2007

1   3   5   7   9   10   8   6   4

Copyright © Michael A. Stusser, 2007
Illustrations copyright © Stephen Smith, 2007
On page i : Photo: Kurt Smith,
Montage : Julie DonTigny
All right reserved

Portions of this book appeared in different from in *mental_floss* magazine.
Used by permission of *mental_floss*.

LIBRARY OF CONGRESS CATALOGING IN PUBLICATION DATA
Stusser, Michael A.
The dead guy interviews: conversations with 45 of the most accomplished, notorious, and
deceased personalities in history/Michael A. Stusser.
p. cm.
ISBN 978-0-14-311227-3
1. Interviews—Humor.   2. Imaginary interviews.   I. Title
PN6231.I63S78 2007
813'.54—dc22   2006052883

Printed in the United States of America
Set in Else
Designed by Sabrina Bowers

CONTENTS

CONTENTS

INTRODUCTION

"The report of my death was an exaggeration."
—MARK TWAIN

THE GENESIS OF *The Dead Guy Interviews* came about after running into Beethoven at a Rite Aid. I was trying to use one of those damn photo machines (straightforward, my ass) and the Boy Genius was refilling the batteries in his hearing aid. Well, it looked like Beethoven, anyway (must have been the ruffled collar and bouffant that threw me off). Point is, it got me to thinking, what if I could track down the most famous folks in history and ask obnoxious and intrusive questions about their lives? Did Mary Lincoln really blow the entire defense budget on shoes? Did Frida Kahlo actually sleep with Tolstoy? Was Crazy Horse really crazy, or just bipolar? And how 'bout picking the brains of the greats about the here and now—global warming, iPods, Internet porn, Flavor Flav!

Turns out the hardest part of the process wasn't getting ahold of these icons (you'd be amazed how many of the deceased have profiles on MySpace), but obtaining clearance from their demanding and over-aggressive agents. Mozart would need to plug his new album, Napoléon wouldn't appear without his high chair, Genghis Khan was pushing a helmet law, of all things, and Cleopatra refused to discuss her son with Caesar or her reported fling with Mark Anthony (not the Roman one, but J-Lo's husband).

Quite a few folks simply refused to be interviewed: Apparently, Jesus has been too frequently misquoted (he was also miffed at my request to turn my water filter into a wine dispenser), Hitler was tied up (in hell, no doubt), and Gandhi was all set to chat when my idiot intern offered him a foot-long sub. And Helen Keller—don't get me started. The reason Elvis wouldn't appear? He's not dead yet. (Hint: The Golden Nugget, Reno.) Once I got Buddha on board, however, things really did start to fall into place, and then it was a matter of keeping the guests focused. You think Regis and Kelly can gab—try someone without a pulse! They may be dead, but these guys can *talk*!

By the way, if you're dead and you weren't interviewed, don't worry. We'll get to you. My deadline was as serious as a heart attack and not as flexible as the spirit world. As Will Rogers said recently, "Half our life is spent trying to find something to do with the time we have rushed through life trying to save." It'd help if you had e-mail, though, as the séances are a spot time-consuming.

In the end, I learned more from these masters than I ever did in school. Not only does history repeat itself, but apparently, we still aren't paying attention (and MLK, Lincoln, and Mother Teresa aren't happy about it). The individuals herein achieved more than fifteen minutes of fame for a reason—not from a catchy hit single or a reality TV show, but due to hard work, determination, guts, talent, and yes, someone there to write it all down.

A few themes came up repeatedly and should be mentioned: Love thy neighbor, of course, take vacations to reenergize the mind (and when visiting new lands, remember to crush and pillage), and something about flaxseed oil. Oh, and one guy wanted me to mention respecting your elders. Surly old goat. . . .

Speaking of old goats, I'll give Winston Churchill the last words: "History will be kind to me, for I intend to write it."

—MICHAEL A. STUSSER

P.S. I should also thank some of the living: Caroline White, for finding me in the pages of *mental_floss* magazine; the bigwigs at *floss*, Will Pearson, Mangesh Hattikudur, and Neely Harris; and my fab editor at Penguin, David Cashion, who cuts with the best of 'em. Huge kudos to Anne Kaiser, who did the bulk of the research here (not to mention more follow-up questions than the crew of *60 Minutes*); and illustrator Stephen Smith, who not only got to sit in the room during the interview process, but did hair and makeup on the narcissistic ones (yeah, that's you, Mao). I'd also like to thank Oprah (it's worth a try); my wonderful parents (I'll pay you back); JavaBean; the country and crops of Jamaica; my beautiful wife, Vanessa, who let corpses into our living room; and, of course, Dead People everywhere. You may be dead, but you're not forgotten.

THE
DEAD GUY
INTERVIEWS

ALEXANDER THE GREAT

BORN 356 B.C.
DIED JUNE 13, 323 B.C.

I SUPPOSE IF YOUR dad was a king, your mom a princess, and you ruled the known world without ever losing a battle, you'd be able to put "the Great" after your name. Alexandros III Philippou Makedonon was born in 356 B.C. in Pella, the capital of Macedonia (now northern Greece). His father, King Philip II, was assassinated in 336, giving Alex the throne at age twenty. Alex's first move was to execute anyone who even looked at him funny, and he was off to the chariot races without opposition.

During his brief life, Mr. Great conquered most of what was then called the civilized (or known) world, with an empire that stretched from the Mediterranean to India. His expeditions and conquests opened trade and cultural exchanges over a huge territory that included the Persian Empire, Syria, Egypt, India, and Central Asia.

Alexander is widely considered one of the greatest military geniuses in history, for unique tactics, superior training, and innovative motivational strategy. He was famous for jumping into the thick of his battles, often leading the charge against the advice of his soldiers, who suggested the general "hang back a bit."

Alexander treated his army like family, was opposed to the common practice of raping and pillaging, and even allowed many of his royal enemies to continue ruling their people (though under his empire). On the flip side, he trashed famous cities such as Thebes, Gaza, and Persepolis, plundered treasures from those he conquered (there were bills to pay, after all), and periodically sold the citizens into slavery.

Alexander attempted to include many of his conquered cultures in his army and administration. This racial fusion didn't go over so well, especially with long-serving Macedonian military men who were less than excited to take orders from young punks who didn't speak their language.

It is believed that Alexander contracted malaria and died on June 13, 323 B.C., at age thirty-two. He also may have been poisoned, or died from typhoid—it was a long time ago. . . .

MICHAEL STUSSER: You're not nearly as tall as I expected. What are you, five and a half feet tall?

ALEXANDER THE GREAT: You will list me as five foot eight or be without hands to write with.

MS: Five foot eight it is. And I'll just erase this part here about your feet dangling from the throne. Now, one of your teachers was Aristotle. Can you tell us a little about him?

ATG: The parental units thought it would be good to have some home tutoring, so when I was thirteen, they brought Aristotle in for some Greek lessons. Guy was an amazing teacher—taught me ethics, politics, philosophy, even wood shop. Homework was a pain, though. I had to read Homer and memorize *The Iliad.*

MS: At the age of sixteen, most kids are learning how to kiss girls and drive the station wagon. You had bigger responsibilities.

ATG: Yeah, my dad [King Philip] left me in charge of the colonies when he was outta town. One time a village revolted and we had to go in there and bang heads. I renamed the place Alexandroupolis.

MS: In June 336 B.C., you're twenty years old and your father gets killed at the theater. Who dunnit?

ATG: Dad had remarried and things got nasty with the new gal, so it coulda been her. My mom also may have had something to do with it, or it could have also been this guy Pausanias, who Pops had a fling with. Man got around. Either way, I can't complain—it made me the king of Macedonia.

MS: You took the name Alexander the Great. Kind of cocky, isn't it?

ATG: You're lucky I'm a dead guy right now.

MS: How about Alexander the Excellent?

ATG: I was amazing for my time, OK? I had a GREAT sense of humor, I was a GREAT military leader, had GREAT loyalty among men, and GREAT respect for women.

MS: That's true. When you conquered Persia [now Iran], you gave King Darius III's mother a home and treated her quite well.

ATG: Tell me Caesar woulda done that.

MS: You were also way ahead of your time when it came to the idea of the melting pot, but the whole idea of ethnic fusion didn't work out. Why?

ATG: Has it worked in your country?

MS: Good point.

ATG: It got to where I had so many countries under my belt that I needed to smooth things out with some intermarriages, you know?

MS: And you led by example.

ATG: Yeah, my second wife [Stateira] was Persian. I also put foreign soldiers in my army so they'd mix cultures. My Macedonian bros hated the idea, and the second I died, they annulled almost all the marriages.

MS: Your army was often outnumbered, but still kicked ass. How so?

ATG: Well, we were pretty well trained. The guys learned to respond to flags and trumpets, which were new. Plus, we had a *killer* cavalry. The catapults and javelin throwers didn't hurt either.

MS: Ever get hurt in battle?

ATG: Oh, all the time. To inspire the troops I rode up front— sometimes I was the first guy over a walled city.

MS: That's not so smart.

ATG: Tell me about it: I took an arrow in the lung in India, got stabbed in the neck at Granicus, and my leg was totally splintered while invading Turkestan—the fellas had to carry me home. One time a bird even dropped a stone on my head in the heat of battle. I was constantly thrashed. Good times.

MS: Tell us about murdering your trusted commander Cleitus the Black.

ATG: I was drunk, OK? Ever get hammered and kill a guy by accident?

MS: I hit a buddy of mine with a dart once.

ATG: It was one of those over-the-top banquets, and Cleitus started popping off about how tall he was or some ridiculous thing, and before I knew it I'd run him through. I'm not proud of it, believe me. He was one of my best pals. Thinking of getting some anger management counseling, but it's damn expensive.

MS: In 333 B.C., you untied the famous Gordian knot, which was only to be freed by the future conqueror of Asia.

ATG: That was a toughie. Kinda like making a knot out of a cherry stem with your tongue.

MS: So how'd you do it?

ATG: Oh, I cut it to pieces with my sword. There was no other way to untie that sucker. Bold, baby! Gotta be bold!

MS: Your sex life is legendary: princesses, escorts, queens, men, boys. . . .

ATG: Don't forget my lifelong relationship with the eunuch Bagoas. . . .

MS: You were in love with a eunuch?

ATG: Don't knock it till you've tried it. Times were different—my closest friends were all men.

MS: And were you . . .?

ATG: "Don't ask, don't tell." That's always been my policy. But male love was all the rage in my time. We didn't even think about it.

MS: Yes, actually, *boy* love. The thing that's unusual is that you dated men your *own* age, such as Hephaistion.

ATG: Hephie was a childhood friend. I loved him like an alter ego.

MS: But, you had relations with women as well, correct?

ATG: Oh sure. As a youngster my mommy arranged for courtesans to come over for practice.

MS: Lucky!

ATG: And I married a bunch of Persian princesses to sire kids and all that.

MS: Is it true you were crowned at one point?

ATG: After we freed the Egyptians from Persian rule, they crowned me pharaoh. So I got that goin' for me.

MS: Didn't they also name a street after you?

ATG: A whole city, actually. Alexandria, which sits on the mouth of the Nile River. I still have a time-share there. Great spot.

MS: There you go with the "great" thing again. Isn't it true that toward the end you started to see yourself as a god?

ATG: I got a little carried away with the whole *prokynesis* thing.

MS: Is that like Dianetics?

ATG: It's a Persian custom of making people bow down to ya, kiss the king's hand, that kind of thing. I was trying to unite all my territories with a common religion—my own.

MS: Let me guess: The Macedonians didn't go for it.

MS: And these are my own people we're talking about! I guess their problem was that, in their minds, you're only supposed to kiss someone's hand if you're in the presence of a deity. I wasn't too far off, if you ask me.

MS: At this point, some of your countrymen tried to assassinate you.

ATG: Yeah, it's always someone in the inner circle, too. This time it was my pal Philotas, so I had him killed. The plot wasn't his idea, but he shoulda warned me. I always said to my posse, "If you hear of any-one who wants to kill me, let me know—or I'll kill ya."

MS: You died one month before your thirty-third birthday. You fought for eleven years, and never lost a battle. Do you have any regrets?

ATG: Yeah, not making it to forty. I'm also not real happy that my tomb was raided by that bastard Ptolemy IX in 89 B.C., who melted my sarcophagus to make gold coins! Can you believe that! [*He was killed for his deeds.* . . .]

MS: Did you happen to see *Alexander*, starring Colin Farrell [2004]?

ATG: Sucked! I didn't have blond hair, and unlike that drunk Irish-man, I could actually ride a horse. I mean, the punk could barely grow a beard, for God's sake! Now, the one with Richard Burton [1956] I can relate to—he's a winner! Speaking of winners, who succeeded me upon my death?

MS: Philip II's son Philip Arrhidaeus. Your half-brother.

ATG: He's a half-witted bastard child!

MS: Your generals had him share the throne with your son Alexan-der IV.

ATG: Well, that makes more sense. So the empire is in good hands, then?

MS: Naw, they both got murdered within a few years, and things went to hell in a handbasket. But look on the bright side: You're still great!

ATG: Kiss my hand.

END
of Interview

LUDWIG VAN BEETHOVEN

BORN DECEMBER 17, 1770
DIED MARCH 26, 1827

BEETHOVEN WAS THE greatest composer who ever lived. And yes, that includes Bach, Bartók, Beyoncé, and the Beatles. He was also an odd man, perhaps even deranged, who could be found wandering alone in disheveled clothing, humming tunes that would become the most famous symphonies ever written.

Crafting classical music, the German Beethoven showed his genius at an early age. As a young man, Ludwig was celebrated more for his incredible piano playing than for his compositions, and earned money playing gigs all over Germany and Austria. Known for improv, he was a wild man on the keys, racing from soft to raucous, and often moving the audience to tears. Beethoven may have been brilliant, but he was not well paid.

Along the way, Wiggie received work and instruction from Joseph Haydn, Mozart, and others, sucking up their expertise like a sponge and interpreting their music in new and innovative ways.

Eventually, Beethoven was able to make some extra cashola by selling compositions to various symphonies and rich Viennese patrons (many of whom had quartets on call in their ballrooms).

In one of nature's oddest ironies, Beethoven was slowly growing deaf. His symptoms appeared at age twenty-eight, and by 1819, at age forty-nine, he had lost all his hearing. Ludwig knew the world needed his art, however, and it was during the last decade of his life that he wrote some of his most important works—without being able to hear a single note.

It is said that Beethoven was the transitional figure between the classical and romantic eras of musical history—whatever the hell that means. His sonatas and concertos are longer and more ambitious than any that had come before, and his odes and soaring hymns can break down even the most hardened tough guys. He was also out of the box, adding vocal choruses to symphonies that had previously been only instrumental, and improvising rowdy transitions.

Ludwig ended his piano-playing career in 1808, stopped composing in 1826, and heard music only in his mind for the last year of his life. After a nasty bout of pneumonia, Beethoven passed away in 1827, at age fifty-six. Thirty thousand admirers attended his funeral.

MICHAEL STUSSER: Da da da daaah.

LUDWIG VAN BEETHOVEN: What?

MS: I say, Duh-duh-duh DUUH!

LVB: I'm deaf, you fool, but I get that you're humming the first bars of my Fifth.

MS: Oh, right. [*Yelling*] SO HOW SHOULD WE DO THIS INTERVIEW THING?!

LVG: It doesn't help to scream. We'll use conversation books: You write down your little questions, and I'll read 'em over, and give you stupendous replies. [Upon going deaf, this was actually the method Beethoven used to communicate.]

MS: Would you like a bath before we begin? You're a bit . . . ripe, shall we say.

LVB: I shower the world with my musical genius, and that should cleanse us all. Begin!

MS: OK. Your dad, Johann, wanted you to be a little piano boy wonder. How did that work out?

LVB: Not so well, thanks for asking. People were still very much aware of Mozart's amazing talents as a kid, but it took me a few more years to mature.

MS: Does Beethoven take lessons?

LVB: Sure, sure. My father hired all sorts of fools: First one of the court's musicians, then this actor, Tobias Pfeifer, and then a Franciscan monk, Willibald Koch. It was like a revolving door at our house.

MS: Well you must have learned from *somebody*.

LVB: Christian-Gottlob Neefe, the musical director of the National Theatre, was my first real instructor. I was around twelve when we met, and he became a friend and mentor for all my days.

MS: Any other mentors?

LVB: Meteors? I can't read this. Does that say *meteors*?

MS: Sorry. M-e-n-t-o-r-s. Teachers.

LVB: Oh, I studied with Haydn for a year, but he split to London. I trained with other composers from Vienna, but you wouldn't know them.

MS: Try me.

LVB: How about Antonio Salieri?

MS: Sure! Salieri! From the movie!

LVB: If you say so. . . . He taught me vocal composition—how to write musical tragedy.

MS: Is it also true you actually gave private piano lessons for a while?

LVB: The horrors! I hated that. Mostly I taught rich young girls till they got married, and then they'd abandon the whole business. Can you imagine? Beethoven offers to teach you piano, and you decide to have tea parties instead! That is *not* hot.

MS: But you did tend to do a little trolling with the lessons. . . .

LVB: *Trolling?*

MS: Ya know, a countess here, somebody's daughter there, and before ya know it, they've fallen for Ludwig the Lover Man!

LVB: You're lucky I didn't hear that.

MS: Let's talk about your temper.

LVB: Let us not!

MS: There's a story about some guy making a mistake during a concert and you going ballistic.

LVB: December 22, 1808, the Theater an der Wien. A clown clarinet player had the balls to repeat an eight-bar count during my Sixth Symphony. I let him know it was unacceptable, and made the orchestra play it *from the beginning.* The audience deserved to hear it as I intended. That is all.

MS: But you've got to admit, you had quite the attitude.

LVB: I am a brilliant virtuoso!

MS: With the ego to prove it. There's a famous quote that's attributed to you after telling off some prince. How's it go?

LVB: "What you are, you are by accident of birth; what I am, I am by myself. There are and will be a thousand princes; there is only one Beethoven."

MS: So, if I've got this right, you're a brilliant, egotistical, moody nutcase?

LVB: You remind me of a whiny violinist who once complained about an unusually difficult passage in one of my compositions. Do you know what I told him?

MS: To shut up and play?

LVB: I told him, "When I composed this, I was being inspired by God Almighty. Do you think I can consider your puny little fiddle when He speaks to me?"

MS: Yes, but Maestro, you teed off on pretty much everyone—yelling at waiters, berating conductors, quarreling with your teacher, Joseph Haydn—even screaming at good friends when a blue mood kicked in.

[There is a long pause in the interview, during which Ludwig drums his fingers on the coffee table and pouts.]

LVB: At times. For this I apologize. It's the lead in the water that's made me crazy, I tell you!

MS: Speaking of which, must have sucked going deaf, eh?

LVB: No, it was great. . . . Come on! Clearly this was a downer of enormous proportions. And there was a time I considered suicide.

MS: Because you couldn't hear your music?

LVB: No, in fact, my depression had more to do with my constant trouble with the ladies. I tried to date married gals, as well as those above my station—aristocratic types.

MS: But you're the best composer of all time!

LVB: Genius is rarely recognized in its era. Damn shame in my case. I never married.

MS: But what of the famous letter to "My immortal beloved?" There's been so much conjecture—was it your sister-in-law, Johanna? A young student, perhaps, or an aristocratic widow? Or was it Countess Julia Guicciardi, to whom you dedicated the "Moonlight" Sonata? Who was this mystery romance?

LVB: My cat, Beloved, you rube.

MS: So you were a bitter and angry fella?

LVB: I was disheartened for a long while, and irritated, with the lack of success in the dating world, you understand. It didn't help that I was poor as a pauper most of my doggone life.

MS: How does Beethoven not make bank on his genius?

LVB: If we'd had a system of royalties in those days, I'd have made this Donald Trump look like a hobo. They didn't exactly have iTunes in 1790, you know? For the Ninth Symphony? My little ditty "Ode to Joy"? One hundred lousy pounds!

MS: So how'd you get any cash?

LVB: I played for rich people. Also concert halls, even saloons. The real money would have been in concessions—Beethoven T-shirts, crop-tops, posters. Oh, to do it all over again.

MS: In addition to money woes, I understand you wore filthy cloth-ing and had—have—some hygiene problems.

LVB: That is untrue! I wash compulsively!

MS: Well, you missed a spot—from your head to your toes. Seems you were a bit of a diva, if I may say so: impatient, grumpy, intolerant.

LVB: People look at me funny! Talk behind my back!

MS: Need I remind you, you're deaf. You have no idea what people are saying behind your back.

LVB: Backstabbing fiends!

MS: Let's get the lead out: A recent analysis of a lock of your hair shows you may have died from lead poisoning—coulda been the water. This may have caused your hearing loss, the wacky mood swings—

LVB: Stupid old wives' tales! Jabberwocky!

MS: Music snobs talk about your work having "intellectual depth" and "highly personal expression." Does that make sense?

LVB: Of course! My structured phrasing transfers weight from early movements to grand sonata finales! The symphonic poems are designed to invoke soulful themes; my vigorous, whirling scherzos and explosive finales progress—arousing harmonic tension and release!

MS: We're talking about music, right?

LVB: Allow me to simplify for the untalented: Like my life, my mu-sic often begins with struggle and ends with triumph. I created master-pieces in the face of obvious personal difficulties. "Music should strike fire from the heart of man, and bring tears from the eyes of woman." I did that.

MS: Bach was great. Haydn was amazing. Mozart was also a virtu-oso. What sets you apart?

LVB: Much of the music of my time was about the art of pleasant sounds; "the pleasure principle," they called it. Nice, classical music to snore by. I turned it all around, you see. My music was evocative, expressive, emphatic! I put feeling back into the art of music. Understand?

MS: It helps when I listen to your stuff.

LVB: I blew the doors off old forms of classical music. I was an innovator on the scale of the Sex Pistols or Pink Floyd.

MS: Wow! Really? The Floyd?

LVB: Do you realize I was the first person to include choruses and vocal soloists? I added Turkish marches, double fugues, trombones, winds, percussion, crescendos—you name it, I made it magic. Unexpected accents! Syncopation!

MS: Calm down. . . .

LVB: And my symphonies had themes that blew people's minds—they inhabit their own WORLD! Rustic life, revolution, heroic ascent! I made players AND the audience work for their triumph. It was a brand-new day, man. Happy endings! Victory!

MS: The last eight years of your life, you were completely deaf, and yet you remained productive, doing some of your best work.

LVB: Shutting out the sounds of the world definitely gives you time to think. And I believe my mind was able to soar without the distractions of outside sounds. As I said on my deathbed, "I shall hear in heaven."

End
of Interview

FRENCH GENERAL, EMPEROR, and diminutive master strategist, Napoléon I is the poster child for egotistical tyrants of old (well, maybe more like a post*card* child). After a meteoric rise through the ranks of the French army, he led his troops to a series of surprising victories over the British and Italian armies (and a less-publicized debacle in Egypt). In 1799 he returned to a hero's welcome. Soon Napoléon took part in a successful coup d'état and dominated the new government through his military dictatorship. At age thirty, the megalomanical midget proclaimed himself the emperor of France, and rather than laugh or ask him where his pony was, people fell in line.

As far as tyrannical monarchies go, Napoléon actually had some democratic ideas. He separated church and state, created the University of France, and crafted the infamous Napoleonic Code, a French civil policy that embodied many ideals of the French Revolution. He also executed plenty of innocents, imprisoned the pope, and had an ego as large as his desire to dominate the entire world.

At one time or another, almost all of Europe united against Napoléon's troops. He earned his reputation as a military genius in brilliant campaigns throughout his reign: Superb performances against the combined armies of Europe, outthinking the massive armies of Russia and Austria at Austerlitz (1805), as well as a victory versus the much larger Allies (1814). His bungled campaigns were equally grandiose, losing over 90 percent of his army in one Russian winter, then failing badly in an attempt to colonize Egypt (1798–1801)—only to try and save face by calling it a "scientific expedition."

In the end, his arch-nemesis became the Duke of Wellington. Fighting the British navy and the Prussian army simultaneously was a losing proposition, and Napoléon's dreams of rebuilding his empire bit the dust when his troops were crushed at the battle of Leipzig in 1813. Napoléon was banished to Elba, off the Italian coast, in a very small room with really tiny chairs.

Squirrelly as ever, he escaped in 1815, returning to France and to power. His last reign lasted one hundred days, with the final battle taking place at Waterloo, Belgium. The Brits imprisoned the emperor on St. Helena, a small island in the south Atlantic, where he died of cancer in 1821.

MICHAEL STUSSER: Your mother called you Rabullione—"the disrupter." Seems you were a spunky little brat from the start.

NAPOLÉON BONAPARTE: I was rambunctious, but zis was necessary, monsieur. I was one of eight children. And I was often hungry. C'est la vie. . . .

MS: That's not true—you got plenty to eat. The only thing you've got to cry about was being sent away to boarding school.

NB: *Oui*, at age ten I was admitted into a French military academy, zen to zee elite École Royale Militaire in Paris, where I graduated in half zee normal time required. I was commissioned as a second lieutenant of artillery in zee French army at zee age of sixteen.

MS: Do you think you had a Napoleon complex?

NB: If zis means zat I am an incredible man with a fan-tast-ic mind, then *oui*, I have zis complex.

MS: Well, it's really about overaggressive short guys who feel insecure and want to conquer the world.

NB: *Oui*, zat too. But for the record, I was not so short.

MS: Five foot two.

NB: And a half. Touché.

MS: OK, five foot two-and-a-half inches. That's not exactly Shaq. According to those who knew you, you were quite a control freak.

NB: "If you want a thing done well, do it yourself." Zat is mine.

MS: Good one. You also said, "Since one must choose sides, one might as well choose the side that is victorious, the side which devastates, loots, and burns. Considering the alternative, it is better to eat than be eaten."

NB: *Belle!* Well said!

MS: You had a photographic memory, could keep track of dozens of initiatives at once, and seemed never to tire. How so?

NB: Snuff. Tis *magnifique*, and I had enough to fill zee Eiffel Tower, eh? Today you have your stupid Amer-i-can Star-bucks, but we needed to be jacked up as well.

MS: Any organizational tips?

NB: Routine! Habit! When I traveled, I liked everything to be arranged exactly as it was at zee palace: furniture in zee same place, same desks, a duplicate travel library, personal belongings in precisely zee same location.

MS: You'd love Holiday Inns.

NB: I don't care much for holidays. I'm a serious person, monsieur.

MS: Speaking of serious, you made several blunders while in power.

NB: OFF WITH HIS HEAD!

MS: Easy there, Nappy. One mega faux pas: The Louisiana Purchase. [Thirteen states were carved out from the Louisiana Purchase in 1803, doubling the size of the United States and making it one of the biggest nations in the world.] You sold 828,000 square miles to the United States for $15 million. Why would you do that?

NB: I needed zee cash, Monsieur Fool. Cashola. Moola. *Comprendez-vous?*

MS: Another megablunder was invading Russia in 1812. You lost over 570,000 troops.

NB: And we killed 400,000!

MS: Yeah, but ya lost 570,000. See where this is going?

NB: See where zis is going?

MS: That's what *I* said. Look, everyone agrees you were a great leader and would have been killer in Stratego or Battleship.

NB: Merci! It was like a game to me. You know I constructed my battle plans in a sandbox? I used the first telecommunication system as well [the Chappe semaphore line in 1792], and had many spies at my disposal. I also liked to sneak up on my enemy from behind, very quietly—then POUNCE!

MS: Clever little bastard, aren't you?

NB: I was five foot six, idiot! [An account of his autopsy claims he was five foot two in French feet, or about five foot six in English feet.]

MS: OK, Wilt, what were some keys to battle?

NB: First, you must read those great generals before you, *oui*? Alexander, Hannibal, Gustavus, Turenne, Frederic.

MS: And then?

NB: Encore! Read zem again! But I must be honest, it is soldiers who win wars, and generals who receive credit for zem. And to have good soldiers, a nation must always be at war. C'est la vie.

MS: Anything else?

NB: Never interrupt your enemy when he is making a mistake.

MS: Speaking of interruptions, let's talk *briefly* about your love life.

NB: *Mon cheri amour!*

MS: And, according to several mistresses, a three-minute limit in the sack, and a two-inch schlong.

NB: Guard! Take this id-i-ot away!

MS: After your wife, Josephine, couldn't bear your children, you said, "I want to marry a womb."

NB: *Oui.* 'Twas not my best moment.

MS: You forced your old enemy, Emperor Francis I of Austria, to give you his daughter's hand in marriage.

NB: Marie Louise was a beauty. Mmmwah!

MS: She was nineteen. The two of you had a mini-Napoléon, though that may be a bit redundant. . . .

NB: She bore me the son I always wanted: Napoléon II, zee king of Rome [who died a few years after Napoléon, at age twenty-one].

MS: After your son was born, you pretty much forgot about the empire, there, Napster.

NB: Listen to meee! When you are a family man, you cannot exactly be ruling zee world—it's tough enough with all zee diapers.

MS: So is it true that your brother's marriage put you in an odd situation, relatively speaking?

NB: "Relatively." American humor. *Très drôle.*

MS: Tell me if I got this right: You married Josephine, and your brother, Louis, married Hortense, who was Josephine's daughter from a previous marriage. So Josephine was both a sister-in-law and a mother-in-law to Louis, and you were *both* Louis's brother *and* his father-in-law. Does that cover it?

NB: I'm sorry, I was distracted by a snail. What did you say?

MS: Never mind. Have you seen *Napoleon Dynamite* [2004]?

NB: I have not, but I heard zee kid, zee star of zee cinema, he is ze same height as *moi.*

MS: He's much taller, but, shockingly, even more of a dork than you.

NB: Stupid Am-er-i-can.

MS: Gosh! Why do so many people hate the French?

NB: When I was Corsican, *I* hated the French, too. [France acquired the island only fifteen months before his birth.] But you learn to love zem. . . .

MS: Not really. Au revoir.

END
of Interview

GAUTAMA BUDDHA

BORN 563 B.C.
DIED 483 B.C. (APPROXIMATE DATES)

BUDDHA WAS BORN a privileged prince named Siddhartha Gautama in Nepal. He lived a luxurious life with his wife, Princess Yasodhara, till the age of twenty-nine, when he realized he'd never stepped foot outside the palace gates and might actually like to take a look around. Seeing poverty and death for the first time, he began to wonder not only how the other half lives, but how to attain a state beyond birth, death, or even desire. (If it were me, I would have run back inside to the grand buffet.)

Leaving the palace behind, he dabbled for six years in meditation, extreme asceticism, and self-mortification, rejecting them all for moderation. After one particular stint of mind-blowing contemplation under a tree, he attained Enlightenment, and became known simply as the Buddha. His spiritual awakening gave him brilliant insight into the nature and cause of human suffering, and a knowledge of how to become happy. The Buddha's goal, then, was to teach his new philosophy to the masses—or at least a few good men along the road.

The aim of Buddhism is to attain true enlightenment, or nirvana: a peaceful state where the individual is free from desire and self-consciousness. Passed down by oral tradition for hundreds of years after his death, Buddha (whose name literally means "enlightened one" or "awakened one") had a message of love as the eternal rule, common sense, and focusing the mind on the present moment.

For the last fifty years of his life, Buddha spread the word throughout India to pretty much anyone who would listen: nobles, outcasts, common folk, and leaders of other religious faiths. His philosophy was open to all, and he made thousands of converts during his travels.

The largest concentration of Buddhists in the world today resides in eastern Asia. In India, Hinduism has absorbed many of Buddha's ideas, and many Muslims believe Siddhartha is a prophet of Islam. Point being, there's plenty of Buddha to go around. . . . In fact, estimates put followers at around four hundred million, making Buddhism the sixth largest religion on the planet.

MICHAEL STUSSER: I gotta say, you are one happy fella.

BUDDHA: And for good reason: All that we are is the result of what we have thought. If a man speaks or acts with an evil thought, pain follows him. If a man speaks or acts with a pure thought, happiness follows him, like a shadow that never leaves.

MS: That explains why my back is killin' me, huh?

B: Those who are free of resentful thoughts surely find peace.

MS: Speaking of peace, what do you think of all the statues and key chains and T-shirts of you in hipster gift shops?

B: If they bring about spiritual enlightenment, I'm happy to be the icon for self-reflection.

MS: But did you see the Buddha tankini from Victoria's Secret?

B: So long as it is not toilet paper, I am at peace.

[There is a long, awkward silence. Two more hours pass.]

MS: Ever hear of the band Nirvana?

B: A band of enlightened brothers?

MS: No, a hard-rock group from Seattle.

B: I have many devoted followers in Seattle.

MS: Try and make 'em give up coffee, we'll see how long they stay enlightened.

B: Teach this triple truth to all: A generous heart, kind speech, and a life of service and compassion are the things which renew humanity.

MS: Point well-taken. Say, odd question, perhaps, but are you a god?

B: I consider myself a guide—a teacher. But try and understand that there is no intermediary between mankind and the divine. People create distinctions out of their own minds and then believe them to be true. In the sky, for example, there is no distinction between east and west.

MS: Let's say I wanted to take a beginner's Buddhism class. Where would I start?

B: The secret of health for both mind and body is not to mourn for the past, nor to worry about the future, but to live the present moment wisely and earnestly.

MS: To be honest, I'm thinking about all the errands I need to run this weekend. I've got this bum lawnmower that—

B: Focus here, young man. The quiet. The tea before you. The sun as it streams into this room.

MS: But so much of your focus is on suffering. You're like a Jewish mother. . . .

B: Think of the suffering as identifying the disease. First we diagnose the problem, and more importantly, we prescribe the cure.

MS: More suffering?

B: Now it is you who are kvetching like a Jewish bubbe. The road that leads out of suffering is the Noble Eightfold Path.

MS: All right, give 'em to me.

B: The Eightfold Path: proper understanding, proper thought, proper speech, proper action, proper livelihood, proper effort, proper mindfulness, and proper concentration.

MS: I'm sorry, what was that last one?

B: Proper concentra—HA! A joke from a young mind. This is a beautiful example of proper effort, but your understanding is faulty. This will take time.

MS: So the Buddha goes into a pizza shop and says, "Make me one with everything."

[There is a long pause. Like, painfully long.]

MS: As a prince, you had it all. Your father, King Suddhodana, even arranged a marriage to a wonderful gal. But you left it all behind. Why?

B: At the age of twenty-nine I finally looked beyond the walls of the palace. There I saw the four sights.

MS: An old crippled guy, a diseased dude, a decayed, nasty corpse, and an ascetic, right?

B: The truth of life: that death, disease, age, and pain are inescapable. Poor outnumber the wealthy, and the pleasures of the rich eventually come to nothing.

MS: That is deep. Though I'm not sure if I saw these things I'd leave all my possessions—and inheritance—to become a monk.

B: You may or may not choose to walk in my footsteps. Remember that thousands of candles can be lighted from a single candle, and the life of the candle will not be shortened. Happiness never decreases by being shared.

MS: Apparently—Buddhas crop up like weeds. Some say you're the seventh Buddha, others the twenty-fifth, and maybe the fourth. Which are ya?

B: The incarnation of a Buddha begins long before his birth, and continues moons beyond his death. In fact, millions of lives have walked the Bodhisattva path on the road to nirvana. If you want a number, simply pick one, and I'll wear it on the back of my Buddha uniform.

MS: OK, more importantly, who's the next one?

B: Like I'd tell you. I can share this: His name will be Maitreya, and he'll appear after Shakyamuni's teachings have disappeared from the world.

MS: Yeah, that helps. Listen, I hope you're not offended by this, but I keep reading about how you were competent in martial arts and hiked for miles each day. So how come you were, ya know, so fat?

B: Yes, you are mistaking me for someone else.

MS: The jolly, laughing Buddha with the potbelly. That's not you?

B: I'm afraid you are describing a character called Hotei, usually seen in China. He is a representation of an obese, medieval Chinese monk. I was quite fit.

MS: Really? Well, can you clear up any other misconceptions about yourself?

B: My eyes were blue, I had fine, curly hair—yes, hair—and rather than being the chowhound you may have imagined, I was indifferent to hunger, environmental conditions, and all bodily appetites.

MS: So, no Pringles, then?

B: No, thank you.

MS: And if I rub your belly?

B: Our interview will cease.

MS: There are a lot of "nightstand Buddhists"—freelance Buddhists looking for a quick fix. Some inner peace. Is that cool with you?

B: There are only two mistakes one can make along the road to truth: not going all the way, and not starting.

MS: You really are the real deal.

B: Remember: Health is the greatest gift, contentment the greatest wealth, faithfulness the best relationship.

MS: I'm OK with a lot of this, but you were celibate from the age of twenty-nine until your death. Is that part completely necessary?

B: Believe nothing, no matter where you read it, or who said it, no matter if I have said it, unless it agrees with your own reason and your own common sense.

MS: Uh, it doesn't.

B: And it doesn't mean that you will ever awaken from the slumber of ignorance in this life or the next.

MS: Sex just seems like one of those things that's on my mind a lot, that's all.

B: However many holy words you read, however many you speak, what good will they do you if you do not act upon them?

MS: Or *don't* act, in this case.

B: Remember this: What we think, we become.

MS: Then right now I'm a triple tall vanilla latte. I'm going to assume you don't want one. . . .

[The Buddha is still and quiet.]

MS: Your last words were, "All things must pass away. Strive for your own salvation with diligence."

B: Yes.

MS: Well, dude, that was a George Harrison tune! From the Beatles?

B: Beetles, boars, men, and women can all learn from my inner peace.

MS: All right, but I gotta get you this CD. There are some things even *I* can teach the Buddha.

B: And let me turn you on to a state beyond suffering, called true Nirvana.

MS: So you *do* dig music! That's awesome!

B: You have much to learn. Of this I'm sure.

END
of Interview

MICHELANGELO'S PAINTINGS AND sculpture define great art—not only during the Italian Renaissance, but for all times. Famous in his day for perfecting the human form, Michelangelo is best known for creating the masterpiece *David* out of a giant chunk of marble, a not-so-little painting called *The Last Judgment*, and one you might have seen where God's outstretched finger is reaching for Adam's. . . .

Michelangelo was brilliant from the start, seeing shapes in his toy building blocks (not to mention his marbles) and quickly outperforming other famous painters of Florence. The elaborate churches of the Renaissance needed excellent artists as decorators, and Michelangelo was quickly in demand from the top brass.

Though he thought of himself primarily as a sculptor, Michelangelo could do it all—painter (*The Doni Tondo*); imaginative architect (Palazzo Farnese and St. Peter's); romantic poet; and even war engineer, helping to fortify besieged Florence in 1528.

Michelangelo left his beloved Florence in 1534 and spent his remaining years in Rome, where he worked primarily as an architect, a job he could do while resting his weary bones. The Capitoline Square and dome of St. Peter's Basilica, though neither was finished at the time of Michelangelo's death, are mind-blowing monuments that still stand in modern Rome for all to take digital pictures of. . . . Plus, we copied St. Peter's for our own Capitol in D.C.

Michelangelo died in Rome from a fever at age eighty-nine. He was working till the very end, and had a pretty good run, eh?

MICHAEL STUSSER: Master painter, extraordinary sculptor, the ability to draw anatomical parts to perfection, and an amazing poet to boot. Is there anything you *can't* do?

MICHELANGELO: I have trouble with a . . . how do you say . . . folding laundry. Can never get the shirts right, with the little arms folded just so. *Dificile*, eh?

MS: You once said, "What good I have is because I sucked in chisels and hammers with my nurse's milk."

M: *E vero*. As a bambino, my father owned a marble quarry, and also a farm. Of course, though I was around stone, I was not training at this time.

MS: For a genius, you kinda got a late start.

M: I become apprentice at age of thirteen, as my father would prefer I work as a banker or government official.

MS: Yeah, my parental units wanted me to go to med school.

M: Do not compare yourself to great Michelangelo.

MS: It must have been intimidating to work in Florence, following Leonardo da Vinci and Verrocchio.

M: Does the *David* look intimidated?

MS: Was there tension between you and Leonardo?

M: I believe that perhaps he was tense, yes. I am rising star when he returns to his Florence in 1500, after many years away. He is already near the end, yes.

MS: He was only fifty.

M: And I am thirty, with many commissions.

MS: I hear you guys had a little fight.

M: We run into each other on a bridge [*Santa Trinità*] and Leonardo asks if I wish to recite a passage from Dante. I reply that perhaps *he* should do it, as he must break habit of running away from unfinished works.

MS: Kinda the pot calling the kettle—

M: End of interview?

MS: It's well-known that you had a nasty temper.

M: Madonna!

MS: That was beautiful, but did your temper hinder your relations?

M: This relationship we are having may soon come to an end with these questions.

MS: See, that's what I'm talking about.

M: Listen to me. Painters are not in any way unsociable through pride, but either because they find few pursuits equal to painting, or in order not to corrupt themselves with the useless conversation of idle people, and debase the intellect from the lofty imaginations in which they are always absorbed.

MS: It's just that you couldn't work with *anyone*—no pupils, no collaborators, no love—

M: *Siamo finito!*

[Michelangelo storms out and the interview seems over until he returns for his glass of grappa.]

MS: I apologize, divine master of the arts. May I continue?

M: Gently. *Andiamo.*

MS: The *Pietà* [1499] looks so real it's amazing. How'd you do that?

M: As I have said many times, the figure is already in the marble. In this case, it was two figures in one block. All I must do is free the Jesus and Mary from inside.

MS: You made it look easy.

M: If people knew how hard I worked to get my mastery, it wouldn't seem so wonderful at all.

MS: On Mary's sash, you inscribed MICHELANGELO BUONARROTI, FLORENTINE, MADE THIS. It's the only work that you ever signed.

M: Yes, I regret this egotistical flourish, but a few days after *Pietà* is placed in the church, I overhear someone say the work is done by Cristoforo Solari, a lesser compatriot, eh? That night I take a chisel and leave my mark. For this I am sorry.

MS: The *David* [1501] is probably the world's most famous sculpture. Gotta ask about his, well, unit.

M: His *pisello*. Tell me.

MS: Well, for a guy that buff, it just looks . . . small.

M: How do you say, *tensione?* Tension, yes, he is about to fight the giant Goliath? Prefight stress made him, uh, shrink up a bit. Contract, eh? You need to think of these things.

MS: Not to question your brilliance, but the *David*'s proportions are a little out of whack. His head is a bit too big for the body, his hands too big for his arms.

M: Yes! This I know. The piece was supposed to adorn the facade of the Duomo in Florence. To be seen from *below*, you understand? At a distance! I calculate this perspective perfectly, and they decide to set him in the middle of the room. *Stupido!* Now my figure looks "out of whack" as you say.

MS: After finishing the *David*, you took on some huge projects, most of which you never got around to finishing.

M: If I'd had some decent assistants, perhaps I could have finalized many.

MS: You yourself rejected the use of helpers on almost all your projects.

M: Yes, and if I'd had some, I could have used them. This is what I am now saying.

MS: And I'm saying you coulda used some help.

M: Not only do I require more hands—but more money, yes? Many patrons become broke, or die, during projects. Also, I require much stone, so I try to open a new quarry at Pietrasanta. We don't find what we're looking for, eh? *Garbaggio*.

MS: Pope Julius II wanted you to carve forty large statues for his own tomb. Kinda garish, really.

M: It was the style at the time, but this Pope is *pazzo*—crazy—and not sure what he really wants. First he says carve, then he changes mind, wants a *grande* bronze statue of him for Bologna. Then he wants that I start in on the Sistine Chapel. You think *I* have temper?! This one is always threatening to throw me from the scaffolding! Makes me tired just thinking about it now.

MS: The Sistine Chapel. There you are, on your back, painting the ceiling for four years. Amazing!

M: Not on my back. This is myth created by Charlton Heston. I design scaffolding, yes? Allows me to stand and paint, but I still get much paint in my beard—looks like wild mosaic.

MS: Originally the pope asked for only twelve figures—the apostles—but by the time you finished, there were over three hundred.

M: I alone determine the scope of my genius. Now, get me a cappuccino!

MS: For some reason you stopped painting the ceiling for a year.

M: No pay, no paint. He marches off to war, I rest. I resume in 1511 and finish things up.

MS: You were a bit of a cheapskate.

M: If this brush was a blade, I would paint your neck.

MS: You slept and worked in the same pair of boots until they had to be cut off. . . .

M: Frugal is *molto bene*! I give until it hurts when it comes to my own *famiglia*—with dowries and loans. I even gave them my home, Casa Buonarroti! Maybe *you* are the cheap one!

MS: You put yourself in a few paintings.

M: As a sinner, of course.

MS: Are you in *The Last Judgment*?

M: Look closely in the face on the flayed skin of Saint Bartholomew.

MS: I'm gonna yak. Did you also put the pope's Master of Ceremonies into the painting?

M: *Certo!* This little man, Biagio da Cesena, says that my work is more suited for public baths and taverns than the sacred church, so I put his face on Minos, the judge of the underworld.

MS: How'd he take that?

M: He goes a-crying to the pope, and Il Papa says to him that his jurisdiction does not extend to hell, so the painting must stay exactly as I have created it!

MS: So, have you seen your paintings since they did the restoration of the Sistine Chapel?

M: *Si, ho visto.*

MS: What'd you think?

M: Bright. *Too* bright, eh? My color palette is dark, somber. They remove all the grit—I smear some of this into the fresco myself! Restoration makes me look like I am artist of *Pink Panther.*

MS: Hear me out on this one: You did a lot of male nudes. You wrote poems professing your desire for other men. Heck, you even used male models to sculpt your female figures.

M: I will admit to dabbling in the Greek traditions rather than Christian ones. I prefer the company—and superiority—of men.

MS: Good thing you're dead.

M: Because of my view of masculine love?

MS: No, because you're a sexist. What of your affectionate letters to Tommaso Cavalieri?

M: I was getting on in years, and had no *famiglia.* What I was looking for was a surrogate son, and I would have been proud to have the *bello* Tommaso take on the role. *Capisce?*

MS: *Certamente.* But you dedicated over three hundred sonnets to him, that seems a bit—

M: You doubt the great master!

MS: In fact, your wicked temper could have been because you had to hide your homo—

M: *Basta!* Enough.

MS: And the way you sculpted women was a bit, well, masculine, with their muscles all—

M: Arrivederci!

MS: Hold on, hold on, please. Before you died, you burned many of your drawings. I'd love to know why.

M: Was not finished, eh? Not perfect for the eyes of God.

MS: Ever feel bad you never married or had kids?

M: I have too much of a wife in this art of mine, which has afflicted me throughout my life, and my children shall be the works I leave.

MS: It's good enough for me, my man. *Piacere*.

END
of Interview

JULIUS CAESAR

BORN JULY 12, 100 B.C.
DIED MARCH 15, 44 B.C.

CAESAR'S WELL-KNOWN Julii family claimed to have lineage going all the way back to the goddess Venus, but not the money you might expect for a deity's dowry. Though Julius wasn't born with a silver spoon in his mouth, he had the drive to rule the world, which will get you far—especially if you've got soldiers to back you up.

Think of Caesar as an early maverick independent and you'll get the picture. He sponsored bills to pay soldiers and veterans and punish misconduct by governors, he gave Roman citizenship to new groups (more taxes!), planned a mega building program (aqueducts!), and adopted a spankin' new calendar. And if the Senate didn't go along with his whims, he had no trouble rewriting the constitution to suit his needs.

A brutal commander, Caesar's estimated to have left three million dead on the battlefield, conquered eight hundred cities, three hundred tribes, and sold another million into slavery.

Using the adage "Keep your friends close and your enemies closer," Julius formed the First Triumvirate—three guys ruling—by getting Rome's richest man (Marcus Crassus) and a leading general (Pompey the Great) to join his political ambitions. Julius even threw his daughter into the deal, marrying her off to the older Pompey.

Caesar, of course, wouldn't have been Caesar if he'd shared power; eventually, it came down to civil war. Against the Senate's orders, Julius marched on Rome on January 10, 49 B.C., leading to a civil war that lasted four years. In case you hadn't heard, Caesar came out on top, and was appointed dictator for life; "Father of his Country." Heck, they even named a month after him (July, from the Latin "Julius").

Caesar's problem? Too nice. Gaius Cassius Longinus and Marcus Junius Brutus, both former enemies, were forgiven for trying to plot against him, and wound up stabbing Caesar in the back. Of course, if it hadn't been them, it would have been one of the other sixty conspirators that were in on his murder.

MICHAEL STUSSER: Hail Caesar!

JULIUS CAESAR: You may stand down. Please, sit.

MS: I always wanted to say that. HAIL! I also like to say, "I came, I saw, I conquered."

JC: Veni, vidi, vici!

MS: Yeah, what was that about?

JC: I said it in regard to a particularly quick battle against King Pharnaces II of Pontus. I showed up, looked around, kicked ass. Came, saw, conquered. *Capisce?*

MS: Well I guess, but it's sort of mean-spirited. So what's with the laurel crown?

JC: Between you and me, I'm losing my hair, so I do sort of a comb-forward thing. The crown keeps the long strands in place. Tell no one.

MS: Say, is it true you got your name after being delivered by caesarean section?

JF: Are you a fool?

MS: I don't think so.

JC: I would suggest perhaps you are. Birth—by C-section, as you say—was not possible in my time, and certainly not done if the mother had any chance of surviving, eh? My mama was alive and well at my birth. Caesarean!

MS: How does a guy get to be emperor, anyway?

JC: Like many of your politicians today, I started as a prosecutor, accusing sleazy governors of corruption and making the headlines. Voters like to see you work on their behalf, even if you don't actually have their interests in mind.

MS: Do you need a college degree to be Supreme Ruler?

JC: At least a GED. I was actually going to study oratory at Rhodes with Apollonius Molo, the famous maestro, but on the way I was captured by pirates.

MS: Say what?

JC: *Ho detto* "pirates." Captured by Cilician thieves—a grave mistake on their part.

MS: No doubt.

JC: Once I arranged for my ransom to be paid—I had them increase it, by the way, from twenty talents to fifty—I gathered some men, and we overpowered the beasts.

MS: Is this the part where you toss 'em to the lions?

JC: No, but I did have them crucified.

MS: All in a day's work. What made you a great political leader?

JC: Build an army, yes? And speak at as many funerals as possible.

MS: Yeah, right. . . .

JC: *Realamente.* It's a good place to look solemn and win over those on the fence. I personally used my wife and aunt Julia's funerals for political gain, and my polling numbers went through the roof.

MS: OK.

JC: Another goodie—and this was before I became the emperor—was organizing all kinds of sporting events for the public.

MS: Serious?

JC: *Sono seriouso!* I was in charge of the Roman games in the Circus Maximus in 65 B.C., and we had a helluva time! Of course, we ended the fiscal year in bankruptcy, but you fudge some numbers and get back on top.

MS: When it comes to military genius, you're mentioned in the same breath as Alexander the Great and Napoléon.

JC: *They* should be mentioned in my breath—when I belch!

MS: What made you so successful?

JC: A great infantry with colossal artillery, and an unequaled cavalry—we could cover forty miles in a day. Sometimes we'd sneak up on the enemy and attack from the rear; I loved the rear assault.

MS: We're talking about war, right?

JC: Don't get cute with me, scribe. Wanna know the key to succeeding in war? Have veteran soldiers who are willing to fight and die for you.

MS: Well, you did kill any soldier who didn't follow orders.

JC: *That* is discipline!

MS: You weren't always the most prepared fellow.

JC: I am Caesar!

MS: Yeah, and your troops coulda used a Caesar salad from time to time—they were barely fed and never had adequate supplies.

JC: My desire was to conquer the world! Getting the men corn and good boots was beneath me. Fighting—this I understand.

MS: No offense, Great Caesar, but you also used sex for political gain.

JC: Yes, *grazie,* of this I am very proud.

MS: And it seems you went both ways—Cleopatra on one hand, King Nicomedes on the other. In fact, you were once called "every woman's man and every man's woman."

JC: It was a different time. Remember, we had vomitoriums, for God's sake.

MS: Let's talk a bit about Cleopatra, Pharaoh Cleopatra VII, Egyptian queen.

JC: Oh, yes. Let's talk about my little Cleo kitty. Woman made me feel *young* again!

MS: I bet. You're fifty-six, she's maybe eighteen and rolls out of a rug.

JC: Talk about shag carpeting!

MS: OK, settle down.

JC: I'd been chasing Pompey all over God's creation and wound up in Alexandria. That's when I met the bella donna—she was fighting against her brother at the time.

MS: Her husband, Ptolemy.

JC: Husband, brother, co-ruler, same deal. As I say, weird times. And obviously I was on her side—I mean, just look at her! *Foxy* Cleopatra! So we crushed Ptolemy, had a roll in the hay—or ten! [*Wink*]

MS: Too much information, oh Great One.

JC: And I put Cleo in power.

MS: Your affair in Alexandria was one thing, but bringing her to Rome in 46 B.C. was politically a risky move.

JC: She was the mother of my only son [Ptolemy XV Caesar, aka Caesarion]. It was one of history's great love affairs.

MS: Not to be indelicate, but you were already married [to Calpurnia].

JC: Lest I remind you, I AM CAESAR!

MS: Right, but the Romans found it scandalous that you'd live with Cleopatra and your bastard son for two years.

JC: My wife had twelve years to give me an heir. Twelve years! *Basta*—that's enough—it was time to move on.

MS: How'd the whole "et tu Brute" come to pass?

JC: I give my own opponents *so* many chances. They try and *kill* me? I give them hugs and kisses. They stab me in the *back*? Not only do I pardon a bunch of treasonous murderers, but I give them jobs in my new government. It's just not *worth* it.

MS: But, you were warned, after all. A few days before your death a fortune-teller told you, "Beware the Ides [15th] of March."

JC: Yes, and I thought she said, "Beware the Heels during March." Remember the knee-high red boots I wore? They *kill* your feet.

MS: Speaking of killed, you were stabbed over thirty-five times. Clearly, a lot of people wanted in on your murder.

JC: Try naming yourself "Dictator for Life" and see how your friends and family treat you.

MS: Ever seen Caesars Palace?

JC: *Non capisco*. I *lived* in Caesar's palace.

MS: No! The one they made in Vegas. It's awesome, man.

JC: Did it have hundreds of rooms? Hot tubs? Banquets a mile long? Ladies-in-waiting?

MS: Oh my God, it's got, like, four thousand suites and more hot tubs than Caligula ever had! As for the gals, there are plenty, and what happens at Caesars *stays* at Caesars!

JC: I must conquer this traitorous land of Caesar!

MS: Come with plenty of cash. Oh, and bring the toga. You'll fit right in!

JC: I must ask, what became of my Roman Empire? Did we conquer Babylonia, Mesopotamia, and all the lands beyond?

MS: Let's have some wine and chat. It's early, Emperor. Rome wasn't built in a day. . . .

END
of Interview

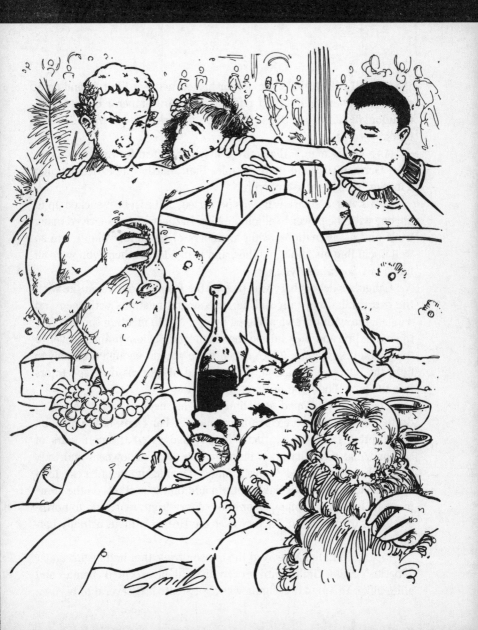

CALIGULA IS KNOWN more for his extravagant lifestyle and cruel despotism than for his brief reign as the third emperor of the Julio-Claudian dynasty (A.D. 37–41). And for good reason: He was a sadistic freak.

As a young man, Caligula lived in constant fear for his life—his father, Germanicus, had more enemies than Martha Stewart, including Tiberius, who became emperor.

Gaius was as smart as he was perverted, and as a boy, sucked up to anyone with the power to eliminate him. In this way, he survived many trials and assassinations, while members of his family didn't fare so well (including his father, mother, and two older brothers who were all taken out *Sopranos* style).

Caligula's debauchery was par for the Roman course, but he went the extra mile—not only did he have sexual relations with men and women, but with his own siblings. Ewww. Not to mention shoving it in the buffet line and then hitting the vomitorium before prancing over to the gladiatorial games. (Once, when there weren't enough criminals to fight the tigers in the arena, Caligula had his guards drag spectators into the pit.) Blood and hurling. Good times.

The man went mad sometime after his beloved sister Drusilla's death, and became more corrupt and morally bankrupt, not to mention bankrupting the treasury that Tiberius had saved through years of economizing. (Caligula often murdered wealthy landowners and took their riches to keep his festivals running. Then again, he often executed people who stared at his bald spot.) In addition to brothels on the home front, he led lousy campaigns on the military front, marching to northern Gaul, then declaring victory over the British without actually battling them.

In A.D. 39 Caligula revived the treason trials that had begun under Tiberius's reign. Guilty until proven disloyal, he executed enemies and allies alike. In A.D. 41, Caligula was assassinated by several of his own guards and a number of senators. If they hadn't, someone else would have; twisted perv had it coming.

MICHAEL STUSSER: Look up "sexually perverted glutton" in the dictionary and there's your face. What was wrong with you, man?

CALIGULA: It was a time of excess. Care for some chocolate-dipped pearls and caviar?

MS: No, thank you, and could you put some clothes on?

C: How 'bout taking yours off, handsome?

MS: Although there was plenty of debauchery going on during the Roman Empire, you kicked it up a notch. What's your secret?

C: I was always part of the "in" crowd, you know? My folks were totally famous—Dad was the grandson of Tiberius Nero, and my ma [Agrippina] was a granddaughter of Caesar Augustus and a top model in her day. That résumé will get you into pretty much any party. Have you tried the gladiator-blood truffle soup?

MS: Caligula is a nickname. What's it stand for?

C: "Little soldier's boots." When I was about three or four, my dad made me the mascot of his army. They'd dressed me in a miniature soldier costume and put me on a horse. Got the name Caligula for the tiny little boots I wore.

MS: Aw, that's cute.

C: I hated that frickin' name. Can I offer you a whore? Man, woman, or child?

MS: You had a very close relationship with your three sisters.

C: What are you implying?

MS: I'm implying that you had sex with them. Incest.

C: Ya got that right, reporter boy. Get used to the madness!

MS: You had great fondness for your horse, Incitatus. How far did that go?

C: Well, you're as sick as I am! And I *like* that in a man. Or in a youngster, for that matter. Listen, I loved that horse, I built him a marble stable and a gave him a jeweled collar, but if it's bestiality you're implying, I did *not* have sexual relations with that horse.

MS: But you did nominate him to a senatorial post.

C: He got invited to a few banquets, yes.

MS: Where did the depravity start?

C: Tiberius turned me on to some wild stuff on Capri, where he had a villa. Orgies and gorging and the like. I went out there without my normal posse [Augustus, his brother Drusus, and best friend, Nerva], so there wasn't really anyone to keep me in line, ya know? I just went wack-a-doo on wine, women, men, and song . . . plus some great snuff these Persians brought. It was swingin', baby!

MS: Tiberius was a sort of mentor, as the years went on. Of you he said, "There was never a better slave nor a worse master than Caligula."

C: Well, I helped him out as he got old, and the old fart appreciated the gesture. I also was a damn fine actor—pretended I was his little pool boy to get what I wanted from the crotchety coot.

MS: When Tiberius died, he named you the emperor in his will.

C: Me and his pint-sized grandson [Tiberius Gemellus]. Joint heirs! That's more twisted that a lot of my orgies. I didn't go for that action.

MS: Ya killed him.

C: What comes around goes around. Hell, murdering a natural descendant of a previous emperor is a Roman tradition!

MS: You pulled quite a bizarre stunt for your inaugural party: You had a three-mile floating bridge built by using ships as pontoons, then rode a chariot of racehorses across the thing into the resort town of Baiae. What was up with that?

C: Payback! A Roman astrologer once predicted that I had "no more chance of becoming emperor than of riding a horse across the Gulf of Baiae." Showed that little bastard!

MS: Perhaps that was a sign you'd started to go mad. In October 37, you really did begin to lose it.

C: I may have come down with a little something, yes.

MS: "Something" as in insanity, brought on by encephalitis or "brain fever." You were, in fact, described as having "emerged as a monster of lust and diabolical cruelty."

C: Mmmm. I like the sound of that, too. Hand me those golden handcuffs, won't you?

MS: You set up brothels for senators and their wives—

C: Nothing that doesn't happen today.

MS: Stole brides from the altar and forced them to marry you—

C: A better life.

MS: And demanded that you be worshipped as a sun god.

C: I was misunderstood.

MS: Please help us understand.

C: Well, I had a painful childhood, ya know? Lots of pressure. I was the beloved son of Germanicus, a descendant of Augustus, related to Julius Caesar, for God's sake, the great-grandson of Marc Antony. That's a lot to live up to.

MS: And the way you dealt with it was by . . .

C: Throwing some blowout bashes. And getting stabbed to death at the age of twenty-eight, of course.

MS: Yes, you ruled for only three years, ten months, and eight days. But your partying spirit lives on, dear Caligula. Albert Camus wrote a play about your decadence, there have been dozens of novels, plus Malcolm McDowell played you in the movie version [1979].

C: Should have been P. Diddy.

MS: Or George Michael, perhaps. We thank you, Emperor, for your time.

C: Let's all take a bath, shall we?

END
of Interview

GEORGE WASHINGTON CARVER

BORN 1864–65
DIED JANUARY 5, 1943

SOMETIMES YOU ACT like a nut, sometimes you're known for one. George Washington Carver, American inventor, botanist, painter, and researcher, is recognized from his work with the peanut and is often credited with freeing the South from its dependence on cotton. (And let's not forget his work with the sweet potato!)

Born into slavery at the close of the Civil War, he was raised in Missouri by Moses and Susan Carver. Slavery was abolished when George was twelve, and he set out on his own to get an education, attending high school at Minneapolis High in Kansas, then on to Simpson College and Iowa State University, where he earned bachelor's and master's degrees in 1894 and 1896, respectively. Booker T. Washington asked Carver to teach at the Tuskegee Institute in Alabama, where he became director of agricultural research, and remained there until his death.

Carver gained fame as "the Peanut Man" after speaking before the House Ways and Means Committee in 1921, listing over 150 possibilities for the peanut—everything from instant coffee to linoleum.

Though recruited by big shots such as his friend Henry Ford, Carver kept it real, turning down an annual salary of over $100,000 to work for Thomas Edison and refusing to consult with Stalin on agricultural matters.

Carver died at the age of seventy-nine, but not before being honored by the NAACP, FDR (who donated thirty grand to build a monument in his honor), and the National Inventors Hall of Fame. His birthplace of Diamond Grove, Missouri, became a national monument, the first honor given to an African American in U.S. history.

MICHAEL STUSSER: Not sure how to say this, but tell us about your owner.

GEORGE WASHINGTON CARVER: Mr. Moses Carver. German immigrant, owned my ma and brother, too. Mr. Carver wasn't all that keen on slavery, but bought my mom to help on the farm, see.

MS: You were both kidnapped at one point.

GWC: Bands of bushwhackers took us and Mr. Carver hired a neighbor to hunt us down. Mister got me back—had to give up one of his best horses for ransom.

MS: And your mother?

[Carver is silent for a long while, outlining a flower on a notepad.]

GWC: After slavery got abolished, Mr. Carver raised me as his own, so I got nothing but good things to say 'bout him. Coulda been a lot worse, for sure.

MS: In the fields they called you "the plant doctor."

GWC: I wasn't the healthiest of a youngster, see, so I couldn't work like the others out there. Instead, I walked 'round and took notes on plants and all. Got to know a thing or two and helped Mrs. Carver in the garden. Kitchen as well. People started bringin' me plants from all over and I figured out how to make 'em grow better.

MS: How'd you get your name?

GWC: Funny thing, that. I wanted to rent a room near my school, and told the woman there I was Carver's George. That's what I always said, and she done told me from now on I'd be George Carver. Added the Washington later, on account of another kid with the same name. There it is.

MS: How'd you get so into the peanut?

GWC: When I was young, I said to God, "God, tell me the mystery of the universe." But God answered: "That knowledge is for me alone." So I said, "God, tell me the mystery of the peanut." Then God said, "Well, George, that's more nearly your size."

MS: It must not have been easy to get southern farmers to grow crops other than cotton and tobacco.

GWC: Heck, it's all 'bout money, right? They woulda been happy to grow tumbleweeds if there was a market. So that meant I had to find viable uses for soybeans and peas, you know?

MS: Such as?

GWC: Well, today you're running cars on the stuff! Heh! Wish I'd been able to convince folks of that back then. *Hoo*—woulda been rich!

Instead, we made flour and sugar from sweet potatoes, along with paint and stains from soybeans.

MS: How about hemp?

GWC: Another multi-use doozy! Make fuel from the pulp, sew yourself a shirt with the cannabis plant, and smoke the flower buds just for the fun of it, if it pleases ya.

MS: And did you . . . partake?

GWC: Like my namesake, George Washington! How do you think I came up with all these ideas? Ha-heh!

MS: But it was the peanut that made you famous.

GWC: Love the peanut!

MS: And why is that?

GWC: Well it's easy to grow, for one. And it enriches the soil and is loaded with protein—somethin' poor folks need when they can't afford a T-bone.

MS: Is it true you came up with over three hundred uses for the peanut?

GWC: Yes indeed, everything from glue to printer's ink. Course, they're edible, too.

MS: You made a meat loaf from peanuts.

GWC: Cooking oil, ice-cream flavorin', cosmetics—

MS: Really?

GWC: Aw, I'm just getting started, now: gas, all kinds of punch, shoe polish, hand lotion, even medicine.

MS: From peanuts.

GWC: I'm telling you, the peanut's got healing powers! Massages using peanut oil can cure all sorts of things—including paralysis from polio.

MS: Luckily we don't have to worry about that anymore.

GWC: Because of the peanut!

MS: More likely because of the polio vaccine developed in the 1950s.

GWC: Well now, I'm glad to hear 'bout that. Next thing you'll tell me they made a chocolate peanut-butter cup candy of some sort that made millions!

MS: How'd you get along with Booker T. Washington?

GWC: Couldn't be that bad—I'm buried next to him.

MS: But you had your differences.

GWC: He was a hyped-up dude—didn't like my pace, the more casual way I dressed, or the fact I was a bit of a dreamer.

MS: A lot of scientists were surprised you didn't keep any lab records.

GWC: You sound like Booker with all the paperwork, schedules, and the like. Sometimes I just wanted to tinker in the lab, or get the brush out and paint, or play the accordion. But he was the boss. . . .

MS: Washington also wanted you to teach more than you liked.

GWC: He had a point: We were there for the students, and eventually we settled on me teaching summer school. Thing is, more important than teaching botany or math classes was showin' these kids how to survive in the world—during the hard times when racism and poverty's gnawing away at their souls, hear? And that's not classroom learning.

MS: Whose idea was the Jessup wagon?

GWC: Booker had the notion. Figured if poor farmers couldn't come to our school, then we should bring school to *them*. We got some money from Morris Jessup [a New York banker] and I helped put together the classes. Thing took off, too, and pretty soon we had wagons all over the place.

MS: Agricultural education, you said, was "the key to unlock the golden door of freedom for our people."

GWC: Too bad the youngsters didn't agree.

MS: For what reason?

GWC: Most of 'em saw education as a means of *escaping* agriculture and the farm, I suppose. Too many boys sick'a the cotton. There are plenty of other uses to a degree in agriculture, students just didn't see the big picture.

MS: Many African Americans were upset by you. Why do you think that is?

GWC: They don't like peanut butter?

MS: Try again.

GWC: Naw, I think they didn't like that white folks were comfortable 'round me. They saw this quiet, hardworking scientist shufflin' around in his ratty lab coat tryin' to make plants grow healthier, and they wished more blacks were like me. If there's something wrong with wantin' to serve humanity—poor sharecroppers—well, I don't wanna be right.

MS: What was your view on black advancement?

GWC: Rising or falling, I believe, is practically inherent in an individual. Races and nations, too: They progress or are held back by the number of individuals who do the right thing. God works in the hearts of men, and the so-called Negro problem will be solved in His own good time, and in His own way.

MS: So African Americans had themselves to blame for not achieving higher status in the South?

GWC: Ya know, I try and avoid public statements on my philosophy and mainly stick to peanuts. It's what I know best. Fact is, if I used my energy struggling to right every wrong, I'd have no energy left for my work.

MS: Sticking with peanuts then, did you ever get bummed out that your products never made much money?

GWC: It would have been fine if they had—I might have had more money at the end to donate to good causes. But I did well enough to get by—and keep in mind where I came from.

MS: You only patented three of your inventions.

GWC: All that darn paperwork took time away from my work. I also wanted my ideas to be free in the public domain, ya see. God gave them to me, how can I then sell 'em to someone else?

MS: Is it true you talked to plants?

GWC: Well, sure. But in order to talk to flowers, you need to be relaxed and quiet—approach 'em with love and wonderment. It was the only way they'd reveal their secrets to me.

MS: Think I can hear them?

GWC: I think of nature as an unlimited broadcasting station, through which God speaks to us every hour, if we will only tune in.

MS: Umm, my antenna seems to be a bit out of whack at the moment. . . .

GWC: Come take a walk with me, now. We'll dial that thing in. Eat some peanuts on the way, too.

END
of Interview

Born SOPHIE AUGUSTA Fredericka, Catherine the Great ruled as empress of Russia for thirty-four years. With a much-deserved reputation as a sexual dynamo, she'd make Christina Aguilera look like a saint, and should have tied a bed to her back.

Cat came from royal blood: the cousin of Gustav III and Charles XIII of Sweden (you're familiar with them, right?). She married Peter III in 1744, became Russian Orthodox, and soon was far more popular than her odd hubby.

Peter could have had the throne for himself if he hadn't been such an arrogant fool. When he left St. Petersburg for a summer retreat in 1762, Catherine proclaimed herself empress, and had Peter killed eight days later.

Inbreeding at the time made some of the royalty dimwitted, but Catherine was smart as a fox; well-read, she followed the news in Russia and throughout Europe. Catherine crushed a Cossack revolt in 1773, but the whole affair made her lose that lovin' democratic feelin'. Instead of land giveaways, freeing the serfs, and less taxation, she reorganized her regime to have greater control over those unruly peasants.

Still, Catherine made positive changes in Russia's system of government, including a legal process to petition the throne (even if most cases were thrown out and the petitioners beheaded), social programs, and relaxed censorship laws.

It wasn't all a happy-go-lucky monarchy hug-fest. Catherine kicked ass in the Russo-Turkish War (1768–74) against the Ottoman Empire and came out the major powerhouse in the Middle East. She got hold of the north shore of the Black Sea, took back parts of the Mediterranean, crushed a revolution in Poland in 1792, then annexed most of the western Ukraine. In the end, Cathy the Great added over two hundred thousand square miles to the Ruskie territories.

It was sexual conquests, however, that made Catherine famous. Cat kept men like the kings before her kept harems, preferring handsome and young men of all shapes and sizes.

Though she had a son (the half-witted Paul), she did not love him—or perhaps know who his father was—and wanted her eldest grandson, Alexander, to take the throne. Contrary to bizarre rumors, Catherine died suddenly of a brain aneurysm while on the toilet at the age of sixty- seven.

MICHAEL STUSSER: Gotta ask: You? The Horse? Yay or Nay?

CATHERINE THE GREAT: Though I have a great libido, I do not wish to have sex with animals. Is this the type of interview you wish to conduct? Because I am considered the Enlightened Monarch, and this is hardly an elevated conversation.

MS: Sorry. Wanted to get that off my chest. Still, and not to obsess here—but why would that rumor persist?

CTG: I liked horses. Do you have any pets?

MS: I've got cat named Mittens.

CTG: And do you sleep with her?

MS: Well sure. I mean, not *that* way.

CTG: And this is how rumors get started, Kitty Lover. I believe my own nonsense came about because men at the time couldn't handle a strong, bold woman—much less one who dethroned her hubby. To them, I had to be some sort of aberration—a freak of nature who'd sleep with animals.

MS: It might also have something to do with the sex room you had built. The walls were painted with pretty graphic stuff: rapes, pedophilia, bestiality . . .

CTG: And from the same craftsmen who decorated Russia's churches. Go figure.

MG: I mean, even the furniture was made to look like sexual organs!

CTG: I had a serious sexual appetite, all right? I think that's clear.

MS: Let's talk about your marriages.

CTG: My first marriage was a setup. Tsarina Elizabeth, bless her soul, thought her nephew Peter would be a good choice, and we were wed in 1744. He was a complete dolt. A hunchback, really. Not to mention he had a problem bathing.

MS: Says here in my notes that your husband Peter was a virgin nine years into your marriage.

CTG: He was all talk, no action. It's the entire reason I roamed.

MS: But you had three kids.

CTG: I am not exactly sure who their father was—I had thirteen lovers at the time—but we got Peter drunk occasionally so he didn't have a clue. Even a broken clock's right twice a day.

MS: When Empress Elizabeth died in 1762, you put on quite a show.

CTG: I cried, if that's what you mean.

MS: For all six weeks that they displayed her body. And then some.

CTG: The Russian people needed to see my grief. And yes, it helped me politically.

MS: Especially when Peter laughed at his aunt's funeral, mocked the priests, and threw a bunch of parties right after. But he did become emperor.

CTG: Not for long.

MS: Official cause of death: hemorrhoidal colic. Someone poisoned him.

CTG: I'm sure whoever did it had to stand in a very long line.

MS: Let's be clear: You had your husband offed.

CTG: I did nothing of the sort! My lover of the moment, Grigori Orlov, did the deed. It's true I benefited, but I am not a murderer. Or a horse whore, for that matter!

MS: A lot of the monarchs of your day were less than bright. You stood out for being one of the sharper tools in the shed.

CTG: Thank you. I tried to keep abreast of what was going on in the world, and it's not easy if you stay within the castle walls. I kept in touch with some of the brighter minds I could find: Voltaire, Diderot, and others throughout the commonwealth.

MS: For a monarch, you were pretty popular. Well, with rich folks.

CTG: The nobles liked some of my policies. Land giveaways, granting them serfs, eliminating taxes.

MS: Sounds like a Republican.

CTG: You could say I was an early compassionate conservative. I encouraged foreign investment, tried to modernize our agriculture industry, and got folks to go colonize Alaska.

MS: It's *still* not colonized.

CTG: I said I tried . . . I was also big on education.

MS: For nobles.

CTG: And the middle class.

MS: You wanted to be regarded as a "philosopher on the throne."

CTG: Better than a barbarian, dear.

MS: Patron of the arts?

CTG: Yes, I dabbled. Wrote a few comedies, in fact, along with my memoirs, and encouraged the arts to blossom.

MS: Unless you didn't like the message.

CTG: Hmmm?

MS: In *Journey from St. Petersburg to Moscow* [1790], Radishchev wrote about peasants held as slaves, and horrible social conditions.

CTG: Did he?

MS: You had him banned to Siberia.

CTG: It's lovely this time of year.

MS: You toured the Crimea in 1787, stopping in the little towns along the way. What for?

CTG: I came into the royal family without a penny to my name. These were my people, and I wanted to promote Russian culture, encourage the sciences. We also established new schools in the territories. We had a ball.

MS: My God, you sound like Oprah.

CTG: Well I don't know her—perhaps she's from the Ottoman Empire? But set up a meeting. I'd enjoy sitting with her.

MS: A lot of politicians put their friends into high positions. You put lovers there.

CTG: It's a excellent way to get to know someone's character. Putting Stanislaw Poniatowski on the Polish throne was a good idea, regardless of how he was in the sack.

MS: Normally you didn't mix business with pleasure, but you made an exception for Grigory Potemkin. Tell us about him.

CTG: Great military leader. Great in bed. He also had a brain, something I respected. Grigory complemented me, in a way. I was a simple German princess, and he wanted to conquer the world. We got along famously.

MS: Unlike many of your conquests—

CTG: Dear man!

MS: Sorry. I'm just saying that, unlike many of your relationships, you and Potemkin remained friends until his death.

CTG: Not only that, he led my foreign affairs and interviewed several of my favorites.

MS: "Favorites"?

CTG: That's what we called them. My boys.

MS: Here we go again.

CTG: It was all very up-and-up. They performed official duties, and were given luxury suites below my own. I'm serious about the duties part. Not just sex: I made these men—battle tested, mind you—generals and ministers.

MS: Quite a training program. Wish I could apply.

CTG: Well, you would have first been screened by one of my ladies-in-waiting. Trial run and all. Vigor! Looking for vigor! Oh, and you probably don't meet all the criteria.

MS: What!? I'm vigorous!

CTG: All my ministers had to be thirty-two or younger. Sorry, steadfast rule. But thanks for coming!

MS: How would you like to be remembered?

CTG: As a fair and noble ruler who saved Russia from being invaded by aggressive neighbors, and made her country prosper like never before. I'd also like to be remembered for preferring affairs of the heart. And for being hot. Write that down. Hot till the end.

END
of Interview

FRENCH DESIGNER COCO Chanel started out far from fashionable. Dirt-poor and orphaned at the age of six, she worked for years as a seamstress until she could get enough money together (thanks to several male suitors) to open her own hat shop in 1909.

Fashion took a backseat to World War I, where Coco served as a nurse, returning to open a second, larger store in Paris in 1924. Using elements from the nurse's uniform in her comfortable line, Coco was all the rage in the Roaring Twenties, revolutionizing haute fashion with casual, sporty clothes and flapper-wear for "active ladies." And this gal could accessorize! Hats, scarves, bathing dresses, costume jewelry, and don't even get me started 'bout the perfume, girlfriend! (Chanel No. 5.) Coco was, in fact, the first designer to sell not only a collection, but a lifestyle, liberating women from the corset, and at the same time, freeing their inhibitions.

Fame and fortune followed, and soon Coco had four stores, a social life that would make Paris Hilton's look dull, and clients from Berlin to Broadway. But when World War II broke out in 1939, sales slowed; she closed the House of Chanel and retired. Shacking up with a German officer during the occupation of France proved less than popular, and Coco moved to Switzerland for a decade.

Unable to stay away from the runway (and in an attempt to boost her perfume sales), Chanel came back with a bang in 1954, wowing American fashionistas with her timeless (and spendy) designs: turtlenecks, blazers, pleated skirts, and the Chanel suit—a status symbol as well as a fashion statement.

Chanel worked till the end (and lived large, with an annual income of $150 million), passing away in her private room at the Ritz at the age of eighty-eight. Coco may be long gone, but The House of Chanel in Paris is still goin' strong (and run by iconic designer Karl Lagerfeld since 1983).

MICHAEL STUSSER: Mademoiselle, I went to get my girlfriend one of your "little black dresses" and they were gonna charge me five grand.

COCO CHANEL: Oh, if you are so lucky, *cheri.* Quality costs. You are talking about zee world's best fabric, hand-stitched, combined with zee perfect design, eh? Crème de la crème!

MS: But it's just a simple black dress.

CC: Simplicity is zee keynote of all true ele-gance. If you want to dress your lover in rags, go to zee Wal-Mart.

MS: People are impressed that someone born without a silver spoon in her mouth could be so classic and graceful. Who did you steal from?

CC: As a youth, my aunts were quite well-appointed.

MS: These "aunts" you speak of were actually nuns at the boarding school you got put in after your father abandoned you and your sisters, right?

CC: I do not like to speak of zis.

MS: Gig's up. You're dead. Might as well just admit you came from a destitute beginning.

CC: All right! Touché. It is true I was raised in a poor orphanage, yes? And zee austere dress of zee nuns stayed with me. Plainness, purity, and intelligence as well.

MS: What's "the Chanel look"?

CC: French, above all. Zis means good taste . . . perhaps you would not understand.

MS: Try and educate a simpleton.

CC: Fashionable but not forward, you see. Also chic and professional. Breaking zee rules, you know? The rich don't always have to *look* rich.

MS: But the poor have to look poor, eh?

CC: I think not. I always said, "There are people who have money and people who are rich." I, of course, have zem both, but am brilliant exception to zee rules. A true origin-al.

MS: And modest.

CC: It is you who asked, imbecile!

MS: The name Coco is unusual.

CC: Yes, well, I am born Gabrielle Bonheur Chanel, but I was given the Coco.

MS: Let me guess: you ate lots of zee Cocoa Puffs, eh? Huh HA!

CC: I performed as cabaret singer at La Rotonde, in Paris. After doing my signature song, "Qui qu'a vu Coco," audiences would call out "Coco," and the name sticks, yes.

MS: So, no Cocoa Puffs.

CC: Zere are no puffs.

MS: How were you able to open your first store?

CC: With older men's money, of course.

MS: As a mistress?

CC: I had romances, *oui*, with wonderful, generous gentle-men, and we both got something out of zee deal, you see.

MS: I do. You had affairs with a number of these "gents," starting out at age sixteen with Étienne Balsan, the fabulously weathly French textile heir.

CC: I will tell you that Étienne let me use his apartment in Paris for my first studio, and was very kindhearted man.

MS: Next rendezvous was with Arthur "Boy" Capel, wealthy English socialite and polo player .

CC: Zee love of my life, he also helped me finance my fashion line and get zee new studio in Rue Cambon. Sadly, he passed in his car acci-dent.

MS: You almost married the Duke of Westminster.

CC: I told him, NO! There have been several Duchesses of Westminster, but only one Chanel.

MS: Then there's the Grand Duke Dmitri Pavlovitch of Russia.

CC: *Oui.* You know he killed Rasputin? The point is, zey all inspired me with their fashion sense.

MS: But you designed for women.

CC: We can wear trousers and suits and ties as well, you know.

MS: That's an odd choice for haute couture.

CC: Zis started when I was cold, yes, and put a man's sailor jumper around my neck as a, how you say, shawl. *Belle!* Many women remarked how wonderful I look—of course—and a trend is begun. I realize zis is a look I can sell, even zo I am buying many of zee clothes from the boys' department.

MS: One of your materials was tricot. Isn't that like the woolen jersey used in men's underwear?

CC: Stroke of zee genius! Yes? It is soft and inexpensive, but chic, when I use it for my tunics and clinging dresses, eh? *Moi!*

MS: Was the idea for women to look like men?

CC: No no no! I want women to be able to move in zee clothes, and still be sexy, you see. Active and attractive, yes? But more zan free from zee gauche corset or zee bustled bottoms, also free *mentally* from zee restraints of zee old style.

MS: What was the *new* style?

CC: It is many things, yes? It is dancing zee Charleston, eh, working— if you must, playing zee sports, smoking, zee travel, zee sex, of course, and divorce, if need be. I choose not to marry, so I have not zis problem, but we are *free* to do as we please. Our clothes must also be zis free.

MS: You liked to model your own clothes.

CC: With zis body, yes, it is the waif that men desire.

MS: I don't know. . . .

CC: Not so much zee face, but the adolescent body, zis I haff. *Magnifique.*

MS: How did you stay so thin?

CC: I am French. I am also from a peasant family, and zer are not many croissants to eat, OK? Plus, I smoke like zee chimney.

MS: Chanel No. 5. Why five?

CC: We had tried four other perfumes, yes? And zey were all unacceptable to me, until I smell zee number five, in 1923, and it was perfect. Voilà!

MS: But perfume's perfume, right?

CC: Nonsense, *garçon.* Before my No. 5, perfumes had been based on natural flower fragrances, yes? Make me want to sneeze at zee dandelions, eh?

MS: Thank god for that. If I want potpourri, I'll go to grandma's.

CC: I instead used eighty ingredients, very distinct and not so flowery, yes?

MS: In 1953, Marilyn Monroe said the only thing she wore in bed was a drop of Chanel No. 5. What'd you pay her to say that?

CC: I was not aware of her saying zis, but it is nice fringe benefit, no?

MS: Let's talk about the Chanel suit.

CC: *Oui!* Let's.

MS: Ya gotta admit, $15,000 for a custom Chanel suit in 1970 was a bit much.

CC: Again, you have brain size of pea! This is elegant—without rival! The skirt is slimming, and lined beautifully, eh? Zer is a ribbon sewed into zee waist, you see, so zee blouse will never slip.

MS: Hate for that to happen.

CC: Boxy lines for my jacket, made of zee wool, woven, of course, hand-sewn for perfect fit. It has zee gorgeous, braided black trim and gold chain sewed into zee hem so it hangs flaw-less-ly, yes, and zere are gold buttons as well.

MS: Let's not forget the pearl necklace.

CC: Costume pearls are fine for you, monsieur.

MS: You liked to mix fake jewelry with the real deal.

CC: I love zee fakes because zee jewelry is pro-voca-tive. I find it disgraceful to walk around with millions around zee neck just because you are rich. The point isn't to make a woman look rich, but to adorn her; not zee same thing.

MS: For over thirty years you lived at the Hotel Ritz. Must be nice never to have to make your bed.

CC: Oh, *oui*, zee room service was excellent!

MS: When the Nazis occupied Paris during World War II, one of your lovers was a German military officer, Hans Gunther von Dincklage. Think sharing your suite with a Nazi was a good idea?

CC: Monsieur, a woman of my age cannot be expected to look at his passport if she has a chance of zis quality of lover.

MS: Nice try. You were an anti-Semite and basically exiled from Paris after the liberation [1944].

CC: I spent my last years in Lausanne [Switzerland], but, of course, had villas on the French Riviera.

MS: Even after being disgraced, you came back in '54 at the age of seventy. Why?

CC: Dior and his perfumes [Miss Dior; Diorissimo] were cutting into my Chanel. To this I say, "No no no!" Also, zee designs were once again getting too stiff for zee woman. I came roaring back, to save zee world.

MS: You dressed quite a few Hollywood stars.

CC: The best, darling. Audrey [Hepburn], Princess Grace, Ingrid [Bergman], and Liz [Taylor], of course.

MS: And Jackie Kennedy.

CC: To be honest, she had horrible taste, and spread it all over America.

MS: Still, you must be flattered she wore your pink suit the day JFK was killed.

CC: What I wish is that she'd taken it off after the shooting. It was covered, you know. Not to be, how you say, rude. . . .

MS: It's OK, you're French.

CC: *Oui.* What I am saying is that everyone should have a spare suit, in the event something is spilled on zee first.

MS: Finally, any tips for the stylistically challenged?

CC: Fashion passes. Style remains. For you—oh, where to start? So many faux pas. . . . I would begin by buying a pair of shoes that are not for zee tennis.

MS: Oh, yeah. Well, I . . .

CC: And fashion is not simply a matter of clothes. Fashion is in zee air, born upon zee wind. One intuits it. It is in zee sky and on zee road.

MS: Wow. I think I'll start with the shoes.

CC: Yes, OK. And come back, monsieur, when you have zee money, we will talk more of what you need. It will take much time, yes? But now I must take my leave. Bon voyage.

MS: Where ya heading?

CC: I am judging ze *Project Runway.* Zees idiots also have much to learn from zee *professeur.*

MS: Don't we all.

END
of Interview

SIR WINSTON CHURCHILL

BORN NOVEMBER 30, 1874
DIED JANUARY 24, 1965

PRIME MINISTER OF England when it really counted, Sir Winston led the Brits to victory over the evil Nazi Empire in World War II—no easy task, especially when many thought the British would wave their white hankies, grab a pint, and call it quits.

Churchill gained fame as a reporter during the Boer Wars and World War I, attracting a large audience with his top-notch writing, and serving in nine British regiments. Using the publicity from his high-profile exploits, Winston won a seat in the general election of 1900, the first victory in a political career that would last sixty-two years.

Churchill lost elections as a Liberal free trader and Independent anti-Socialist and won under the Conservative label of "Constitutionalist." The public gave him more lives than a cat, and he proved his political mettle time and time again with leadership, patriotism, and fresh ideas.

On one issue, Churchill never wavered: the growing threat of an aggressive Germany. Opponents accused him of warmongering, for promoting disarmament, but his instincts were dead-on. In 1940, at the age sixty-six, Churchill was finally appointed prime minister. He forged a fierce union during World War II by teaming with Franklin D. Roosevelt and unlikely ally Joseph Stalin to fight the Nazi war machine.

Churchill's public broadcasts and fiery oratory kept spirits high during the Blitz bombings, and his popularity allowed him to survive several confidence votes in Parliament.

You'd think Churchill's position as prime minister would be safe after leading his country to victory, but noooo. The masses loved him as a war leader, but failed to see him as leader of the party; two months after VE-day, Churchill and his Conservative cause was out the door.

Bouncing back as usual, he got the top spot in 1951 and remained prime minister until 1955, when strokes forced him from office. In 1953 he received the Nobel Peace Prize for Literature, along with being knighted by the queen. He died in London in January 1965, and anyone who was anyone came to the great statesman's funeral.

MICHAEL STUSSER: Sir, you're in your . . .

WINSTON CHURCHILL: Jammies! PJs! Bloody well right. Man's got to be comfortable—and in my right hand is a fine glass of bubbly. Care to join?

MS: Champagne? No sir, it's not even . . .

WC: It's cocktail hour somewhere, my dear man.

MS: Would you say you had a drinking problem?

WC: All I can say is that I have taken more out of alcohol than it has taken out of me. Truth be told, I watered my whiskey—just wanted the Ruskies to think I could drink them under the table.

MS: And your interest in cigars. Where did that start?

WC: Havana, 1895. Went down there to see some live military action and got hooked on Cubans! We pretty much lived on cigars and oranges—bee's knees!

MS: Think you were addicted?

WC: I had my oxygen mask outfitted so I could smoke while airborne. If that's not addiction, I don't know what is. Now let's begin this blasted tête-à-tête, shall we? What say I talk and you listen?

MS: Go right ahead, sir.

[Churchill works furiously, scribbling notes onto a pad.]

WC: One moment, son, I'm just preparing my impromptu remarks. There we are. And let's begin.

MS: Maybe you can talk a bit about your upbringing.

WC: Happy to. My father, Lord Randolph Churchill, was a politician as well. Fancy it's in our blood. Royal blood, I might add—my pops was a descendent of John Churchill, the first duke of Marlborough, and he had some successful wars indeed, taking it to Louis XIV of France. Aces!

MS: Right. Um, not to be indelicate, but it's been speculated that Lord Churchill was not actually your . . .

WC: We did not have the sort of relationship that father and son might want, and for reasons I cannot explain. In terms of who did what to whom in the boudoir, I will not be going there.

MS: Your mother?

WC: The lovely Jennie Jerome, from New York City. Lady Randolph. Her pappy was filthy rich, though we earned our own loot. They put me up in boarding schools—it's how we did it back then, and even though my mum rarely visited, I worshipped her, really did. Thing is, I was quite the underachiever in school. Lazy, total lack of effort, not my cup of tea. Took me three blooming tries to pass the entrance exam to the Royal Military Academy.

MS: Well, you made up for that, sir.

WC: Damn right. I was a helluva writer as well, did you know that?

MS: Yes, you wrote—

WC: Penned dispatches from Cuba, India, and campaigns in the Nile. Could have avoided politics altogether, and made a good go of it living by the pen. But I got the fever, in 1900, I did. Maybe it was because my father was such a prominent politico, but I felt I had to run for Parliament, and eventually won a spot with his old slogan, "Tory Democracy." Got a nice ring to it.

MS: Probably helped that you were loaded.

WC: Loaded? As in drunk on a bender?

MS: No, loaded, as in rich.

WC: You've got the wrong man, I'm afraid. Though I may have had an aristocratic birth, I didn't inherit a pot to piss in. My mum spent whatever loot there may have been. In fact, the reason I wrote my historical pieces was because I needed the coin. The writing allowed me to be my own man as a politician.

MS: Were you always a great speaker?

WC: Heavens, no. I worked at it. Had a speech defect that held me back a bit.

MS: You're kidding.

WC: Not at all; had a bit of a lisp. I was fine for set speeches—good as they get—but in the impromptu, I had to be careful. Practiced like the dickens.

MS: I've heard about a conversation you had with Nancy Astor about women's rights that turned nasty. Was it true?

WC: Oh, Lady Astor was a beauty. She was visiting Blenheim Palace and we disagreed a bit on things, to the point where she told me that if she were my wife, she'd put poison in my coffee. And I told her that if she were my wife, I'd drink it!

[Laughter]

WC: She went on to become the first female MP in the House of Commons, by the way. Fancy that!

MS: You were often accused of crossing party lines for political gain.

WC: And both sides of the aisle hated me with equal vigor. What really mattered was my popularity with the regular blokes.

MS: Back in 1920, you had a bit of trouble in Iraq.

WC: Doesn't everybody? I really thought we could just pound away at them from the air, but the uncivilized bastards are impossible to get at.

MS: What was the best decision you ever made?

WC: Marrying Clementine Hozier. No question about it—after taking on the ball-and-chain, I was a winner no matter what happened. We went on for fifty-seven years. Here's to beating the average. Cheers!

MS: What about your best political decision?

WC: So many to choose from—but probably putting [friend and industrialist and newspaper baron] Lord Beaverbrook in charge of aircraft production in 1940. He was a fabulous businessman, and that allowed us to gear up in a hurry, don't you know, with both engineering and production.

MS: It helped that you had the best pilots in the world.

WC: Righto—when I said, "Never in the field of human conflict was so much owed by so many to so few," well, the "few" were the Allied fighter pilots, god bless 'em.

MS: When did you first start worrying about the Germans?

WC: Oh dear, early, early in the game. Back in 1911, if I've got my years right, the Germans sent a gunboat to Agadir [a Moroccan port to which France had claims] and I knew then that if push came to shove, we'd have to be at France's side. I started getting the navy ready, lickity-split, then got the cabinet to shell out the largest naval expenditure in British history.

MS: Not to sound morose, but you were kind of made for World War II.

WC: I was ready, of that there's no doubt. I'm old school when it comes down to values and what we Brits stand for. One of the last believers in Whig history.

MS: Forgive me if I'm not up on obscure English history.

WC: It's the belief that we British have a unique greatness—imperial destiny! This wasn't a time to sit back and have a spot of tea; we needed action, Jackson! And I thrived on the conflict, loved a challenge, daresay even a crisis. Tests the soul, challenges the ol' noggin. September 3, 1939, the day England declared war on Germany, Neville Chamberlain put me in my old naval post and the word went out to the fleet: "Winston is back." Back, baby!

MS: "I have nothing to offer but blood, toil, tears, and sweat."

WC: My first speech as prime minister [1940].

MS: Pretty inspiring.

WC: That was the idea. We were about to take on the enemy full force—needed balls the size of battleships.

MS: Before the Battle of Britain.

WC: Spot-on. That's when I said, "We shall defend our island, whatever the cost may be, we shall fight on the beaches, we shall fight on the landing grounds, we shall fight in the fields and in the streets, we shall fight in the hills; we shall never surrender." Bracing ourselves for our finest hour, and, as it turned out, it truly was.

MS: The turning point?

WC: Our bravery throughout. But it helped to be fighting an uneducated, maniacal tyrant.

MS: Hitler?

WC: Daft dolt forgot about winter! Went into Russia in 1941 and simply forgot that it got blooming cold as the queen's bum on a sleigh ride over there—freezing temps, snow. Ha! I never made a blunder half as bad!

MS: When the Japanese attacked Pearl Harbor [December 7, 1941], you immediately went to Washington, D.C.

WC: Everything was changed that day. Roosevelt and I pooled all we had for the common good—military and economic resources, even combined chiefs of staff and command. We were in it together, and not a minute too late.

MS: Describe your relationship with FDR.

WC: Asked her to marry me, she turned me down flat.

MS: No, that was actress Ethel Barrymore. I asked about Franklin D. Roosevelt.

WC: Oh! Righto! Well we were mates, but, more importantly, we understood what our countries needed. I remember after he was re-elected in 1940, we started our joint effort.

MS: "Give us the tools, we'll finish the job."

WC: And this was before Pearl Harbor, remember, that we had a lend-lease program going. I'd give him a ringie-dingie on the ol' tellie and he'd lend—not give us, mind you—military supplies and such. Key being, 'course, that we didn't have to send him a million pounds every bloody time we needed ammo.

MS: Were there disagreements?

WC: Stalin was the problem, all right? Today everyone knows he was a mass murderer, but I tell you I had a feeling. FDR thought he could handle him—thought he could keep him from taking Poland or the Czech Republic. I was way ahead of everybody on that one.

MS: Modest, too.

WC: Ultimately, I called FDR the greatest American friend we'd ever known. But Stalin I could never relate to. Too many awkward pauses. Bloody bonkers.

MS: V-day musta been incredible, huh?

WC: As I rode around London I was proud, but I also had foreboding feeling in my belly.

MS: About having to rebuild?

WC: No, about the Soviets with Stalin at the helm.

MS: You're like a broken record with that. . . .

WC: He was an aggressive Ruskie if ever there was one, and I warned anyone who'd listen that the Communists were bad news.

MS: Right. The iron curtain speech. Did anyone listen?

WC: Not so much.

MS: You weren't treated so well after World War II. In fact, it's been said that the great man who led the nation at war was not the man to lead it in peace.

WC: Bollocks! The Labour Party coined that little slogan and it worked like a charm. In my not-so-humble opinion, the reason we lost was due to the Conservative Party's record ten years prior, with nitwits Baldwin and Chamberlain, and I never had a bloody chance.

MS: Were you bored after the war?

WC: Bored and brimming with ideas, chappie. My ideas on the European Common Market were ahead of their time, and much needed. It's not always easy being a visionary, my boy.

MS: What vision do you have for the world today?

WC: Same vision I had: We need a world government, my friend, a League of Nations. One that is made up of irresistible force and inviolable authority for the purpose of securing peace and preventing war. With it, there are no limits to the blessings which all men enjoy and share. That, and we need to prevent the Iron Curtain from taking over the entire world.

MS: Uh, the Cold War's over. The Soviet Union kind of went bankrupt and faded away.

WC: Really? Well thank goodness for that. Too much vodka and missiles, not enough chow on the table, eh? Knew it!

MS: Sir, this has been a most interesting interview.

WC: Remember that all the great things are simple, and many can be expressed in a single word: freedom, justice, honor, duty, mercy, hope.

MS: Well said, sir. I'm afraid we've run out of—

WC: A few closing words are in order. First, I am prepared to meet my Maker. Whether my Maker is prepared for the great ordeal of meeting me is another matter.

MS: Well you oughta—

WC: And lastly, remember, many forms of government have been tried, and will be tried in this world of sin and woe. No one pretends that democracy is perfect or all wise. Indeed, it has been said that democracy is the worst form of government—except all those others that have been tried from time to time. Let's move this into the parlor room, shall we? I'll tell you about my escape in South Africa, keep the chin wag going a spot longer.

MS: Thanks for your time, sir. I think I need a nap.

END
of Interview

CLEOPATRA

BORN 69 B.C.
DIED 30 B.C.

CLEOPATRA VII WAS the most famous of seven same-named queens and the last Pharaoh of Egypt. Upon her father's death in 51 B.C. (Pharaoh Ptolemy XII), the throne went to his son, then ten years old, and Cleopatra, age seventeen. Instructed to rule Egypt as husband and wife (odd, to be sure), young Ptolemy threw a temper tantrum and sent his sis into exile. Using her sex appeal and political skill, Cleopatra took back the throne with the aid of her new lover, Rome's Julius Caesar. Together, they tossed her brother on his ear (and deathbed) and continued their famous love affair.

Caesar was fifty-four when their romance began, and Cleopatra soon gave birth to his only son, Ptolemy Caesar. While Caesar allowed Egypt to remain independent, he left behind three Roman legions to protect the country's treasures (including his sassy new girlfriend).

After Caesar was murdered, Marc Antony summoned Cleopatra to determine her role in Julius's demise and to see if she could be trusted. As happened with most men who encountered Cleo, the general fell madly in love, and the dynastic duo spent the winter of 42 B.C. together in Alexandria. Antony and Cleopatra (has a nice ring to it) had twins, and made Alexandria their permanent home. The Romans thought the romance was scandalous (Caesar was still warm in the grave, after all), and Octavian rallied the Senate to wage war against Egypt in 31 B.C.

Together, the couple attempted to oust the ruling Octavian (Caesar's grandnephew, if anyone's doing a family tree), but were defeated in the battle of Actium. Marc Antony escaped with Cleopatra to Egypt, but as Octavian's army approached, he committed suicide by falling on his own sword.

Taken prisoner by Octavian, Cleopatra knew she'd be stripped of her title as Queen of Egypt and paraded through the streets as a slave. Cunning (as well as beautiful) Cleopatra had a cobra hidden in a basket of figs delivered to her quarters. She died of a ritual snakebite at age thirty-nine and was buried beside Antony.

MICHAEL STUSSER: You're really one of those one-named wonders, like Prince or Oprah.

CLEOPATRA: Actually, I was Cleopatra VII. Two of my sisters were named Cleopatra, and there were others before that. The name means "father's glory" in Greek.

MS: No offense meant here, but it's said you had a hook nose and were not so beautiful as sexy.

CLEO: Let's just say I learned to use my feminine wiles to great effect.

[Cleopatra places hand on interviewer's thigh.]

MS: I'll say. You had two very famous lovers: Julius Caesar and Marc Antony. Who was better in the sack?

CLEO: I don't kiss and tell. But what I can tell you is that once you go Roman, you never go back.

MS: Shakespeare wrote this about you: "Age cannot wither her, nor custom tale." [From *Antony and Cleopatra*.] What did he mean by that?

CLEO: I had a great plastic surgeon. Plus, by the time I was born, the Egyptians had been working on beauty creams for three thousand years. I also used sunblock. Gotta use sunblock.

MS: Word is you were quite smart about money.

CLEO: Well, I made money. Literally. I devalued the metal content in our silver and bronze coins and was the first ruler to stamp the numerical value on the actual currency. No one was going to say a Cleo Coin was worth fifty cents when it was actually worth a dollar.

MS: You'll be happy to know that Hollywood's most gorgeous actresses have played you on the silver screen: Liz Taylor, Theda Bara, and Claudette Colbert, to name but a few.

CLEO: Problem is, they always make me fair-skinned. I'm Greek-Macedonian, and part Iranian and Syrian. I've got an olive complexion. Get that right for this interview, won't you, sweetheart?

[She leans in for a kiss.]

MS: Consider it done. Is it true you spoke seven languages?

CLEO: Nine, actually. Hebrew, Aramaic, and several African and eastern dialects. I was looking to rule far beyond the shores of Egypt, my shy boy.

MS: Upon meeting Caesar, you made quite an entrance.

CLEO: Oh, right, the rug trick. [An aide wrapped her in an Oriental carpet and unrolled her at Caesar's feet.] At the time, I needed Caesar's help with the civil war against my brother. He'd put guards all around the palace to keep me out. We kinda pretended to be room service. And I was dessert.

MS: When you dated Caesar he was twice your age. How did that go?

CLEO: Julius gave me Cypress as a gift, and ransacked pretty much every other country in the known world while leaving my Egypt alone, so I'd say it went well. He also put up a golden statue of me in the Temple of Venus, though I would have preferred a honkin' diamond.

MS: Did he have any pet names for you?

CLEO: He called me his "sister." That was a term for Royal Wife in my country. He already had a hag back in Rome—the little money-grubbing—

MS: You and Caesar had a son.

CLEO: Caesarion—Little Caesar. After his father was killed I had to take him back home, or he would have been murdered by Octavian. Together we shared the throne, and he took the name Ptolemy XV.

MS: So, if you don't mind me asking, how long did you wait before sleeping with Marc Antony?

CLEO: What is this, *60 Minutes*? Long enough, thankyouverymuch.

MS: Two years is hardly a long time. The day you met Marc Antony, you sailed in on your famous barge full of sea nymphs, dressed as Aphrodite, the goddess of love, and were fanned by boys in Cupid costumes. Seems like you were looking to bed the man.

CLEO: Egypt was on the verge of collapse, and I was her leader. I did what I had to do, not that it was much of a challenge.

MS: What do you mean?

CLEO: Well, unlike Caesar, Marc was dumb as a post, unimaginative, and a bit of a drunk little beast, at times. Ripe for the picking, as they say. I did love him, though, if anyone cares.

MS: While you were wining and dining Antony, you made an interesting wager. Tell us about that.

CLEO: The bet was on who could host the most expensive feast ever, and I won hands down.

MS: Lobster for one thousand? No, let me guess: tiger soup!

CLEO: Wrong on both counts: It was pearl wine that put me over the top. I dissolved a giant earring that was worth the value of fifteen countries into vinegar, and drank it with my dinner. Game, set, and match. Not to mention that pearls are an aphrodisiac.

[She removes her ruby-beaded robe and drapes it over the interviewer's lap.]

MS: A tough subject: You had three children with Antony, but he married Octavia.

CLEO: His half sister, no less. These were strange times.

MS: No kidding! Sounds like Appalachia.

CLEO: I had the last laugh. We married in 36 B.C., and I threatened to starve myself if he ever saw his other wife again. Two years later he crowned me "Queen of Kings" and we were inseparable until our deaths.

MS: Octavian and the Roman Senate had a problem with your little love affair.

CLEO: I suppose they'd have preferred Marc be with little boys, eh? More their style. The Senate also had a problem with us calling ourselves gods, and making our children kings and queens. I mean, what did they expect?

MS: When the Romans attacked Antony's navy, you kinda bailed on him, midbattle.

CLEO: His own men deserted him. I was hardly going to stay and watch the action on a lifeboat. Besides, we'd prearranged a meeting place.

MS: That is doubtful, my sexy queen.

CLEO: What did you want me to do, let Octavian sink my battleships? I am not someone who likes to get her dress soaked. Dry cleaning was not cheap in my day.

MS: When Antony came looking for you, you instructed your staff to tell him you were dead. Is that nice?

CLEO: Well, no, but I thought he'd be upset.

MS: He *was* upset. So upset he stabbed himself to join you in the afterlife.

CLEO: And here we are.

MS: During your reign, Egyptians thought you were the goddess Isis. I don't blame them. . . .

CLEO: You're sweet. Bewitching grace and charm have a way of holding folks spellbound. Unlike many, I also bathed.

MS: By the way, did you really make a love potion from opium, figs, and nightshade, and put it on your sails, sheets, and pillows?

CLEO: You're sitting on it.

MS: You really are a beauty.

CLEO: Gotcha!

END
of Interview

CONFUCIUS

BORN 551 B.C.
DIED 479 B.C.

CONFUCIUS WAS A great Chinese philosopher and teacher who created a system of beliefs based on personal morality, and the concept of a government that served its people. (Hey, there's a change!) Though often thought of as a religion, Confucianism had nothing to do with gods or the afterlife, and instead focused on honor, respect, and the Golden Rule: "What you do not want done to yourself, do not do unto others."

Growing up poor as dirt in the Shantung province in northeastern China, Confucius was big on education for the Everyman, and keepin' it *real*—shaping your own destiny. He advocated a mentoring system for young and old, poor and stinkin' wealthy: Find a good, older teacher, study his manner, and imitate his words and deeds. Better yet, if you're hanging around *two* people, pick out the good habits of one to follow, and the bad points of the other to correct in yourself.

Confucius has influenced billions—yes, billions—of people on the planet, defining and forming a foundation for life and culture in eastern Asia and elsewhere for over two thousand years—yes, two thousand years! In fact, his theories were even taught to civil servants (who were tested in entrance exams) and became the backbone of Chinese government and ethics. His writings on decorum, manners, and overall appearance helped groom Chinese families for millennia and also make the country a darn pleasant place to visit.

The Con-Man's most radical idea was probably an early version of No Child Left Behind. Education should not just be for the ruling class, he proposed, but for all of society. In addition to reading and writing, Confucius also wanted character building to be on the syllabus.

The man himself had knowledge coming out his ears, and a recipe for perfect virtue: gravity, generosity of soul, sincerity, earnestness, and kindness. Try it; might do ya good.

MICHAEL STUSSER: Confucius say, "He who eats crackers in bed get crummy sleep."

CONFUCIUS: Of this I did not speak.

MS: How about, "Man who have feet firmly planted on ground have trouble putting pants on?"

C: Confucius say, he not have much time for foolish games in a world with so much time for intelligent conversation.

MS: Yes! This is what I was hoping for. You were big on leading by example. Is that a good idea?

C: Taking a moral high ground is difficult in an era of greed, ego, and instant gratification. Many should not lead, this is a certainty. Others should not attempt to.

MS: So, you're talkin' about guys like Rush Limbaugh and Don Rumsfeld, right?

C: Or yourself, perhaps. Leadership is a task of utmost importance.

MS: I understand the whole worship your ancestors thing—

C: As well as siblings.

MS: That's not gonna happen.

C: Self-restraint will be required.

MS: As long as I can put my brother in a headlock.

C: These desires are normal. You must reconcile these with the needs of family and community.

MS: So *then* I can put him in a full nelson?

C: Devotion to parents and older siblings is the most basic study in placing the interests of others ahead of your own. It will take time and self-discipline. Then, perhaps, you will become worthy of respect and admiration.

MS: You also emphasized obedience to your rulers. What if your rulers suck?

C: Tyrants should be despised for their conduct. My belief is that the state exists for the benefit of the people. Those in power should not deprive even the humblest peasant of his opinion.

MS: You shoulda been around for Tiananmen Square. . . .

C: Rulers are to govern by moral example and never by force, especially with a peaceful populous. Loving others is a calling—a mission one should be ready to die for.

MS: Your views on women were a bit pathetic, if I do say so myself, Confused One. Not only were they to obey their husbands unconditionally, but they could be divorced for any reason whatsoever.

C: I always felt mothers should be treated with great respect.

MS: And that their main job was to give birth to sons. . . . It's OK, for a guy operating 2,500 years ago, you were a gem.

C: Do not forget *jen* and *li*.

MS: How could I forget *jen* and *li*! Who are Jen and Lee?

C: *Jen!* All-important virtue for conduct—love and concern for your fellow man.

MS: Good one. And *li*?

C: *Li!* All-important virtues of manners: etiquette, ritual, custom, propriety.

MS: Part of your teachings emphasized the "Six Arts." It's kind of a strange mix.

C: Ritual, music, archery, chariot-riding, calligraphy, and computation.

MS: OK, what happened to reading and history?

C: We covered that, small-minded man. My subjects included speech, government, and most importantly, morality.

MS: Did you give grades?

C: The subjects are tools for learning to use your mind. The goal is to create well-rounded gentlemen who speak plainly and who carry themselves with integrity in all things.

MS: In 221 B.C., during the Ch'in dynasty, the first emperor tried to destroy your reputation by burning all your books and trashing your teachings. How'd you feel about that?

C: All things must pass. You still burn books in your own world, and it only brings more interest to the author. In the case of the Ch'in, they crumbled like crumb cake.

MS: Did you just say, "Crumbled like crumb cake?"

C: I am trying to relate my wisdom to your experience, cake-eating one.

MS: Yeah, I do like cake.

C: The succeeding dynasty [*the Han*, 206 B.C.–A.D. 220], not only made scholars free to teach my principles, but Confucianism became the official Chinese State philosophy.

MS: In fact, your ideals were hugely popular all over China for two thousand years [100 B.C.–A.D. 1900]! How'd you do that?

C: Sincerity, for one. I did not attempt to sell my ideas in motivational books or tapes.

MS: But if you change your mind on that one, I'd be happy to represent . . .

C: I was also a practical being—my lessons were not beyond those of the Everyman. My people were already honorable, peaceful, respectful folk. I simply restated our ideals.

MS: That's it?

C: In addition, I believed in expressing gratitude through toasts, ceremonies [including sacrificial rites done at ancestral temples], and gift exchanges that have a magical, feel-good effect. Like your toastmasters, or Mother's Day perhaps.

MS: Sounds more like Saint Paddy's Day. Any thoughts on heaven and hell?

C: I believe in a Supreme Being, and spirits from the beyond, but my emphasis is what we do here on earth. Men are responsible for their actions and how we treat others. We may not be able to alter our fate, but we determine what we do—and are remembered for—here and now.

MS: You were extremely modest about your ideology, saying the concepts came from antiquity, and that you were "a transmitter, not a maker." But we know better.

C: Much of what I taught reflected love for the ancients. I passed on much knowledge from the height of the royal Zhou [the first half of the millennium B.C.], and put a little twist of my own on some practices. Gotta keep current, you know.

MS: Speaking of current, the Chinese Communists have taken some cheap shots at you and your ideas over the last century.

C: In my own day, politicians who wielded power made claim to titles for which they were not worthy. We can do little or nothing to alter our fated span of existence, but we determine what we accomplish and what we are remembered for.

MS: In Taiwan, they celebrate your birthday—a national holiday called Teacher's Day.

C: Of this I am quite pleased. Teachers are the key to our future.

MS: Too bad they don't get paid squat.

C: Choose a job you love, and you will never have to work a day in your life.

MS: Perhaps some words of wisdom to part with.

C: I once said, "A journey of a thousand miles begins with a single step." But more apt for times of war might be, "If your desire is for good, the people will be good. The moral character of the ruler is the wind; the moral character of those beneath him is the grass. When the wind blows, the grass bends."

MS: Give us one more for the road, Confucius.

C: Our greatest glory is not in never falling, but in rising every time we fall.

CRAZY HORSE

CRAZY HORSE (AKA Tasunka witko, pronounced *tashúnka uitko*) was chief of the Oglala Sioux tribe and the fiercest warrior the white man ever met. In addition to teaching the Lakota people the importance of their Native American traditions, he fought to save their land and way of life.

Crazy Horse led his tribe in the 1850s and 1860s, fighting mainly against other Plains tribes in and around the area now known as Rapid City, South Dakota, and proving himself a fierce warrior.

For ten years, Crazy Horse led a series of engagements against U.S. troops in what was known as the Indian Wars, often using crafty military strategy. (The Trojan Tepee trick was amazing!)

Crazy Horse's main claim to fame came at the battle of Little Bighorn (1876), where he outwitted one of the Civil War's most outstanding generals, George Custer (thus making it Custer's Last Stand).

The main problem for Crazy Horse and his braves was never the army or other tribes, but the rapid disappearance of the buffalo. (Overhunting by new settlers eliminated the hairy beasts in no time.) Upon realizing they would soon starve or freeze, Crazy Horse surrendered to troops in Nebraska on May 8, 1887. With him were several thousand Native Americans.

Though the Lakotas agreed to give up their guns, hunts, and horses, the government never lived up to their part of the bargain, and life on the reservation sucked. (Casinos wouldn't be open for business for another hundred years.)

After rumors swirled about Crazy Horse plotting to escape, he was stabbed at Fort Robinson in a scuffle with army guards. He died at the age of thirty-six and was buried in a secret grave in the Badlands.

MICHAEL STUSSER: You guys have a lot of silly names: He Dog, Cloud Shield, Crow King, Big Road. What's up with that?

CRAZY HORSE: I will call you Inquisitive Rat.

MS: Hoka hey! How'd you get the name Crazy Horse?

CH: Lakota tribe have custom of changing name as one gains in years. I am named Curly Hair at birth, then Horse Stands in Sight after I become good at catching untamed horses.

MS: So, let me guess: You caught a wild horse at one point and they switched your name again.

CH: Wrong, Kemo Sabe. My father's name was Crazy Horse. After I fight with great bravery with the Arapahos, he pass name on to me.

MS: Clear something up for me: In 1870, Black Buffalo Woman moved in with you, but she was already the wife of No Water. How does that work?

CH: Lakota custom allow woman to divorce husband at any time.

MS: We have that custom. I'll show you my bank account.

CH: Woman signals divorce one of three ways: Move in with relatives, move in with new man, or toss husband's belongings outside lodge. Husband that is dumped expected to accept wife's decision for good of tribe.

MS: Is that what happened with No Water?

CH: No, he track me down and shoot me in shoulder.

MS: My God!

CH: I want to kill him, but elders convince me no more blood must be shed. No Water give Crazy Horse three horses as compensation for owie shoulder.

MS: You were one of the youngest men in Lakota history to receive the title of Shirtwearer. Does that mean the rest of the tribe went shirtless?

CH: Shirtwearer is translation by white fools! The Lakota term is *Ogle Tanka Un*—highest honor and great responsibility. Shirtwearer must be ultimate protector of tribe and provider of people.

MS: Sorry, it's just a funny-sounding name in English. One of the great Indian warriors—a guy named Hump—kind of took you under his wing.

CH: Great Teton Sioux warrior and friend.

MS: Yes. That's what *I* just said. Why did he like you?

CH: I save Hump's hide in battle against Gros Ventres when I am sixteen years of age. Hump lose horse in combat, I circle back and pick him up in hail of arrows—ride to safety on pony.

MS: They should call you Crazy Pony!

[There is a long, uncomfortable silence.]

CH: When we return to camp, Hump pronounce me next great warrior.

MS: When you were sixteen, you had your first run-in with the white man.

CH: First encounter with U.S. Army. Lakota tribe members capture abandoned cow, and officer tell us to return beast. Push come to shove, and we kill thirty soldiers. Army return one year later, kill many Lakota—not only warriors, but women, children. Lesson learned.

MS: You have a reputation as an amazing warrior. But there's a gentle side, isn't there, crazy?

CH: AAAHHHYIIIII!!!!!

MS: OK! Fierce and crazy!

CH: I am a man of honesty and integrity, above all. The battle is to assure my people are safe.

MS: Is it true you sometimes spared the life of your enemy?

CH: I often refrain from killing. Instead of striking with weapon, I strike with switch, showing enemy I do not fear their weapons, nor do I wish to waste hatchet on their skull.

MS: What was the turning point where you finally said, "Enough of Whitey, we're at war?"

CH: Year of 1864, Teton Sioux chiefs gather to discuss actions against invader. We believe country is wide enough for all. White traders made welcome. Even agree on Oregon Trail.

MS: But somehow we didn't live happily ever after.

CH: White invader build forts! Build fences to enforce territory. One does not sell the land upon which people walk. Our bands no longer willing to make new treaty. In 1866 White Bull, Two Kettle, Swift Bear all agree—time to defend rights and land by force.

MS: What was your role?

CH: I lead warriors to raise arms against settlement. Sword, Crow King, Touch-the-Cloud [a seven footer!]—we attack forts and trespassers. Ten years of war begins.

MS: Gotta ask about the whole Custer thing. Why did they come after you in the first place?

CH: Army not like that we enjoy such large encampment. Probably not surprise that our lands include Black Hills full of gold.

MS: How'd you manage to wipe everyone out?

CH: Understand, we not wish to massacre Long Hair [Custer]. First impulse is to escape, but surrounded, so we fight. Kill or be killed.

MS: And well, I might add.

CH: We outnumber white man five to one. Not so smart to attack us. Plus we upgrade from bow and arrow to repeating rifle.

MS: A few years later you surrendered voluntarily to General Crook. It seems like you'd be one of those warriors who'd fight to the death.

CH: I think first of my people. Hunger set in. Cold. I wish for Lakotas to live on, not die in winter, always hunted like dogs.

MS: The army wanted you to meet the new president of the United States, Rutherford B. Hayes.

CH: I refuse offer. I refuse to sign treaties. I refuse to be Chief Sellout Photo Op!

MS: In 1877, General Crook asked you to help him when the Nez Perce broke out of their reservation and headed toward Canada.

CH: I was a reluctant warrior.

MS: And a misunderstood one, apparently.

CH: Yes, I have trouble with idiot translator. [Official interpreter Frank Grouard, who disliked Crazy Horse, intentionally misreported what he had said. Instead of conveying that he would "fight till all the Nez Perces were killed," he switched the quote to "fight until not a white man is left."]

MS: Word got around that you were going to kill not only white soldiers, but General Crook.

CH: I try to set record straight by confronting him at Fort Robinson. This not go so well.

MS: I'll say.

CH: Guards try to arrest me. I not like hands on Crazy Horse. I push little man who ranks only as private [William Gentiles], and he have nerve to stab great warrior with bayonet.

MS: Kidney shot. That was the end, eh?

CH: My father sing Death Song over me and I pass into greater world.

MS: Big Picture question: Aside from taking your land, forcing you to abandon your language and customs, and killing off your best men, what do you really have against Whitey?

CH: How many moons does Man with Little Pencil have?

MS: We've got time.

CH: We did not ask you white men to come here. Great Spirit gave us this country as a home. You had yours.

We did not interfere with you. Great Spirit gave us plenty of land to live on, and buffalo, deer, antelope.

But you have come here, you are taking my land from me, you are killing off our game, so it hard for us to live.

MS: Let me apologize for all—

CH: Now, you tell us to work for a living, but the Great Spirit did not make us to work, but to live by hunting. You white men can work if you want to. We did not interfere with you, and again you say, "Why do you not become civilized?" We do not want your civilization! We would live as our fathers did, and their fathers before them!

MS: Maybe I can offer you a peace pipe to patch things up.

CH: Crazy Horse give up smoking, but could go for nice buffalo feast.

MS: This isn't gonna be easy. . . . Say, have you heard about the giant carving they're making of you in the Black Hills mountain?

CH: I understand Lakota elders want likeness of me and horse on mountain to show red man also has heroes. I demand to be larger than your presidents at Rushmore!

MS: Oh, no worries there. If they ever finish, Mount Rushmore would fit inside your head. The thing's over 550 feet tall!

CH: What take so long?

MS: Well the original sculptor worked on it for over forty years before he died. Guy musta be *crazy*, huh?

CH: Crazy like fox.

END
of Interview

DALÍ: LOOK IN the dictionary under SuperFreak and you get this guy's (surrealist) picture. Painter, sculptor, filmmaker, and dark dreamer, Dalí makes Nike marketers look shy and Warhol normal.

You've seen Salvador Dalí's trademark work: melting clocks, pictures within pictures, skeletor-cyclists riding nowhere fast, scenes of necrophilia and decay, all tossed into vast landscapes from Mars. It's wacky stuff: part reality, part Freudian fantasy, part paranoid symbolism.

Dalí hoped his work would ". . . systematize confusion and thus to help discredit completely the world of reality." Yeah. What he said.

Salvador's best creation was quite possibly his calculated eccentric persona. From 1940 on, Dalí and his wife worked on self-promotion, making his wide-open eyes, silver cape, and waxed handlebar mustache as famous as any artist on the planet.

Moving to the United States in 1940, Dalí became an instant celeb, working with Hitchcock and Walt Disney, designing ballet sets, jewelry, chic shop interiors, and objets d'art.

Though many questioned Dalí's integrity and commercialism (jealous bastards), there is no doubt that his provocative, dreamlike paintings are powerful displays of imagination and original talent.

MICHAEL STUSSER: How would you best describe your work?

SALVADOR DALÍ: I've said I do hand-painted dream photographs, but that doesn't give the full picture of my genius.

MS: Seems you have a healthy amount of self-confidence.

SD: Modesty is not my specialty. At the age of six, I wanted to be a cook. At seven, I wanted to be Napoléon. My ambition has been growing ever since.

MS: Where do you think this self-assurance came from?

SD: My parents worshipped me. In fact, they saw me as the reincarnation of my brother [also named Salvador], who died nine months before I was born.

MS: Having to live as both yourself and your dead bro, that's gotta be tough.

SD: It's a challenge. I'm glad I was able to channel some of my thoughts on death and decay into my work, or I'd really be messed up.

MS: I'll leave that one, for now. Is it true you hate spinach?

SD: I despise its aesthetic! I eat only items with well-defined shapes. Things like shellfish, with its beautiful armor. How wonderful to crunch a bird's tiny skull.

MS: Blech!

SD: Delicious! The taste of truth is in the marrow of a bone!

MS: OK, let's not get too revved up. What's with all the melting clocks? [*The Persistence of Memory* and *Dream of Venus*.]

SD: The omnipresence of time, obviously. Time devours itself, and everything in its path.

MS: You're an odd bird.

SD: Frankly, I'm flabbergasted about the normality of everyone else. I always said, "Nothing of what *might* happen ever happens!" There's so little fantasy. Why are bathtubs always the same shape? Why, when I ask for grilled lobster, am I never served a cooked telephone?

MS: What's the key to being so weird?

SD: The desire to do the opposite of what everybody else does. Ask me to paint a statue of the Virgin, I'll paint a pair of elephants on scales.

MS: Did that attitude get you thrown out of school?

SD: Affirmative. I was about to give my oral exam at the San Fernando School of Fine Arts when I got this insurmountable feeling of indolence. "I'm sorry," I said, "but I'm clearly more intelligent than these three professors, and refuse to be examined by them." Tossed!

MS: Some titles of your work: *The Great Masturbator* and *Young Virgin Auto-Sodomized by the Horns of Her Own Chastity.*

SD: Well what did you expect: *Still Life with Pears*? Dalí is an innovator!

[Dalí begins to climb the couch and attempts to hook his leg on the chandelier.]

SD: Plus, I stand on my head a lot to induce hallucinations.

MS: Please get down from there.

SD: Please get up from there.

MS: Who influenced your work?

SD: Who didn't? Miró, Picasso, the classics, the avant-garde, I took it all in and made it mine. Mine! I also liked Harpo Marx.

MS: What did you learn from Harpo?

SD: How to hit your head without being hurt.

[Dalí falls from the chandelier with a thud that sounds like an eggplant hitting a table.]

SD: I sent Harpo a Christmas present once—a harp, with strings of barbed wire. Brilliant!

MS: While many surrealists embraced Communism, you were fascinated by Hitler. Are you a fan?

SD: We were both masochists. I wouldn't say I was a "fan"—my own moral role model was more along the lines of the Marquis de Sade, hmmm? I was obsessed with Hitler's personality, no doubt about it. But not in a political way—it was more paranoiac. He attracted me as an object of my mad imaginings—a man uniquely capable of turning things completely upside down.

MS: This obsession must have gone over well with the French surrealists, huh?

SD: No, obviously not, you scribomatic goof-gazoo. When the war started in Europe, I felt it best that I head for the States. Upon my arrival, I told André Breton I'd found three great American surrealists: the Marx Brothers, Cecil B. DeMille, and Walt Disney.

MS: When it came to self-promotion, you really were a machine.

SD: And I thank you for noticing. That's really the whole point—do incredibly bizarre things, and make sure the public sees your amazing work.

MS: In the '50s, you were constantly pitched on ideas for collaboration—furniture, Alka-Seltzer ads, even "Dalícatessens." What was your favorite?

SD: *Spellbound* [1945]. If the fool running the studio [David Selznick] had let me and Mr. Hitchcock have our way, my dream sequence would have been mind-blowing. We were going to zoom in on a colossal statue. Suddenly it breaks open—cracking like a shell! Inside, thousands of ants. Close up: They crawl in unison toward Ingrid Bergman and cover her, swarming! She screams! Well, we can cut right there. No star was going to allow herself to be covered in red ants. Shame, really.

MS: Talk about meeting your wife, Gala.

SD: She was someone else's wife at the time [poet Paul Éluard], but I wooed her in my own particular way.

MS: I'm sure.

SD: First I dyed my armpit blue, then I wore a geranium on my head and rubbed myself with a layer of goat dung.

MS: How romantic.

SD: I was so taken with her that every time I saw her, I burst out laughing.

MS: You said that if not for her, you'd have had an early death.

SD: She saved me, there's no doubt. Under this cocky exterior, there lies an insecure and disorganized madman. Gala was my go-between— she was my agent, my business manager, my muse.

MS: And she slept around.

SD: We had an open marriage, and so she did what she wanted. Gala liked young artists, and I honestly didn't care; sex, for me, was overrated. I masturbated a lot while looking at—

MS: Too much information, huh?

SD: Each morning when I awake, I experience again a supreme pleasure: that of being Salvador Dalí.

MS: When you moved back to Catalonia after World War II, you were criticized for living in Spain while it was ruled by Franco.

SD: And I could say the same thing about you and your president. Pick any one of your warmongering heads of state—and yet you live among them!

MS: But you praised Franco when he signed death warrants for political prisoners. Were you a Fascist?

SD: All these labels and no clothes to put them on! I'm an anarcho-monarchist. That clear things up for you? Point is, I loved it in Spain, and wanted to wind up there.

MS: After Gala died you tried to kill yourself.

SD: It was an attempt to put myself into a state of suspended animation.

MS: You refused to eat, Salvador, or receive visitors.

SD: And later, I lit my bed on fire—and yet the grand Dalí survives.

MS: True enough. Remember wanting to do something with Walt Disney?

SD: We worked on an animated cartoon, *Destino*, in 1945, sort of like *Fantasia*, but with my own weird twist. Never did get around to finishing it.

MS: Good news! They made it in 2003. Helluva show. Won Best Short at the Melbourne International Film Festival and was also nominated for an Academy Award.

SD: The grand Dalí lives on *again*! Revel in the me.

MS: One last question: The famous mustache—any weird story about that?

SD: No, not really. It's just the way I receive messages from aliens in outer space. Now, if you don't mind, I'm going to take my pet lobster for a walk.

END
of Interview

CHARLES ROBERT DARWIN was a British naturalist with a radical new theory about where we came from. Darwin attended Edinburgh University in 1825 and studied medicine. His attention soon moved to naturalism, and he began learning about evolution and acquired characteristics under Robert Edmund Grant.

It was a trip aboard the HMS *Beagle* in 1831 that allowed the twenty-two-year-old Darwin to circumnavigate the world and develop hands-on hypotheses while encountering flora, tropical rainforests, fossils, and untamed civilizations.

His theory of evolution by natural selection, *The Origin of Species*, was published in 1859; it laid out the argument that the traits of living organisms change from one generation to the next, and include the emergence of new species over time. This theory rocked the world and changed the way we saw ourselves.

The possibility now existed that human beings no longer originated from divine design, but shared a common ancestry with animals! Men from monkeys! Goodness gracious!

Right or wrong, Darwin's greatest accomplishment was to begin the debate and move the concept of evolution into the realm of serious scientific thought. He died at age seventy-three and was buried at Westminster Abbey, London, a rare honor for a scientist.

MICHAEL STUSSER: How'd you get into the whole field of naturalism?

CHARLES DARWIN: Like many youngsters, I used to collect stuff: coins and birds' eggs and rocks and flowers.

MS: I had a baseball card collection. Didn't give me any grand theories on the world, though.

CD: Well, then I got into shooting game, which was damn fun. Brilliant, really. Started looking at their anatomy, the innards and all, and that's what got me to thinking, you know.

MS: You went to school in Edinburgh for medicine, but soon switched majors. How come?

CD: Aw, the anatomy lectures sucked canal water, mate, and the surgery at the time was complete butchery. Blood and gore and a hacksaw. I couldn't stand it. Made my stomach turn.

MS: What did your father think of you giving up on med school?

CD: He thought I'd be a disgrace to myself and the family.

MS: Nice fella.

CD: Pops actually did me a favor by enrolling me at Christ's College [at Cambridge, in 1827]. The only real way for an English naturalist to make a quid at the time was to be a clergyman by day and "explore the wonders of God's creation" in their spare time.

MS: How'd you wind up in the tropics, then?

CD: I kissed up to Robert FitzRoy [the captain of the HMS *Beagle*], and he let me carry his bags on what was supposed to be a two-year expedition along the coastline of South America.

MS: Sounds a little like *Gilligan's Island*.

CD: We wound up being out there five years [1831–36], but I don't think we charted any island called Gilligan, and I took copious notes.

MS: You got incredibly seasick. How'd you deal with that?

CD: I vomited a lot. Just plain hurled overboard. I also spent as much time as I could on land writing in my diary [a 770-page whopper, with 1,750 pages of notes and twelve catalogs of 5,436 bones, skins, shells, and carcasses]. All told, I only spent eighteen months aboard that damn ship.

MS: You kinda lost religion on the boat. How did that happen?

CD: You start observing the nasty state the natives of Tierra del Fuego lived in, or the horrific cruelties of slavery, and I fancy you'll start doubting all sorts of things. Not sure God would allow that to exist in this world.

MS: Does the theory of evolution mean there is no God?

CD: No, I think it's compatible with a belief in God. It's quite possible God made the earth and let the natural laws of evolution take over. No need to be a complete control freak 'bout it.

MS: But you are agnostic.

CD: I am, but I'm well aware that the mystery of the beginning of all things is going to remain as such.

MS: This whole theory of evolution was quite radical. How'd it start?

CD: With my grandfather, Erasmus Darwin. Old coot was a wild card, I tell ya—total freethinker who spoke his mind. He always hypothesized that all warm-blooded animals sprang from a single living filament, going way back. Then there were the kids from Edinburgh— the English Dissenters—crackpots barred from Oxford and Cambridge. They'd get loaded and talk about animals and humans sharing traits.

MS: This thing about acquired characteristics. Does it mean humans will lose their little toes at some point?

CD: The theory is that, over time, new generations' individual traits become enhanced with repeated use—

MS: Like opposable thumbs.

CD: Righto. And that they can be removed if we don't use 'em. So perhaps your great-great-great-grandkids will have one less toe. But I doubt it. More likely, they'll be playing video games with their feet, talking on the phone, and driving with their bloody noses!

MS: I thought your theory of sexual selection was quite interesting.

CD: How'd you come across that, I wonder.

MS: Let's just say I was surfing the Internet looking for something, um, less evolved, and ran into it. Anyway, I want to make sure I've got it straight: If I'm a peacock, the bigger the plumage, the better chance I've got of getting laid.

CD: Up to a point, my fair-feathered friend. Experiments show that offspring of males with more "eyes" on the tail are actually bigger at birth and have a better chance of surviving in the wild.

MS: So bigger's better.

CD: Not so fast, speedy. If a peacock's train becomes too big or too colorful over time, it might not be an advantage. In fact, a gigantic train may attract a new predator, or become too damn heavy to carry around and go all to pot. Moderation, me boy. The evolutionary wheel keeps turning, and a new cycle begins.

MS: Let's talk about the theory of creationism—

CD: Bible stories.

MS: Well, today they're calling creationism "Intelligent Design." Any thoughts on that label?

CD: I guess I'd have to say that any intelligent designer who made 99.9 percent of every organism he or she designed go extinct, couldn't be all that intelligent.

MS: You really did piss off some Bible-thumpers with your theory of evolution.

CD: I can understand that. If you want to keep telling the Adam and Eve story—creationism—it's hard to allow for evolution. We either got put on the earth by God as fully formed people, or we evolved from something a little less human.

MS: On a personal note, you found an odd way to decide whether or not to marry.

CD: Oh, the list!

MS: Go on.

CD: Well, you know, I was quite the cataloger, so I drew up a little cost-benefit analysis on the concept of marriage. Pros and cons, that sort of thing.

MS: How'd that turn out?

CD: The advantages clearly outweighed the disadvantages, and I asked Emma Wedgwood [1808–96] to marry me.

MS: She was your first cousin. Talk about evolutionary theories. . . .

CD: If that's meant to be a slight, I do not appreciate it. We had ten kids (three who died young), and several became distinguished scientists.

MS: The apple doesn't fall far from the tree, eh?

CD: That was not one of my theories.

MS: No, but one was that males are more evolutionarily advanced than females. Maybe you need to evolve a spot yourself.

CD: Blimey! Nobody's perfect.

MS: You once said that believing in evolution was "like confessing a murder."

CD: At that time I was under a lot of . . .

MS: *Guilty as charged!* Sorry. Just got excited there. Ya think your theory should be taught in schools?

CD: Do apes crap in the woods?

MS: Speaking of apes, if one accepts that humans were descended from animals, it's also true that humans are animals.

CD: Arrrgh.

MS: So, in the end, my great-great-relative's some sort of ape?

CD: That's a misconception, dear man, and the reason everyone ran around at one point looking for the missing link. It's also the reason I waited twenty years to publish my book.

MS: So, am I a monkey or not?

CD: You're not an anthropoid ape. Our relationship to chimps is through a common ancestor, not through direct descent. And we're talking about something that happened ten million years ago, so you can stop looking in that family tree you have there. . . .

MS: How did your last book, *The Formation of Vegetable Mould, Through the Action of Worms* [1881], come about?

CD: I was suffering from angina and figured I should learn about my future roommates.

MS: Ever hear of the Darwin Awards?

CD: No.

MS: You'll like this: They give an award each year to commemorate individuals who protect our gene pool by making the ultimate sacrifice of their own lives.

CD: They kill themselves? Go Caddywampas? Bugger right off?

MS: Yeah, but in an extremely idiotic manner, thereby improving our species' chance of long-term survival. Dolts who eat anthrax or jam forks into light sockets, that kinda thing.

CD: Evolution in action—trial and fatal error. I *like* it. Now put down the chainsaw, sonny.

END
of Interview

LEO DEFINED THE Renaissance man, and not in a well-rounded, metrosexual kinda way: He painted *The Last Supper*; played a wicked violin; sculpted with the best of them; was an amazing architect, geologist and engineer; and anticipated some of the greatest inventions and scientific observations of modern times. To quench this man's thirst for knowledge you'd need a Big Gulp the size of an ocean—and three straws to go along with it (talk about a "brain freeze").

Even a whiz like Leonardo needed some help getting up on two wheels, and he apprenticed with the best Florence had, Andrea del Verrocchio (1466–72). Studying with other brilliant painters including Botticelli, Perugino, and Lorenzo di Credi, young Leo absorbed the scene, learned how to mix colors, and blew his mentor and studio-mates away with his detailed drawings.

As a painter, Leo was an Italian master who invented new styles; he created brilliant transitions between colors, contrasting light and shadow, and introduced atmospheric perspective—kinda like 3-D, but without the glasses. His knowledge of anatomy gave him an upper hand when it came time to draw gestures, posture, and facial expression. His backgrounds were innovative as well, giving the landscape new hues and a depth never before seen—so good, in fact, High Renaissance artists copied the technique.

As a scientist, he was light-years ahead of his time on subjects as varied as circulation, meteorology, and geology. He began predicting the tides (it's the moon, stupid!), figured out where fossils came from, knew what it would take to fly, and understood circulation of the blood and elements of the eyeball before anyone had a clue, much less an eye chart. This guy was good.

And did I mention he painted the *Mona Lisa*? But then again, you knew that. You read *The Da Vinci Code.* . . .

MICHAEL STUSSER: Leo, you were quite the Renaissance man!

LEONARDO DA VINCI: Yes. *Veramente.* I lived during the height of the Renaissance.

MS: No, what I mean is . . . well, you wore many hats, ya know? Painter, sculptor, scientist, engineer. How'd you get into all this stuff?

LDV: My folks putta me in a, how you say, program for the apprentice.

MS: "You're fired!"

LDV: No. Notta fired. At the age of-a fifteen, I became apprentice to famous Andrea del Verrocchio. He had a work-shop, they do-a painting and-a sculpting and I learn to do a little of-a this and a little of-a that.

MS: You were a Jack-of-all-trades, but you also jumped around a lot—started one sculpture, didn't finish it. Devised brilliant architectural drawings, none of them got built. Made incredible scientific observations, then didn't finish your experiments. Did ya have attention deficit disorder?

LDV: I grow-a tired of this interview, I can-a tell you that much. You won't be able to understand, eh, but when you have a mind as fertile as-a my own, you move into-a new subject areas as you learn-a more about the world we live in, eh?

MS: We'd know a lot more about the world *you* lived in if you hadn't used that weird mirror script. [Leonardo wrote in a reverse script that could be read when held up to a mirror.] Very hard to read. . . .

LDV: *Scusi.* I'm-a left-handed and it-a came naturally. Also, it's kind of a cool trick to hold a mirror up and-a be able to read-a the notes. *Capisce?*

MS: In your later years, you were into scientific experimentation and mastered anatomy. How'd you know so much about the human body?

LDV: I dissected corpses.

MS: Ewww.

LDV: The way to-a true knowledge is to observe and then draw the world as it is. Form-a! Structure! Function! Painting is a *science!*

MS: You spilled your cappuccino, there. . . .

LDV: I was-a centuries ahead of-a my time! In-a 1495, I was a-working on a, how you say, robot—eh? Mechanical man, yes, before anyone had this clue. I am *Homo universalis*! Universal man!

MS: OK, Mr. Universe, is there anything you *couldn't* do?

LDV: Fly. I made-a some rough drawings of a helicopter ["helical airscrew," c.1487], but I never got offa the ground.

MS: Well, don't beat yourself up about it. They didn't even have a combustion engine for another four hundred years.

LDV: *Combustamente! Certo!* I have-a drawing of a this in-a notepad somewhere.

MS: You painted *The Last Supper.* [From 1495–98 Da Vinci worked on his epic wall painting.]

LDV: *Si.* All twenty-seven feet of it.

MS: So I gotta ask: *The Da Vinci Code*—true or false?

LDV: Puh-leeza.

MS: So there's no . . .

LDV: No. No secret society, no-a Tom Hanks, no-a line of-a French kings fathered by Jesus or-a Mary or-a *anybody.* Just a really long painting of your basic *Last Supper.* Maybe-a somebody looks like-a girl. Maybe I forgetta the wine cups. Speaking of which, my fettuccini's gettinga-cold. You have-a one minute.

MS: OK, tell me about the *Mona Lisa.*

LDV: I like to call it by the *nome Italiano, La Gioconda*—the name of her husband. Let's just say I took a liking to this-a bella donna.

MS: I'll say. You carried the painting with you on all your travels.

LDV: She has a nice smile. *Giocanda* is also a, how you say in the English, it-a means "jolly lady." So we play on-a the name of the husband, and-a the fact-a she's-a jolly. I just wish-a I receive a nickel every time some idiota put her on a coffee mug or a mouse-a-pad.

MS: But people want to know the story behind the smile. Does she know something we don't?

LDV: *Certamente.* She-a knows you're-a supposed to smile for the camera, eh? It's a obvious. And she's gotta gigante cheekbones-a.

MS: Some scientists recently did a study on emotion-recognition software and the results showed her 83 percent happy, 9 percent disgusted, 6 percent fearful, and 2 percent confused.

LDV: And-a that makes me 100 percent-a pissed off. It's-a *ridiculoso.* She's a smiling for her pictura.

MS: People think of you as a painter, but you were an amazing inventor. You even came up with swim fins.

LDV: That's not all: I single-handedly originated the science of hydraulics, devised a way to putta rivers in canals, created my own-a paint, built a *vrroom* with a bomb-a—

MS: Tank?

DLV: Yes, *e vero*! And I also invented the underwater diving-a suit, cranes, and-a contact lenses. It's a all in my notebooks.

MS: Speaking of which, did you know [Microsoft founder] Bill Gates bought one of your sketchpads [*The Codex Leicester*, a notebook of scientific observations] for like $30 million?

LDV: *Molto bene!* I'm-a going to need-a that to build my newest creation: a phone, yes, that takes pictures, is-a compass, gets-a movies, and-a does not even need to be plugged into a wall. Incredible, eh? Of this you are amazed!

MS: We need to talk. . . .

EMILY DICKINSON MAY be one of America's best-known poets, but she barely published a word in her own lifetime. And though she spent her days hiding away in her family's home in Amherst, Massachusetts, somehow Em had an exciting enough life to be the subject of endless biographies and speculation about her sex life.

The Dickinsons were a prominent religious family, very involved in the educational community (her grandfather was a founder of Amherst College). Emily studied at the Amherst Academy, and, at seventeen, attended Mary Lyon's Mount Holyoke Female Seminary, a strict, evangelical school that didn't sit well with the open-minded waif. Due to bad health and a worse vibe, Emily split after less than a year.

Her innovative poetry broke the rules of grammar and was probably the first modern verse ever crafted. Using imperfect rhymes, daring concepts, and changing the meter on a whim, Dickinson may have simply been over most editors' heads to get a fair shot at publication.

The bulk of Dickinson's 1,700 some-odd poems were kept in the bottom drawer of her dresser, and only seven were published during her life (all, perhaps, against her wishes). Lucky for the rest of us, Emily's sister found a way to get the masterpieces to print, and time told the tale; by the twentieth century, Dickinson took her place as one of the country's greatest poets.

Dickinson's poetry originally became popular in the 1890s, but was heavily edited to fit a more traditional style. (Emily had a weird way of laying out her poems: all dashes, weird caps, and thought rhymes.) Republished in 1955 the way she would have wanted, *The Poems of Emily Dickinson* fit right into the time—modern, bold, and setting the standard for where poetry can go.

MICHAEL STUSSER: Where'd you get your love of language?

EMILY DICKINSON: My father used to read the Bible to us like it was theater, and I loved the rhythms of the passages. We also read [Ralph Waldo] Emerson's poems, Shakespeare, Keats, and the Brontë sisters.

MS: Your dad has been described as basically a hard-ass. Is that how you remember him?

ED: Oh, not in the least. Let's remember the time: Nineteenth-century fathers were, by definition, a bit removed. Less than affectionate, you might say. But mine was respectful, and most important, he valued education for his children. I remember Daddy buying me all sorts of books, then begging me not to read them lest they joggle the mind!

MS: You Dickinsons didn't stray far from home, did ya?

ED: Why would we?

MS: I don't know. Branch out. See the world?

ED: I went away to school.

MS: Ten *miles* away!

MS: Amherst is a perfectly lovely community. Austin [her older brother] moved next door, and my sis, Lavinia, lived with me and the folks. I saw no real reason to venture out too far. . . .

MS: Tell us a bit about your friendship with Abiah Palmer Root.

ED: She's a dear. We were good friends until she got all religious on me, and then we grew apart.

MS: Because you wouldn't publicly convert?

ED: In the end, I had to let her know that, while I was religious, I wasn't convinced hers was the only way. "Saved" is overrated.

MS: How so?

ED: I simply refused to think badly of the world, or believe that greater pleasures can be found in heaven than on earth. It's why I came back to visit. . . .

MS: Resisting conversion, refusing to change your writing style, questioning the traditional roles of the sexes. Feminists love your feisty independence.

ED: And I theirs.

MS: How'd you get into writing?

ED: Well, it began with letters, starting around the age of twelve. I loved to play with words, and I'd do it almost in secret to whomever I was writing. Got away with a lot more that way.

MS: People have the impression you were a freakish recluse, hiding behind curtains in the attic of your house in a white dress, afraid of the outside world.

ED: I've read a lot of those descriptions and they make me out to be an agoraphobic ascetic. I was definitely the stay-at-home type, but I had lots of friends, and kept in touch with all sorts of folks. I wrote over a thousand letters, you know?

MS: Come on, now—for your last twenty years you never left the house! You even sent your sister to be fitted for your dresses.

ED: I had all I needed at home: family, a warm fire, books, peace and quiet, and my poetry. We had fourteen acres.

MS: You often "visited" with friends by talking to them through a closed door.

ED: I wasn't fully dressed.

MS: What did you do all day?

ED: Vinny [*Lavinia*] and I did household chores and took care of poor, quiet mother.

MS: How thrilling.

ED: And I could bake with the best of them! I won second prize in the 1856 Cattle Show for my rye and Indian bread.

MS: Dressing all in white was a weird choice.

ED: They called me "the nun of Amherst."

MS: Did you think you were a nun?

ED: I was hardly a Catholic, or even a confessed Christian.

MS: Some suggest you saw yourself as a secret bride to the already married minister Charles Wadsworth.

ED: In case you aren't aware, dear, brides didn't even *wear* white in those years.

MS: A madwoman? A maid? A ghost? *What?*

ED: How about you stop guessing now. It was simply one of my favorite colors. If you must know, it looked quite fetching with my fair complexion and chestnut hair.

[She blushes.]

ED: I also liked to be in control of my visiting guests. I let you in, didn't I?

MS: I've been trying to set this meeting up for over 150 years.

ED: And here we are, my sweet man. Should we sit in the garden?

[We move to the greenhouse, which is dark and covered by shades.]

MS: In the 1850s, you began to have problems with your eyes.

ED: Anterior uveitis, I think they called it. It's intolerance to direct sunlight—made it so I had to garden at night, by lantern light. Thought I might even go blind, and so I dispatched over three hundred poems in a single year.

MS: Why not publish your poems when you were alive?

ED: At one point I talked to a family friend, Thomas Wentworth Higginson, about publishing. I showed him a few poems, and when he tried to "improve them"—for a more romantic style, I suppose—it really took the wind out of my sails.

MS: Delicate little flower, aren't you?

ED: Why, yes, I'm delicate, but more important, experimental and a bit defiant. Thomas said that my gait was "spasmodic," and he's not wrong. My poems were handwritten, and there was no good way to put my phrasing and meter down on the page without my own set of dashes and such.

MS: So you never wanted them published?

ED:

> *Publication is the Auction*
> *Of the Mind of Man*
> *Poverty be justifying*
> *For so foul a thing.*

Let's just say that I wrote for myself and for a few friends—and Thomas was one of them. I always said his friendship and feedback saved my life.

MS: You're not going to like what he did to your poems after you took the big dirt nap.

ED: Let me guess: straightened out the punctuation, took out the half rhymes, and changed my odd capitalization.

MS: Yeah, that, and gave them titles, and even reworded a few so they'd make "more sense." You were damn popular, though—they got great reviews and were printed in dozens of editions.

ED: That's all well and nice, I suppose. I'm not quite as pleased with the brutal edits done by my brother's mistress [Mabel L. Todd]— removing my signature from letters, erasing my sexy stanzas, and even changing pronouns to avoid any mention of love between my sister-in-law and me. Jealous worm—that's a no-no in my book!

MS: Which brings us to the big question, if you don't mind. Folks want to know, are you a lesbian?

ED: I think the best place for you to look for the answer to that question is clearly in my poems.

MS: Any in particular I should reread?

ED: The Master letters would be a fine place to begin.

MS: If I'm not mistaken, those are love letters to a guy you call "Master."

ED: Uh-huh.

MS: So you're not gay.

ED: Gay, bisexual, autoerotic, intimate, romantic friendships—the words only confuse the truth of the matter, and perhaps it's best left that way, my inquisitive visitor.

MS: I'm kinda looking for a more definitive answer here, Em.

ED: I'd suggest you read my poems for the passion and read my unedited letters to Susan [Gilbert] to compare and contrast.

MS: Susan was a "friend" of yours since you were kids.

ED: There are four decades of love notes to look over.

MS: I thought those were burned by your family after your death.

ED: No, Susan's *replies* got burned, but my original letters survived and are quite telling, not to mention articulate. You'll love my penwomanship. Hee!

MS: Well, here's one from April 1852:

> *Sweet Hour, blessed Hour, to carry me to you, and to bring you*
> *back to me, long enough to snatch one kiss, and whisper*
> *Good bye, again.*

ED: Lovely.

MS: But didn't she marry your brother Austin?

ED: Indeed, and it broke my heart. But if I couldn't have her, I suppose it's best to keep her in the family.

[More blushing. Then a knock on the door.]

ED: I am sorry, but I must run, dear. I have a "friend" coming over for tea. Good day—and let's do this again, shall we?

END
of Interview

ISADORA DUNCAN CAME out of the womb running, skipping, and prancing with a modern twist all her own. Born in the bohemian days of San Francisco, Duncan was raised by her mother, a music teacher with little money but a great imagination. Disinterested in the rigidity of classic ballet or "fancy dance," Isadora began dancing and teaching in her own way—and became known for innovative, natural, and simple movement.

After struggling to make it as a dancer in the States, Duncan and her family went abroad in 1899 to seek more avant-garde crowds. Soon she was skipping all over the planet, performing her groundbreaking, athletic dance and leaving ballet in a trail of fairy dust. In addition to performing and teaching choreography, Izzie founded academies in Berlin, Salzburg, and Vienna, with hoards of groupies called Isadorables following her every move.

In Europe she gained fame at a level not seen for a dancer; artists and authors were inspired by her vision, creating sculptures, poetry, and paintings in her likeness. Dancing to composers such as Schubert, Brahms, and Tchaikovsky, Duncan became the mother of modern or expressive dance, interpreting symphonic music on stages the world over.

She married Sergei Aleksandrovich Yesenin, a spry Russian poet, in 1922, and started schools in the newly formed Soviet Union. Returning for a tour in the United States, Duncan was labeled a Bolshevik and assailed by the press. Furious that she could no longer speak her mind in her own country, she left America for good on February 3, 1923.

Going out with a flourish, Duncan choked to death at age fifty, when her trademark scarf became tangled in the spokes of her rented sportscar while motoring in France.

Love her or leave her, Duncan put dance on a level with other arts, and developed a philosophy that moved bodies, feminism, and the debate forward.

MICHAEL STUSSER: Do a little jig for us, won't you Izzy?

[She takes her shirt and shoes off and runs effortlessly across the room.]

ISADORA DUNCAN: And a-one, and a-two, and a one-two, one-two!

MS: You basically just walked quickly across the floor, there, with your arms flailing.

ID: Gorgeous, wasn't it? The breath work. The power from the solar plexus. The haunted gestures.

MS: But, I mean, I can put one foot in front of the other. That's not dancing.

ID: Isn't it? Who's to say? I strode in rhythm, I was gentle and yet primal, and completely conscious of my actions. Dance, little man!

MS: But what does it *mean?*

ID: If I could tell you what it meant, there would be no point in dancing it.

MS: When did you first begin to dance?

ID: In my mother's womb. Seriously, she couldn't hold down anything but iced oysters and Champagne—the food of Aphrodite—and it made me dance.

MS: Your style is quite, shall we say, different. How did your early performances go over with audiences?

ID: Not so well. I don't think the people of Chicago and New York were ready for me or my see-through costumes, and let's just say I failed to impress. So my family and I took the show on the road, so to speak—a boat, actually—and went abroad.

MS: Anybody like you over there?

ID: Goodness, yes! I was a smash in London with the ladies. They were fascinated by my unconventional style and unbound movement! Barefoot and fancy-free!

MS: Scantily clad, too. I like that part.

ID: Yes, I suppose you would. I'm sure you enjoy my emphasis on the pelvis, as well.

MS: Oh, sure.

ID: I think Europe was simply tired of ballet, and looking for something new, and I fit the bill.

MS: What was the problem with ballet?

ID: All the toe dancing and corsets! So unnatural and affected, you know, it deforms the beautiful woman's body. Social gymnastics for snobs isn't what dancing's about—it's unrestrained expression. Not just upright dancing, either, but horizontal. Leap and roll and crawl if you wish, but DANCE!

[She prances over to the hotel bar and pours herself a stiff drink.]

MS: No offense, but you got around.

ID: None taken. I believe in love, and life, and romance.

MS: With both sexes, I might add. Didn't you date the poet Mercedes de Acosta?

ID: As did Greta Garbo, Marlene Dietrich, and about half of Hollywood's leading ladies.

MS: You had a few kids with a few fellas.

ID: Deirdre, my first child, was with Gordon Craig, the famous stage designer. Lovely, brilliant man.

MS: Marry him?

ID: Goodness no. Topsy and I both abhorred the concept.

MS: You had another child with Paris Singer [1910]. Is he from the sewing-machine family?

ID: One and the same—the twenty-second child of Isaac Singer. Paris actually owned Madison Square Garden in New York at one point and was going to turn it into an art pavilion for me. But of course, we had our tragedy.

MS: Yeah, I'm sorry about that. [Duncan's two children and their nurse drowned in Paris in 1913, when their car rolled into the Seine.] Is it true you had a vision about the accident?

ID: The night I found out, I was dancing to Chopin's *Funeral March*. It was like being in a weird trance, and I knew something horrible would happen.

MS: Maybe a happier subject: Your school in Moscow.

ID: I always loved Russia, and in 1921 she was brand new. The communal school seemed right up my alley—revolutionary and activist—and students could attend for free. And of course, I met Sergei there.

MS: Poet and madman Sergei Aleksandrovich Yesenin. *This* guy you married.

ID: It was the only way I could bring him back to the States.

MS: Your timing kinda sucked, with the Red Scare and all.

ID: Tell me about it: The press called us Bolshevik agents! A traitor! I'm a dancer, for gosh sake!

MS: Then you probably should have stuck to dancing, and skipped all the curtain speeches.

ID: My point was simply that America was created from a revolution—why not support more of them, especially if they were more democratic than before?

MS: You wore red costumes, and screamed "This is red, so am I!" Even your hair was dyed red.

ID: The color of passion! Of life!

MS: After the tour, you swore you'd never return.

ID: And I didn't. Of course, things didn't exactly work out for Sergei and I.

MS: Well, poor guy was a drunken nutcase. He trashed more hotel rooms than Ozzy Osborne.

ID: Yes, it made it difficult to get upgrades. He also didn't speak English, and I didn't speak Russian—the whole thing was a mess. [Yesenin went back to the USSR alone; in 1925 he slit his wrists, writing a suicide poem in his own blood.]

MS: I don't mind the communism so much as the racism. You called jazz dancing "the sensual convulsion of the Negro"; polluted, performed by African savages, and unclean.

ID: Too many spasms and angles in their dance. Where's the grace and curve of the fox-trot and the grizzly bear?

MS: Your basic point was that American modern dance is white. So much for democracy, huh?

ID: What I was trying to do was elevate dance from low to high, from sexual to spiritual, from woman to Goddess.

MS: From black to white.

ID: And from profane to sacred. Dancing in my time was considered sacrilegious, and I simply wanted to contrast it with that of African primitives.

MS: And again, I want to point out you're not only an elitist but a racist.

ID: Listen, sweets. I'd been basically exiled from my own country since 1922. It may not seem PC today—but my attempt was to put the authority of modern dance in the camp of upper-class civilization. Perchance this way I'd get more work.

MS: George Balanchine saw you perform and said it was awful to watch "a drunken, fat woman who for hours was rolling around like a pig."

ID: May I have another drinkie, please?

[She quickly sucks down another gin and tonic.]

ID: I was older. [*Slurp.*] It was a later stage, and I'd let myself go a spot, 'kay?

MS: Still, plenty of people obviously thought you were brilliant. You were sketched by Auguste Rodin and Jean Cocteau, and Edward Steichen took amazing photos of you.

ID: I am what I am. One more, please. MAKE IT A DOUBLE!

MS: Is it true you once wrote to George Bernard Shaw and said you should have a child together?

ID: I told him that with my body and his brains, we'd have a wonder baby! You know his response? "Yes," he said, "but what if it had my body and your brains!"

MS: Kind of odd, the way you died, ma'am, strangled when your shawl got tangled in the wheel of your convertible.

ID: I'll say. But I was always about eccentric costumes and Greek tragedies, so perhaps it was par for the course. Life's an odd dance, eh?

MS: I thought you were going to say it's a walk in the park.

ID: I *wish* I'd walked that day. Care to dance?

END
of Interview

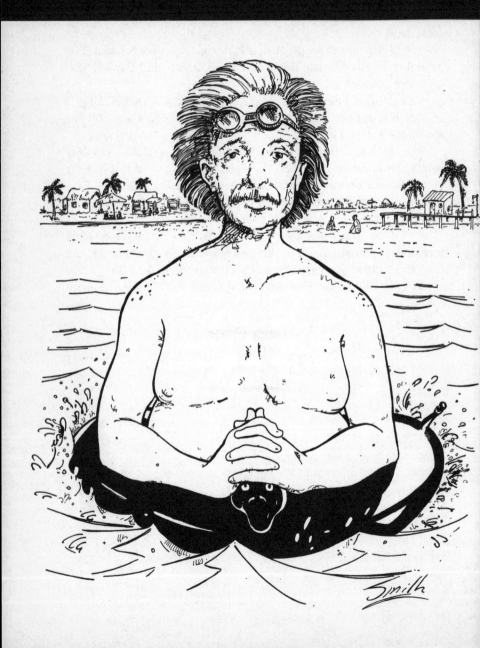

IN ADDITION TO being the poster child for frumpy genius, German American physicist Albert Einstein developed several theories that changed the way we think about space, time, and gravitation. He was also absentminded (where are those damn keys!) and had the all-important shaggy, mad-professor hair.

Brilliant from the get-go, Einstein got the Nobel Prize in 1921 — not for his theory of relativity, but for his work proving the existence of photons (particles of light). In addition to showing us how space is curved and that the universe is (*hello!*) expanding, Al-Baby pioneered quantum mechanics, proved the existence of molecules, and pointed out flaws in Newtonian assumptions about gravity.

His theories led to discoveries of things we now take for granted, including DNA, black holes, vacuum tubes, X-rays, nuclear power, and, yes, TV.

Beyond the brain (and fame—who thought scientists could be cool?), Einstein was a sweet, caring citizen of the world. An outspoken critic of German militarism, he renounced his German citizenship soon after Hitler became chancellor and left for America in 1932. In 1939, he wrote FDR, warning him about the possibility that the Nazis might develop the atomic bomb. (Years later he'd call the letter "the greatest mistake of my life.") Though his name was associated with the creation of the atom bomb, Albert joined scientists in seeking ways to prevent its use and advocated world disarmament.

On the romantic front, Einstein had two failed marriages and more flings than Mick Jagger. His first marriage [1903], to an outstanding physicist, Mileva Maric, lasted sixteen years and produced three children. His second marriage was to his cousin Elsa. Einstein moved with her to Princeton in 1933, where he lived and taught for his remaining years.

Einstein died in New Jersey at age seventy-six. Contrary to rumors, his brain was not frozen or implanted into a wunderkind but preserved by Dr. Thomas Harvey, a Princeton pathologist, who doled slices out to various institutes for further study.

MICHAEL STUSSER: So everyone thinks you're the smartest guy ever. Were you?

ALBERT EINSTEIN: No, I sink not. I actually got lousy grades in zee school.

MS: Get outta here.

AE: Really. Vas boring unt intimidating. I even failed zee entrance exam to study as unt electrical engineer. Der frickin' liberal arts section of zee test threw me for un loop! [In 1895 Einstein failed a test that would have allowed him to study for a diploma at the ETH in Zurich.]

MS: Some people say you may have actually had a learning disability.

AE: Yah, I haff a disability to learn vat *zey* vant to teach me. My problem vas zat I clashed at times vith my professors—unt vas usually correct in my argument, I might add. Zen I began to skip classes to study vat *I* vanted. School vas a bit of, how you say, bust.

MS: Don't let school get in the way of your education, huh?

AE: Zer vas vunce un fifteen-year-old girl who wrote me about how hard her homework vas. I tell her, "Do not vorry about your difficulties in mathematics; I can assure you zat mine are much greater."

MS: All the photographs show you in old moth-eaten sweaters and baggy pants. Why not wear some swank clothes now and then?

AE: Vat is zis swank? I minimize my vardrobe so zat I do not haff to vaste time in zee mornink deciding vat to vear. I get up, put on my two items, and am off to verk. Socks are not necessary. Very important matters must be attended to, yah.

MS: Is it true you were once offered the presidency of Israel?

AE: Tis true, yah, but I turn zis down.

MS: Lousy people skills?

AE: A little of zis, yah, and zee fact zat politics is for zee moment, while un equation ees for eternity.

MS: Speaking of equations, $E = mc^2$. Can you explain that in a nutshell?

AE: It followed from zee special theory of relativity zat mass and energy are both but different manifestations of zee same thing—a somevat unfamiliar conception for zee average mind. Furzzermore, zee equation E is equal to mc squared, in vich energy is put equal to mass, multiplied by the square of zee velocity of light, showed zat very small amounts of mass may be converted into a very large amount of energy unt vice versa. Zee mass and energy vere in fact equivalent, according to zee formula mentioned before.

MS: I said do it *simply.*

AE: Take un physics class, mine frund. Vat I am sayink is zat mass and energy are aspects of zee same thing. Interchangeable, ya?

MS: Nah.

AE: Zey are zee same, yes? Vun can be converted into zee other, unt most objects haff both mass unt energy. Does zis help?

MS: I still don't get it.

AE: It's OK, you see. Many scientists thought zat I vas nuts and just vaited for me to be found out. No amount of experimentation can ever prove me *right,* a single experiment can prove me *wrong.*

MS: I guess my question is, what's it tell me, man? What's it all about?

AE: It's aboot how zee sun vurks! Pure energy is moving at zee speed of light. Understand?

MS: No. But I'm a slow learner. You wrote four articles that basically defined modern physics, and did it in your spare time over the course of one year [1905]. How the hell did you do that?

AE: Quadruple espressos. Yah. Very motivating. Unt I had a year of vunder—a miracle year. It all just poured out of my brain unt I saw zee light. I haff no special talent. I am only passionately curious.

MS: The special theory of relativity. Why so special?

AE: To keep it separate from zee general theory of relativity, you see.

MS: Again, no.

AE: Time unt space are not fixed. As vee speed up, space contracts.

MS: Whoa.

AE: Space unt time are linked, you see. Eef you change vun, zee other changes.

MS: Example, please.

AE: Yah, OK. I am driving my Volkswagen Bug at one hundred miles per hour.

MS: Slow down!

AE: OK, I am drivink at seventy-five miles per hour, and you are driving next to me, also at zis speed. Looking at each other, it seems vee are not moving, yes?

MS: Right.

AE: But vee *are* speeding! It is about perspective! It is relative! Zis relates to zee speed of light, vich does nut change no matter how fast you approach it. Slow down, speed up, zee speed of light is zee same. Zee notion of absolute concepts of time and distance are no longer! Zey are rejected!

MS: Um.

AE: OK. Put your hand on un hot stove for vun minute and it seems like an hour. Now, sit vith a pretty girl for zis same hour and it seems like vun minute. That's relativity!

MS: You'll be glad to know that after you died, some scientists proved your theory that the faster one moves, the slower time passes.

AE: Zis is true?

MS: Yah. In 1971, scientists took an atomic clock around the world in a plane, and, after comparing it to clocks on earth, found it had lost time.

AE: *Alvetizein!*

MS: Gesundheit! But we have one problem, here, genius: It seems like your two main discoveries—relativity and quantum theory—contradict each other. What say you?

AE: Yes. Both cannot be true, and yet both are remarkably accurate.

MS: So, how do you reconcile these?

AE: It makes me uncomfortable. As I said: "God does not play dice," and I spent zee last years of my life vurking on zis ultimate qvestion. It is not easy to unify gravity and electromagnetism.

MS: I'll say.

AE: I can only say zis: No one has a better solution—at least I had a theory, hmm?

MS: That's for sure. Hanging with you is like being with a walking encyclopedia.

AE: Not encyclopedia but artist! I am enough of an artist to draw freely upon my imagination. Imagination is more important zan knowledge. Knowledge is limited. Imagination encircles the vurld.

MS: People know you were a brainiac, but you had a softer side, too.

AE: Yah, zis is true. Social justice and social responsibility, zees are as umportant as any theory of relativity, no?

MS: No?

AE: Yes! Durink my life I denounced McCarthyism and asked for end to bigotry unt racism. I believe in pacifism, liberalism, and Zionism.

MS: And yet your own energy-mass equation—that particle matter can be converted into a huge quantity of energy—led to the creation of the atomic and hydrogen bomb.

AE: Yah, but vith zis I did not help or anticipate. I vas simply tryink to discover zee composition of zee atom—how zee universe verks! Not how to destroy it!

MS: Maybe someone with your smarts could have anticipated the bomb stuff.

AE: I am not all-knowing. I know not vith what weapons World War III vill be fought, but World War IV vill be fought vith sticks unt stones.

MS: Maybe you can find a way to do some reverse time travel, come back and prevent all that.

AE: Eef I came back, my next invention vould be zee perfect headache medicine. Vith all zee varmongering in zee vurld, vee need peace unt quiet now. Yah?

MS: Yah. You know they sliced your brain up and it's probably been studied more than your theories.

AE: I specifically told zem zat I vas to be cremated!

MS: No one listened. This doctor, Thomas Harvey, took it out and kept it in his basement for forty years. Turns out your brain was actually kinda small.

AE: It's not zee size zat matters. It's how you use it, yah?

MS: Yah. You did have a big-ass inferior parietal lobe, though [the center of mathematical thought and spatial imagery].

AE: Vatevah. Now you must tell me somezing: Vat great invention or theory has changed zee vurld since my passink? Vat is zee next great notion? Vat has captured zee world's attention? Invisibility? Cure of all cancer? A machine zat immobilizes nuclear devices? I must know!

MS: Uh, we're cloning sheep. And there's the George Foreman Champ Grill—way less fat! So we got that goin' for us.

AE: Oy. I vill a little think now. Must get to cracking!

END
of Interview

BENJAMIN FRANKLIN

BORN JANUARY 17, 1706
DIED APRIL 17, 1790

FOUNDING FATHER, SUPERINVENTOR, scientist extraordinaire, philosopher, printer, diplomat, and author, Benjamin Franklin had more roles than Tom Hanks and Morgan Freeman combined.

Born in Boston, Big Ben was the fifteenth of his father's seventeen children. Ben quit school at age ten and then apprenticed at his brother's print shop before setting out on his own. In 1729 he bought the *Pennsylvania Gazette* and turned it into the most popular rag in the colonies.

Franklin proved to be the greatest writer of the eighteenth century, espousing common sense and hard work with a healthy dose of humor. In addition to writing one of the first-ever autobiographies, he wrote political essays (many urging fair treatment toward the Native Americans) and *Poor Richard's Almanack* [1732–57]. Full of weather forecasts, jokes, and proverbs, his almanacks were almost as popular as the number one seller at the time, the Bible.

Ben lived in England on and off for eighteen years, mediating conflicts on behalf of the thirteen colonies, before hitting France to gain support for the Revolutionary War. He spent nine years in Paris, chowing croissants, flirting with the ladies, and getting crucial aid to back our bid for independence. Of course, Doc Franklin helped craft both the Declaration of Independence and the Constitution, and his elder-statesman seasoning came in handy when tempers flared and calmer heads had to prevail.

For a man with so many titles he was, above all, a public servant. As French philosopher Turgot put it, "He seized lightning from the skies and the scepter from tyrants."

MICHAEL STUSSER: Poet, scientist, philosopher, inventor—you must have gone to Harvard or something.

BENJAMIN FRANKLIN: Two years of grammar school, the rest was learning on the job.

MS: Get out!

BF: I just got here.

MS: No, it's a phrase that—

BF: Know what it is, young man. In fact, I coined a few phrases in my time: "The worst wheel of a cart makes the most noise." Heard that one?

MS: Not exactly.

BF: How 'bout: "Fish and visitors stink after three days." That's mine. So's: "An ounce of prevention is worth a pound of cure."

MS: Somehow, you *prevented* yourself from getting electrocuted: June 15, 1752, the story goes, you ran around with a key on a kite in an electrical storm—that's nuts!

BF: How else are you going to demonstrate that lightning is electrical? And to be honest, I got the charge from a storm cloud—not full-on lighting. I'm no idiot.

MS: What other inventions did you tinker with?

BF: Well the kite trick led to the lightning rod, which was a good one, but I also came up with an odometer.

MS: But there weren't any cars.

BF: Yeah, we strapped 'em to wagon wheels to clock a horse's road time. That was a big seller. [*He rolls his eyes.*] 'Course there's also the Franklin stove. That kept the little ones from falling on their faces into the fire, so I got a lot of good pub there. And as a kid I invented some flippers.

MS: For swimming?

BF: No, for horseback riding. Of course for swimming! I was a helluva athlete in my day and would do laps in Boston Harbor. I swam the river Thames when I was across the pond—freaked the Londoners out.

MS: The rocking chair and the library step stool were your ideas too, right?

BF: As well as the extension arm and three-wheel clock.

MS: And let's not forget the armonica.

BF: Don't mention it.

MS: It was some sort of glass musical instrument, wasn't it?

BF: Seriously, please don't mention it. Both Mozart and Beethoven composed music for the thing, so you'd think it would have caught on.

MS: And finally, bifocals were your invention.

BF: I was eighty-three years old and could see the peas on my plate, but not the gal seated across from me! So I had a glass-cutter slice my two pairs of glasses in half and clamp 'em together. Problem solved.

MS: "A person's highest duty in life is to serve others." True?

BF: Yep. And God and man are best served by good works. It's the reason I did so much civic improvement and philanthropy in Philly.

MS: You started the first public library there [1731].

BF: At the time, books were quite expensive. Got to read to succeed.

MS: Didn't you also develop the first colonial post office?

BF: And the hospital, insurance agency, and police force . . .

MS: Wow!

BF: As well as the first volunteer fire department.

MS: Did you know you're on the hundred dollar bill?

BF: I am?

MS: Oh, yeah. Franklins are a sign of bling, man.

BF: OK. Bling. Sure.

MS: But Ben Franklin was also Richard Saunders.

BF: Richard Saunders was the pseudonym I used for the *Poor Richard's Almanack*. I'm happy to admit I was also Mrs. Silence Dogwood, the advice columnist in my brother's paper. Never wore a dress though.

MS: Indeed, you were quite the wordsmith. In fact, you wrote a list of 228 slang terms for drunkenness. What were your favorites?

BF: Let's see—*cherry-merry, soaked, biggy*, and my numero uno had to be *nimptopsical*. Beer is proof that God loves us and wants us to be happy.

MS: Your own print shop made a bunch of money.

BF: We were more than a printer—sort of like a modern-day Wal-Mart. Sold food, books and candles, nails, and we even had a post office.

MS: You were married for forty-four years. What's the key?

BF: Living on separate sides of the Atlantic. *Ha!* No, Deborah and I made each other happy. Even when we were apart for years at a time, we kept in close touch—she'd send home-cured bacon to London and I'd mail her silk and pottery.

MS: No offense sir, but you didn't see her for the last nine years of her life.

BF: Well she was afraid to sail, and I didn't get around to coming home. I do feel badly about that.

MS: You're also known to have had a good number of affairs.

BF: "Where there's Marriage without Love, there will be Love without Marriage." Mostly amorous friendships, if truth be told.

MS: Still seems funny that this old, bald, chubby guy got tons of young girls to flirt with him.

BF: It's about using your noggin! My best line was, "If you ladies have any questions, the answer is 'yes.' "

MS: You said, "Early to bed and early to rise, makes a man healthy, wealthy, and wise."

BF: I also said, "There are more old drunkards than old doctors."

MS: At one point you were a vegetarian.

BF: Didn't take, but I stuck to dieting. Moderation's the key in food, drink, and women.

MS: You sound like Dr. Phil. Is it true you were into nudism?

BF: Ah, air baths in the buff! I made a habit of writing in the nude each morning for an hour or so—not so much to be buck naked, but for the cold air, which has excellent therapeutic properties. Same reason I slept with the window open. In fact, think I might shed a few of these—

MS: Please don't, sir. Now, is it true your initial instinct in regard to independence was to make sure you didn't piss off King George?

BF: I wanted to placate the British, but also establish colonial representation in their Parliament.

MS: Plus, you offered to pay for all the tea we dumped in Boston Harbor.

BF: No reason to go to war over tea. "Safety first," I always said.

MS: You lived in London for almost twenty years. Ever think of staying?

BF: Oh, yeah. For the crumpets and dentistry alone. I was at King George III's coronation and really thought we could do well as part of the British Empire.

MS: What changed?

BF: A couple things: First, the Brits were thinking of wringing my neck after I printed letters by the royal governor of Massachusetts that showed how he was screwing over the colonies. And second, a war broke out.

MS: Your own son was on the wrong side.

BF: Illegitimate son, but yes, William had his own strong mind. I also think he wanted to keep his job, which was pretty cush [royal governor of New Jersey], in case the Yankees lost.

MS: You guys ever kiss and make up?

BF: I disinherited the bastard. Does that count?

MS: Moving on . . . the French loved you. Why?

BF: I think I was like Levi's jeans or a Nike commercial at the time. People all over the world wanted what they thought America was about—unsophisticated ruggedness. The last frontier, you know? And, funny as it may seem, they saw me as a patriot ready to go to war for liberty.

MS: Your bald mug was on posters and snuffboxes and busts. I'm surprised they didn't make a Bobble-Head out of you!

BF: They made a Ben doll! I told my daughter that my face was as well-known as that of the moon. Amazing, really.

MS: What was it like to sign the Declaration of Independence?

BF: It was incredible and nerve-wracking. I remember saying, "We must all hang together or we shall all hang separately."

MS: Did you really want the turkey to be the symbol of the United States of America?

BF: What I wrote—to my daughter, mind you—was that the eagle is a bird of bad moral character. He's a bit of a vulture and doesn't get his living honestly.

MS: Still. A turkey?

BF: Hey now, don't knock the turkey. Though a spot vain and silly, he's got courage enough to attack the British guards who would invade his farmyard with red coats on.

MS: By the time you went to the Constitutional Convention, you were eighty-one years old.

BF: Say what, sonny?

MS: I say, "BY THE TIME—"

BF: I heard you the first time. Too bad the youngsters didn't listen to any of my ideas—and I had plenty!

MS: Such as?

BF: I didn't think you should have to own land to vote, that's for sure. I also didn't like the idea of paying government officials salaries: they should be elderly gents, maybe retirees, with no other agenda than helping the citizens, ya know?

MS: That's a bit unrealistic.

BF: And the president should be a one-termer! Serve your four years and get out!

MS: This I can get behind.

BF: In fact, *forget* one guy—there should be an executive council that does the top job. And if there *was* gonna be a president, he shouldn't be able to veto bills passed by a legislature or appoint judges. Gotta be a better way.

MS: Nevertheless, you wrote a statement at the end of the convention that everyone rallied around.

BF: What I did was let them know democracy's not pretty. I said my piece about not having my ideas listened to—*not a single one of 'em!*—and let folks know I understand free men are bound to disagree. Compromise is necessary, and so is acceptance. The will of the majority may not be perfect, but in this case it would have to do.

MS: Only Founding Father to have signed the Declaration, the Treaty of Paris, and the Constitution.

BF: And the oldest.

MS: One of the last things you worked on was the abolition of slavery in Pennsylvania.

BF: We signed that to law, and were well ahead of the time.

MS: Speaking of being ahead of the curve, you wrote your own epitaph.

BF: Ha! Yeah, I was deadly sick when I was twenty, and thought I was going to need it.

MS: May I read it?

> The body of B. Franklin, Printer
> (Like the Cover of an Old Book
> Its Contents torn Out
> And Stript of its Lettering and Gilding)
> Lies Here, Food for Worms.
> But the Work shall not be Lost;
> For it will (as he Believ'd) Appear once More
> In a New and More Elegant Edition
> Revised and Corrected
> By the Author.

BF: Sounds about right.

MS: Thought you'd like to know that it's now a tradition to toss a penny on your grave at the Christ Church Burial Ground.

BF: Didn't anyone hear me when I said, "A penny saved is a penny earned?"

MS: Yeah, but we've got credit cards now. Pennies are kind of a joke.

BF: They add up, son. That's the whole point.

MS: Is there a final quote you'd most like to be remembered by?

BF: I'll give ya two: "Nothing is inevitable but death and taxes," and "The Constitution only gives people the right to pursue happiness. You have to catch it yourself."

END
of Interview

SIGMUND FREUD

BORN MAY 6, 1856
DIED SEPTEMBER 23, 1939

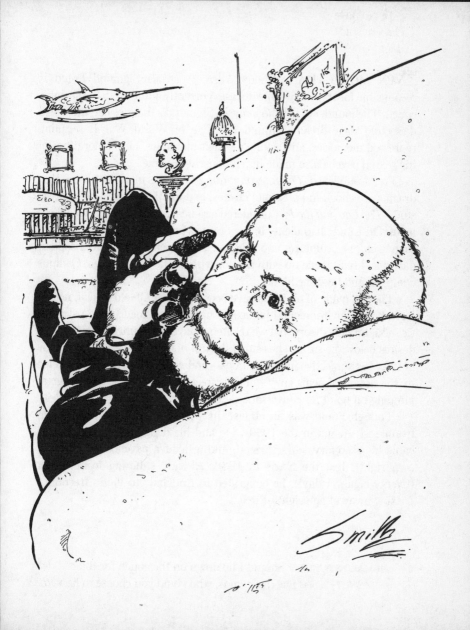

Ｅ̲VEN MORE THAN Woody Allen, Austria's Sigmund Freud is responsible for the neurotic head cases currently addicted to the shrink's couch. The founder of psychoanalysis, Sigmund's theories had the world dissecting their dreams around the time of World War I, recalling repressed memories, and asking for their mommies. His explorations of the sexual psyche also made him a household name.

Freud published *The Interpretation of Dreams* in 1900, posing that dreams are chock-full of sexual desires, and in 1923 he wrote his classic study *The Ego and the Id*. Considered a radical by the scientific establishment, Dr. Libido had plenty to say on everything from homosexuality to sexual mores, sculpture, and religion. Part scientist, part philosopher, part doc, Freud came up with the concepts of the id, superego, Oedipus complex, and big-time libido.

Though many of his ideas have been tossed or altered (social, neurological, and environmental influences have been added to the psychiatric mix), Freud's theory that we're often motivated by unconscious sexual desires below the surface has stood the test of time. Modern shrinks may not like his subjective interpretations—and women surely aren't thrilled by the notion of penis envy—but his free-association method is a great jumping-off point for conversational therapy.

Though Freud was an atheist, he was born a Jew, which meant trouble in Vienna in the 1930s. He and his daughter Anna (who became his secretary, nurse, friend, and a helluva psychoanalyst in her own right), fled the Nazis in 1938. Already suffering from cancer (twenty cigars a day!), he emigrated to England "to die in freedom," passing away at age eighty-three.

MICHAEL STUSSER: Should I lie down on the couch for this?
SIGMUND FREUD: The qvestion is, who vould you choose to lie *with*?

MS: OK, why are you sitting behind me?

SF: So zat you unt I avoid eye contact. It is more likely you vill feel comfortable unt open up this vay.

MS: Listen, I tried to read *The Interpretation of Dreams*, but it was all over the place—the history of Vienna, the technical theory of the mind, autobiographical stories—it kinda made me sleepy. Can you dumb it down for me?

SF: Dumb it? Insights such as zis fall to one's lot but vonce in a life-time! Luckily for you, I also wrote a short version—*On Dreams*—very brief unt easy to follow, yes? Read zis ovah. Zen vee talk again. Goot-bye.

[Session is adjourned. The interview begins again a week later in Freud's office.]

SF: So. Vat haff you learned?

MS: I learned that your goal was to "agitate the sleep of mankind." Now I can't take a nap without a notepad by my bed.

SF: Zee interpretation of dreams is the royal road to a knowledge of zee unconscious activities of zee mind.

MS: Tell that to Lindsay Lohan and the miniature dolphin she was riding in the nightmare I had.

SF: You see, zis is important! Everythink has meanink! Zere is no slip of zee tongue or dream vithout meanink! Zey are riddles zat can be understoot!

MS: You had a few disorders of your own, eh, Herr Doktor?

SF: Yes, OK. I haff fear of dying, unt some ozzer phobias I would like nut to discuss. Depression, you understand.

MS: Fear of ferns. Fear of riding on trains. Fear of visiting Rome.

SF: Not to mention zee anal retention—how you say, constipation. A certain degree of neurosis is of inestimable value as a drive, especially to a psychologist. Let us say I am vurking on some tings, yah?

MS: What did the great Dr. Freud learn from his own self-analysis?

SF: I haff hostility to my father, unt some early sexual feelings for my mother. But she vas very much younger zan my father, very beauti-ful, unt zis is normal.

MS: In fact, you're sort of a momma's boy. She called you her "golden-haired Siggy."

SF: *Mein goldener Siggy*, yah. Listen, zee relationship with zee mother is zee most complete relationship between human beings. I vould add, zat, for zee mother, the little boy brings zee longed-for penis vith him.

MS: Not all your ideas were such winners, there, Siggy. Your seduction theory, for example, kinda sucked.

SF: Yes, OK, I am incorrect here. I had believed that all neurosis came from child molestation, often incestuous. Zis is clearly not so goot a theory. I admit zis.

MS: You also used cocaine both personally and in your practice.

SF: Oh yah! Tis goot, yah? Euphoric for patients—a mood enhancer vith cure-all properties. A vunder drug, yah!

MS: Well, we kinda made it illegal here in the States.

SF: But it is in zee Coca-Cola!

MS: No, they took it out of that as well. We've got other drugs for depressed patients now. You should try Zoloft. You might love it.

SF: I haff heard of zee quick fix zat doctors are now lookink for. Zis is not possible. Vee must listen to zee patient.

MS: You discuss three types of memory. First, conscious memory.

SF: *Conscious* is zat you know vee sit in zis room. You take zee notes, maybe you are hungry, yes?

MS: Just ate. But thanks. Then there's *pre*-conscious memory.

SF: Zee memories of zee past—zee birthdays, zee times you suckle your mother's breast, zee ridink of zee bike.

MS: And finally, *un*conscious memory.

SF: Zees are sings deep in zee mind you are unaware of—but zey are *zere*. Your deepest desires, zee dark secrets even *you* are nut aware of.

MS: Yeah?

SF: Yah!

MS: For example, the Oedipus complex. Aw, if we could just find a gal like dear old Mom. Do you think we marry our mothers?

SF: It is complicated. She is zee primary source of all pleasure, so yes. Zere is definite experience of zee boy being jealous of his father. Do you feel zis?

MS: Not so much, but you're the doctor here.

SF: Zere is also castration anxiety.

MS: Good Lord!

SF: I am atheist. But zis anxiety comes about ven zee son becomes scared zat zee father vill cut his, ah, pee-pee off to stop his son from killing him.

MS: You had to make this stuff up, right?

SF: I go on: Zee son, so as not to haff his pee-pee chopped, he begins to identify vith his father, he lives vicariously through heem, and zen finds his own mother later in life—a wife of his own.

MS: What about girls? Are they worried about their "pee-pees" getting lopped off as well?

SF: Zey have pee-pee—or penis—envy. Zey also vant to haff sex with zere mama, but haff no penis!

MS: Thank goodness.

SF: Yes, goot for *you*! But women must search zere entire lives, zen, for zis penis—to make zem complete.

MS: So they're lesser versions of men, huh? Women must love you.

SF: Zees are *theories*—fixations—to help us understand. Vee can resolve zees conflicts unt desires, eef vee under-stand!

MS: Yeah, well a lot of women aren't so hot on your theories or the fact that you referred to them as "a dark continent," or psychologically castrated.

SF: Yah, unt some of zem are hysterical as vell, unt not in a funny way.

MS: Perhaps women weren't your bag, so to speak.

SF: I vill say this: Zee one question I vas unable to answer during all my years of analysis vas, "What does a woman want?" To zis, I haff no idea.

MS: Why do you think your work is so controversial?

SF: I speak of urges, yes? Zees urges are often in zee unconscious—zee uncharted mind. Zer are many who do not like zis idea. Many religious people, for example, zey do not want to discuss zee possibility zat zey may do things in zere dreams zat are in conflict with zere conscious wishes, you understand. Zis is not a tidy little idea . . . unt zey resist exploring.

MS: And did the controversy bother you?

SF: Vat I say is zat vee are making great progress. In the Middle Ages zey vould haff burned *me*. Now zey are content vith burning my *books*.

MS: So much of your dream analysis is phallic.

SF: No. I do not sink so.

MS: What if I have a dream about a mountain or a branch?

SF: Zis, yes, is symbolic for zee penis.

MS: And if my dream has a fountain or a river?

SF: Again, in zis case it has running vater, it is the penis.

MS: And what about a pen or a balloon?

SF: Oh yah, definitely zee erection. Zee penis.

MS: See?

SF: You haff a dream vith an exploding rocket shooting into a cave or a tunnel or zere is dancing, it is sex. Zis is *true.* You must *see* zis!

MS: And what if I have a dream where my teeth fall out?

SF: Zis is a symbol of castration—punishment for masturbating.

MS: Not again.

SF: Oh, yes, zee castration complex—very common, do not vorry.

MS: Do you think that you are obsessed with sex?

SF: It is a major desire, yes? Anatomy is destiny: You must admit zis. So, vat I am sayink is zat our desire—all the way from infancy—for zee pleasure, is a basic urge. You cannot, however, have sex all zee time. Vee vould like zis, but vee vould get nothing done.

MS: Sorry, I was thinking about this girl on the bus today.

SF: Yes, unt because you could not have sex vith her, you must sublimate zis desire. But it does not go avay. You turn zis sexual energy into somezing else: Interviewing dead people and taking your little notes here, perhaps. Or fondling your pen as you do.

MS: Hey!

SF: You have repressed feelinks. Zis is the unconscious, unt it is OK. Vee are not apes. Vee are civilized. But vee must repress zees things. Let us open your mind vith vat I call zee "talking cure"—some free association. Vhy don't you say zee first thing zat comes to your mind, and vee go from zere?

MS: Let's not. You're the one on the hot seat, for the moment.

SF: I begin: Dress.

MS: Undress.

SF: You *see?* Please, go on. Say vat comes to your mind.

MS: OK, I can't believe you slept with your wife's sister, Minna Bernays.

SF: Zis is not vat I meant by free association, yah? Perhaps vee should continue zis session unt nother time.

MS: Allow me to continue with my free association. Swiss psychiatrist Carl Jung found out about you getting it on with your sister-in-law. Was that part of the reason you two had a falling out?

SF: OK. Enough associating like zis, eh? Carl unt I had many reasons for our fallink: Part of it vas a little, how you say, homoerotic crush, vich I admit to, unt part because he began to move away from zee psychology, unt emphasize zee occult unt ozzer Eastern religions. As you know, I am atheist, unt zis does not sit vell.

MS: Probably didn't help that he was less than critical of Hitler and started to believe in flying saucers.

[Freud takes out his fifth cigar of the interview.]

MS: Would you say that's an oral fixation?

SF: Nein. Sometimes a cigar is just a cigar.

MS: Speaking of which, you couldn't give 'em up even after your jaw was surgically removed because of cancer.

SF: Zere is an erogenous zone in zee mouth vee haff developed since vee are infants. From zee breast to zee cigar, OK. It is stimulation. I see zat zee end of your pen is quite chewed as vell, yah?

MS: Nice redirect. My point is that you may very well have been in denial about cigars causing the cancer in your mouth.

SF: Goot point, yah. Denial unt addiction, unt most importantly, a bad habit I do not vish to abandon. Luckily, now zat I am dead, I can smoke day unt night. Unt I do.

MS: In 1905 you published *Jokes and Their Relation to the Unconscious.* Let's try a few of them.

SF: Shoot.

MS: How many Freudian analysts does it take to change a lightbulb?

SF: How many?

MS: Two. One to change the lightbulb, and one to hold the breasts. I mean, ladder.

SF: Yes. Zis is funny. I've got vun: Man says to his friend, "I've been making a lot of Freudian slips lately." "Like vat?" asks his friend. "Vell, last week I asked the train conductor for two pickets to Tittsburgh."

MS: That is funny.

SF: No! It goes on: "Really?" says zee friend. "I did something similar. My wife and I were having dinner unt instead of sayink, 'Sveetheart, pass zee butter,' I said, 'You miserable vench, you ruined my life!' " *Hee!*

[There is a long, awkward silence.]

MS: OK.

SF: Now, let's get down to zee business of vhy you are here. Tell me about your mother. . . .

END
of Interview

HENRY VIII BECAME the king of England in 1509 at the age of seventeen after his dad, Henry VII (obviously), died of tuberculosis. The second monarch of the Tudor dynasty, Henry is known less for playing a mean harp than for his six marriages, creating the independent Church of England (the other church wasn't big on divorce), and uniting England and Wales (and irritating speakers of Welsh ever since).

Unable to sire an heir with Catherine of Aragon (though it may have been a good political alliance with Spain, marrying his brother's widow was bad form), the king tried for years to divorce her, threatening several cardinals along the way. Supported by the emperor, the pope would have none of the king's nonsense. Undeterred, he broke free of the Catholic Church and privately married Anne Boleyn in 1533, enacting a law a year later that made his marriage to Catherine invalid—and made Henry head of the Church of England.

Like most kings, Henry liked to show his might through war, and in 1512 he invaded France, winning the battle of Spurs. Unlike most kings, Henry actually joined the army and took part in dozens of battles.

1536 was a big year: Downgraded from queen to Dowager Princess of Wales, Catherine died of cancer, and poor Anne Boleyn was executed for infidelity. Not much for mourning, Henry married Jane Seymour. Though Jane died soon thereafter, she gave the king a son and future heir (Edward VI).

Henry married a fourth time, again for political purposes, to Anne of Cleves, in order to grab the Protestant interest in Germany. In fact, he hated Annie's mug, and got hitched only on the condition he could divorce her soon thereafter. There were two more wives, both Catherines . . . one who suffered the same fate as Boleyn, and the last, Catherine Parr, who actually outlived the old goat. In fact, this final wife has the special distinction of being the most married queen of England, taking four husbands in *her* lifetime.

Contrary to public opinion, for most his life Henry was a good-looking, athletic chap, admired for his smarts and courteous nature. Injured in a jousting accident in 1536, he was unable to exercise, and Henry got fat—real fat. His mood changed, and the last decade was a scary one for the king's friends and enemies alike. An irrational temper and insomnia made him the miserable despot history now remembers.

Henry died on January 28, 1547 (a combo platter of nasty leg infections and syphilis, if you must know). In a sick side note, his coffin overturned on the way to Windsor, and sentries found dogs licking his remains the next day. He was buried in St. George's Chapel in Windsor Castle, next to his wife Jane Seymour.

MICHAEL STUSSER: Your Majesty, let's go through your wives, shall we?

HENRY VIII: Good a place as any to begin, dear boy. That is, if you've got the bloody time for it. . . .

MS: "Divorced, beheaded, died, divorced, beheaded, survived."

HVIII: If mnemonics help to remember my fame. But just so you know, I never divorced any of them. Had the things annulled, don't you know.

MS: First off, Catherine of Aragon.

HVIII: Right-e-oh! Lovely gal, good head on her shoulders.

MS: And before he died, your brother's, Prince Arthur's wife.

HVIII: Right as rain. The poor bloke got an infection and keeled. He was only fifteen, for God's sake. I knew if I married her, it would give us a strong alliance with Spain and make France cool her aggressive heels for a bit.

MS: Marrying for political reasons kind of runs in the family.

HVIII: Righto. My pop was no dummy. Mumsy [Elizabeth] was not only a catch, but the sister of Edward V. I only wish it had worked out with Cat as well as it had for my dear old mum and daddy.

MS: What was the problem?

HVIII: Well, her father [King Ferdinand II] was a horse's arse, for one. Wanted to control me and England through his daughter, and I'd have none of it.

MS: Anything else?

HVIII: I needed a male heir, quite obviously. And it wasn't for lack of trying, God bless her—we were married twenty blooming years. In fact, she was pregnant seven times, but only [Princess] Mary survived.

MS: So you ventured out.

HVIII: Jolly right! I was a king, mate! King needs a boy to follow up, carry on, and all that!

MS: Your mistresses included Mary Boleyn and Elizabeth Blount.

HVIII: I don't bloody remember.

MS: Do you remember Mary Boleyn's sister?

HVIII: I'm not a crackpot, chum, so don't treat me like one. Anne and I got flippin' married—that's not something you forget.

MS: But you were *already* married.

HVIII: To a barren wench!

MS: So you requested Pope Clement VII allow you to marry another woman.

HVIII: Aw, I fancy we tried pretty much everything: annulment, legal challenges, secret commissions, and dispensations. Today I'd go to Mexico and it would be over in ten bloody minutes.

MS: You married Anne Boleyn in 1533.

HVIII: Brilliant day for a wedding, everyone had a fine time!

MS: Except Sir Thomas More.

HVIII: Wanker should have kept his mouth shut, and he'd be having high tea with the queen as we speak.

MS: You had him beheaded in 1535 for refusing to acknowledge your union to Anne and for stating that the pope was still head of the Church.

HVIII: 'Bout sums it up. We changed a few laws after that, made it high treason to refuse to acknowledge me as, let's see, "the only Supreme Head in Earth of the Church of England," I think we put it.

MS: Pope must have loved that.

HVIII: Ya know what hurt the chap worse than the title? That we stopped sending him money.

MS: Anne was an attendant of Queen Catherine. It's actually been said that she suffered as a victim of sixteenth-century sexual harassment.

HVIII: That's malarkey! I charmed the pants off her, but she was a willing participant, lad.

MS: Your romance didn't last long.

HVIII: Oh, it was amicable enough with the missus. Just decided to go our own ways, actually.

MS: You had her arrested on charges of incest, extramarital affairs—four of them, in fact—

HVIII: Five.

MS: Battery, attempted murder, and using witchcraft to trap you into the marriage in the first place.

HVIII: Well that was uncalled-for.

MS: Guilty on all charges, what a surprise: she and the five men were beheaded.

HVIII: Damn shame, too. Darlin' gal could have hung, if she'd liked.

MS: A few days later you married Jane Seymour.

HVIII: Finally got my son! Smashing!

MS: Jane gave birth to Prince Edward in 1537, and she died two weeks after.

HVIII: And I got my son!

MS: Touching. Even after Queen Jane, you married again.

HVIII: Yeah, well, Prince Eddie—God bless him—wasn't such a healthy bloke, so I wanted a back up, if ya get my meaning. Someone who might succeed him if things got rough.

MS: Meeting your next wife may have been the first royal blind date in history.

HVIII: And hopefully the last, mate. It was Thomas Cromwell who suggested I engage with Anne, the sister of the Protestant Duke of Cleves—sort of a safety plan in case the Roman Catholics decided to attack, see? In order to get an early look at her, my boy Hans Holbein painted this portrait, but he seems to have fudged the reality of the thing, don't you know. Bloomin' missed the mark by a mile.

MS: When Anne arrived, you were less than thrilled.

HVIII: It's not that I'm so bloody picky, but she had a mug that would make hounds howl, I tell you. When she was born, they slapped her mum! I mean, really. I called her a Flanders mare, and that was a *compliment.*

MS: But you married her on January 6, 1540.

HVIII: I fancy so, but we'd already had papers drawn up to annul the thing in a hurry. Anne didn't mind, really. She got to be called the king's sister, and we gave her Hever Castle.

MS: Who was next?

HVIII: Lord, let me think. Catherine, Anne, then there was Jane, then . . . Oh! Right! Catherine Howard. Lovely dish.

MS: Anne Boleyn's first cousin.

HVIII: Great genes in that family.

MS: You waited all of twenty days to marry her. Still, there was a problem.

HVIII: Well she cheated on me. Hurt my feelings. Hurt my pride, mate.

MS: Executed?

HVIII: First we annulled the marriage, then we lopped her. Poor love was only eighteen, too.

MS: Perhaps it's a technicality, but if the marriage was annulled, she couldn't officially have been guilty of adultery.

HVIII: Hurt my bloody feelings, mate! Heartbroken, I tell you, and I think that's quite enough! She needed to bugger off!

MS: Who's next?

HVIII: Well, we've got to the end now, haven't we? I married Catherine Parr in 1543.

MS: From an eighteen-year-old to a wealthy widow. You really ran the gamut.

HVIII: Love conquers all.

MS: You almost had her beheaded.

HVIII: Oh, right. Well, we argued about religion—she was a radical Protestant. But in the end, this ball-and-chain let me be a Catholic and kept her pretty mouth shut. And she was more a nurse to me at that point than a wife. I was bloody old.

MS: Shockingly, in between all these marriages, you actually enacted some important pieces of legislation during your reign. What are you most proud of?

HVIII: The Acts of Union [1536–43], which made Wales and ourselves one nation, was spot-on. I also fancied anything that severed the ties with the Roman Catholics—that's thumbs-up in my book.

MS: You had a thing against the Roman Catholic Church.

HVIII: It wasn't so much that I had a thing against them, as I had needs of me own. It's simply easier to make yourself the head of the Church [of England] than to have to go through all those blasted cardinals. . . .

MS: Seemed a bit more personal than that.

HVIII: Perhaps you know something I don't?

MS: You sanctioned the destruction of the shrines to Roman Catholic saints in 1538 and a year later dissolved all the monasteries and transferred the land to yourself.

HVIII: We had some cash-flow problems, and it was simply time to split from Rome.

[The king begins to glance at one of the female researchers in the room.]

HVIII: Tell me, who's the lovely lass you came here with?

MS: My assistant, Vanessa.

HVIII: Perhaps she and I . . .

MS: Perhaps we could discuss the Witchcraft Act [1542], which put anyone to death who invoked or conjured an evil spirit. Did that have anything to do with the women in your life?

HVIII: Let's just say it was a preemptive strike.

MS: Given your ego, you've probably seen some of the films and movies about you.

HVIII: Shakespeare's play was accurate.

MS: *Henry VIII; or, All Is True* was the one that was playing the night the Globe Theatre burned down [June 29, 1613].

HVIII: I didn't say I liked it. Also, Richard Burton seems to have had a fair understanding of my struggles with wives. [Burton was nominated for an Academy Award for *Anne of the Thousand Days*, 1969.]

[The figure of a woman glides through the room and causes the temperature to plummet.]

MS: My God! Who the hell is that?

HVIII: Oh, it's the ghost of Anne. She follows me every bloody place I go.

MS: How do you know it's her?

HVIII: She keeps saying, "The executioner was very good," and "I have a little neck."

MS: Guess it serves you right, huh?

HVIII: If I could just get her to sit still, I might be able to put her in a . . .

MS: She's a ghost, Henry. You're stuck with her.

END
of Interview

JOHN EDGAR HOOVER directed the Federal Bureau of Investigation from 1924 until he bit the dust in 1972. In those five wiretappin' decades, Hoover served under ten presidents, from Coolidge to Nixon, and was one of the most powerful men in Washington.

The Big Hoover had a deserved reputation as a ruthless, lawless strongman. Using illegal break-ins and hidden microphones, he collected damaging info and blackmailed anyone in his path. Holding on to the most seedy bits for his own personal use, Hoover kept insanely copious files on the likes of Martin Luther King Jr., John Lennon, and Frank Sinatra—not to mention each and every sitting president, just in case someone had the idea to can him. . . .

Hoover also did his job, taking on America's gangsters during the 1920s and '30s and making a series of widely publicized arrests. He also organized the FBI into one of the best law enforcement units the world has ever seen. Rebuilding from the ground up, he stripped lousy officers of their jobs (political appointees and anyone too fat to be a Special Agent) and hired rookies only after extensive tests and interviews.

Hoover, of course, was a controversial, hit-or-miss kinda guy (and definitely a shoot-first-and-ask-questions-later fella): He supported Prohibition, which only led to the largest development of organized crime in our history. While harassing black activists and suspected Commies right and left (everyone from John Lennon, to JFK, to Eldridge Cleaver were on the enemies list), Hoover was suspiciously soft on the Mafia, denying its existence and allowing the Mob to grow throughout his reign.

We'd know a lot more about Hoover's wheeling, dealing, and oddball sexuality, but he made damn sure his files were shredded the day he died. He croaked in 1972 at age seventy-seven, having served as the FBI's chief for forty-eight years.

MICHAEL STUSSER: What was your first job at the FBI?

J. EDGAR HOOVER: I was a special assistant to Attorney General A. Mitchell Palmer, who was responsible for removing "undesirable elements" after World War I. [*Wink, wink.*]

MS: Right, the Palmer Raids. You helped him round up and deport suspected Communists—and liberals, of course. So you pretty much strong-armed folks right from the start.

JEH: You may wish to harbor Bolsheviks, but I will not.

MS: You hacks deported 556 innocent people, and Palmer resigned after his methods came to light.

JEH: I would emphasize my positive contributions in this interview if I were you.

MS: Here we go. . . .

JEH: Let's remember that I turned a ragtag organization into a top-notch unit. I started the FBI National Academy, where men had to go through background checks, serious interviews, and physical testing in order to become Special Agents.

MS: I had a G-Man Action Figure when I was a kid.

JEH: My G-men were handpicked, highly educated, and abstained from booze, relations with women, and other amoral behavior. Guardians of the civic good!

MS: My G-Man doll wasn't always the good guy.

JEH: And lest you forget, young man: At the age of twenty-nine, I created a centralized fingerprint file as well as established the scientific crime lab.

MS: I watch *CSI: Miami.* Is it kinda like that?

JEH: We know what you're watching. But yes, it's just like what you see on television.

MS: But I bet the coroners aren't as good-looking in real life.

JEH: Some of them are, actually.

MS: Eleanor Roosevelt called your FBI "an American Gestapo." Thoughts? Comments? Criticism?

JEH: I never liked her. In fact, she was on my Custodial Detention list, along with other *Communists* who might be questioned during wartime for their liberal activities.

MS: You had a thing about Commies, huh?

JEH: If you're talking about *Communists* and Fascists—individuals who wish to overthrow our government and way of life—yes, I had a "thing" about them. Un-American activities, son, are un-American.

MS: How'd that all start?

JEH: President Franklin Roosevelt gave me the directive to investigate both foreign espionage and perform surveillance of *Communist* and left-wing activists within our great country's borders. I felt the need to stop what I liked to call "the mad march of Red fascism."

MS: *Communists.* Like Charlie Chaplin, JFK, Einstein, and Marilyn Monroe?

JEH: I see you took a trip to Cuba in 2002.

MS: You are *so* 1940! It's interesting to note that you had almost five hundred agents investigating Communists and Hollywood entertainers in 1959 and only four looking into the Mob.

JEH: My men investigated anyone involved in un-American activities, including the Ku Klux Klan, as well as the Nazis in the '40s and '50s.

MS: I would hope. How'd you establish your moral compass?

JEH: I was taught by my momma—

MS: Here it comes . . .

JEH: —that middle-class Protestant morality is the core of American values. Anything that calls those values into question should be distrusted and possibly eliminated.

MF: How do you feel about using law enforcement as a political tool for revenge and intimidation?

JEH: What is your Social Security number?

MF: What was your problem with the great Martin Luther King Jr.? [FBI files show an obsession with King and nearly constant efforts to bring him down, including mailing tapes of his sexual affairs to King's wife and encouraging him to commit suicide.]

JEH: He was a dissenter. A left-wing activist who may well have been a *Communist* with his "civil rights." And truth be told, I'm a bit of a racist.

MS: All these secret files and dossiers on innocent people, many of them the presidents you served under. Was the whole idea to make sure you had the upper hand when someone tried to finally can your fat ass?

JEH: High-stakes poker is one way to look at it, though I would suggest my database was more about truth and justice—and that you be very careful when you speak of my ass.

MS: I think you just liked to look at all the nudie pics of people.

JEH: It's important to note, in your little analogy there, that no one ever had the balls to call my bluff.

MS: I gotta ask about the cross-dressing.

JEH: I will have you killed.

MS: This interview is being recorded in order to blackmail you later. Shall we continue?

JEH: Why you little *Commie* pinko. . . .

MS: There are reports of you wearing an ill-fitting cocktail dress.

JEH: I did not!

MS: And any photos of you doing such a thing would obviously have been destroyed.

JEH: There are no photos.

MS: OK, we'll chalk it up to urban legend—but it does seem that Clyde Tolson [an FBI associate] was your boyfriend. . . .

JEH: Where do you come up with this information? Who told you. . . ?

MS: There's something called the Internet now. Kind of a sick database like the one you were establishing, only less biased and *way* bigger. Says here Mr. Tolson was your "companion" for over forty years, took vacations with ya, was named the beneficiary of your life insurance policy, and is buried in a grave next to yours.

[Hoover sputters for some time.]

MS: Today we call that a homosexual partner. Not that it matters, but you clearly took this secret to the grave.

JEH: Killed.

MS: Any last words?

JEH: I have a philosophy. You are honored by your friends and you are distinguished by your enemies. I have been very distinguished.

MS: Well, thank you for your time. And your bra strap's showing.

END
of Interview

ＨANDCUFFED AND STUFFED into a straitjacket, tied upside down and submerged into a dunk tank. Who else but the one and only Harry Houdini?

Ehrich Weiss (aka Weisz Erik) emigrated to the United States with his parents and four siblings when the future escape artist was only four. His father, Mayer Samuel Weiss, started out as a rabbi, but eventually moved to the Big Apple, where he struggled to find work.

Seeing famous illusionist Dr. Lynn's act as a boy gave Houdini the magic bug and he soon began practicing sleight of hand (and probably that trick where you pull the tablecloth out from under the dishes). Taking the name Harry Houdini, he started a magic act in 1891. Harry was seventeen years old.

Houdini got his big break in 1899, when promoter Martin Beck noticed his escape act and signed him for his own vaudeville circuit. Within a few years, Beck had made the Handcuff King into the hottest ticket in the world.

Over the years, Houdini added spectacular elements to his act: Performing in front of thousands of spectators, he'd dangle from cranes in a straitjacket; submerge his weighted, shackled box in deep water; and escape from prison cells.

Houdini died from peritonitis at age fifty-two, on Halloween 1926. His motto: "And this, too, shall pass away."

What Houdini passed on was a love of magic, which he promoted all over the world; he helped the Society of American Magicians and left them a good chunk of change in his will so that the act would go on. The organization's crest is engraved prominently on his grave.

MICHAEL STUSSER: Was escapology your first career choice?
HARRY HOUDINI: Hell, we were immigrants. I would have done any-

thing to get out of the poorhouse. Factory work stunk, magic seemed glamorous.

MS: Still, most immigrants didn't tie themselves in knots and dive into the "death tank."

HH: Most kids don't leave home at the age of twelve seeking fame and fortune, but it was in my blood.

MS: The name Harry Houdini—why not Escapo the Magnificent?

HH: Harry was a pet name from my folks. My birth name was Ehrich—Ehrie for short, which rhymes with Harry—and so it stuck. The Houdini part was a tribute to French magician Jean Eugene Robert-Houdin. Escapo Ehrich woulda been good, though.

MS: Wasn't one of your brothers also an escape artist?

HH: My little brother, Dash. His stage name was Hardeen Houdini. Taught him everything I know.

MS: Well, not everything.

HH: Dash did it all except *one* trick—the old straitjacket escape. Ya gotta be able to dislocate both shoulders to get out, and the kid could only do one.

MS: Is it true another brother did a bunch of X-rays on you?

HH: Oh, yeah. I let my brother Leopold X-ray me all the time. We're real proud of him—he was New York's first specialist, and I guess he needed the practice.

MS: FYI, it may have made you sterile.

HH: I always wondered why we never had children. I could tell you how many of my ribs were broken, though. So I got that goin' for me. . . .

MS: At one point you were called the "King of the Birds"?

HH: Ha! Yeah, I started performing with birds and other animals at first. My vanishing elephant act was good stuff.

MS: How'd you manage that?

HH: Well, you're never supposed to give away the tricks, but we had a swimming pool under the stage. It's how Siegfried and Roy did it in Vegas. Poor bastard.

MS: Speaking of giving away secrets, you kinda gave away the store with your book *Handcuff Secrets* [1910]. Isn't that bad form?

HH: I could tell you how to regurgitate a key and pick a lock behind your back, upside down, underwater, and there's no way you'd get out of the straitjacket you were chained to. Takes mad skills, kiddo. The book just made my act more popular.

MS: How'd you escape all those rope ties?

HH: OK, this oughta be fun.

[Houdini begins to lasso and tie the interviewer in a series of knots.]

MS: Um, I can't breathe.

HH: The key is to puff up enough when you're being tied up to create some slack, see? Then it's a piece of cake.

MS: Puff up?

HH: Yeah. If you move your arms out to the sides a bit while I tie you, puff up your chest and hunch your shoulders, then you can find room to squirm.

MS: *Erph.* Arms asleep.

HH: After that, it's all about knowing knots—and how to untie them. Study. Practice. And never give up.

MS: [*Gasping.*] Feel like dead slug. Need help.

HH: Well, I'd also suggest hiding a knife on you somewhere, just in case you start to freak out, see? One of those hook-shaped blades come in handy, especially if you're underwater and running out of breath. Wanna add water to the mix?

MS: Are you insane?

[Houdini undoes all ten knots in less than a minute.]

MS: Thank you. How'd you ever think to use a straitjacket in the act?

HH: I was visiting patients at an insane asylum in Canada and saw this maniac flopping around in a padded cell. He was just rolling around and struggling like mad. Looked like a really masochistic thing to do onstage, and the next day I started experimenting with one.

MS: There were lots of magicians around—how did you get to be the "World's Most Famous"?

HH: First, I'm a master showman. That's important, or people will walk away going, "Yeah, OK, he made a rabbit disappear." I was also the best magician *in the world*, see? For real. I also had a good horror element to my act.

MS: 'Cuz you might drown?

HH: Oh, yeah! Flirting with death is an aphrodisiac! Equally important here: I was a publicity *machine*!

MS: You had friends in the business.

HH: I was good pals with the publishers of New York's main papers, right? But I also worked my ass off. When we had a show, I put up ten thousand posters by myself! I had decals made, did giveaways, great promotions. I made this Trump fella look like a chump.

MS: In your later years you had a war of sorts with spiritualists—people who claim to be able to communicate with the dead.

HH: Had a problem with hucksters. Charlatans. Scam artists calling themselves mediums and mind readers. They're supernatural phonies, see? So I made their tricks part of my act—had ghosts appear and did levitations and crap so people could laugh at their frickin' claims.

MS: Why the anger, Ehrich?

HH: After my mom died, I wanted to debunk all these so-called psychic loons. It just seemed unfair that these frauds charge two bucks to common, grieving folk and tell 'em they can get in touch with a loved one.

MS: So you were upset you couldn't contact your mother after her passing?

HH: That's not what I said.

MS: No, but you really took the whole thing to heart for some reason—attending séances in disguise and trying to be a ghostbuster.

HH: Exposing the fact there is no paranormal ability is right up my alley. Just like I showed people how magic isn't magic; it's art. I didn't dematerialize to get out of a locked crate, I used *natural* means—there was physics involved, see? I wanted the truth to be out there. . . .

MS: You died during one of your performances.

HH: Nope. Burst appendix.

MS: I thought you died doing the Water Torture Cell trick.

HH: Yeah, I get that a lot. Too many people saw that damn movie with Tony Curtis. It was actually a ruptured appendix; peritonitis did me in.

MS: So no one sucker punched you in the gut?

HH: Oh, I got sucker punched, all right—but that happened a few weeks before. It's why I thought my stomach hurt so damn much, and the reason I didn't go to the doc. Think I've just got a sore abdomen, and my appendix kills me.

MS: Even after your death you were messing with the audience.

HH: Course I had a final trick up my sleeve. Made a pact with my wife, Bess, that I'd contact her from the other side. We agreed on a coded message before I died, and every Halloween she held a séance to see if I'd show up.

MS: And did you come back?

HH: Not till now. After a decade of séances, she said, "Ten years is enough to wait for any man." [*Laughing*.] Kept everyone guessing though, and that's part of the act!

MS: You'll get a kick out of this: Charles Dillingham and Florenz Ziegfeld were pallbearers at your funeral.

HH: Glad to hear it.

MS: On the way to the church, Dillingham leans toward Ziegfeld and says, "Ziggie—I bet you a hundred bucks he ain't in here!"

END
of Interview

THOMAS JEFFERSON

BORN APRIL 13, 1743
DIED JULY 4, 1826

JEFFERSON IS KNOWN as a Founding Father and our third president, but his brain was bigger than politics or philosophy: In fact, TJ used equal parts of his noggin on science, inventions, botany, and diplomacy. Oh, and the guy had a way with words. . . .

Young Thomas was born and raised a rich kid, living large on his father's Virginia plantation and schooled by the finest private tutors in the land. Groomed to succeed, he studied Latin, history, the violin, etiquette, and the two-step.

At seventeen it was off to the College of William & Mary, and then law school. Looking for more cash than even a lawyer could earn, Tommy returned to his daddy's plantation, entered politics, and made a name for himself advocating independence from the Brits.

Jefferson married Martha Wayles in 1772, a wealthy widow who died five years later, leaving Thomas heartbroken (and loaded).

In 1774, in response to the Intolerable Acts, he wrote "A Summary View of the Rights of British America." In it, he clearly pointed out that the English had no real right to govern the colonies. The essay was well read and made Thomas a well-known revolutionary. When it came around to writing a draft of the Declaration of Independence, everyone knew whom to recruit.

Jefferson lost one presidential race (to John Adams, by three electoral votes), and served as VP before winning the presidency in 1800, barely beating out Aaron Burr. His first term was chock-full of policy decisions, including the war with Tripoli, the Louisiana Purchase (doubling the size of our country for the low, low price of $15 million), and sending Lewis and Clark on a hike west of the Mississippi (1804–06). Lowering taxes and the national debt, Jefferson won his second term in a landslide in 1804.

Jefferson died on July 4, 1826, exactly fifty years after the adoption of the Declaration of Independence. That same day, his chief political rival, John Adams, also died.

MICHAEL STUSSER: I'm gonna jump right in here, Mr. President. How does a man who wrote that "all men are created equal" own 187 slaves?

THOMAS JEFFERSON: My first draft of the Declaration of Independence had a section calling for an end to slavery.

MS: But—again—you owned slaves.

TJ: Even more powerful that I'd call for an end to the nasty business. We dropped the provision because, obviously, the southern states would refuse to ratify.

MS: Hmm.

TJ: Look, as president, I outlawed the importation of slaves to our great nation. Not a solution, but a start.

MS: If that makes you feel better. Let's cut to the issue on everyone's mind: You fathered four children with your slave Sally Hemmings.

TJ: That's absurd! It's a rumor that was around before I was even president.

MS: They look just like you.

TJ: It was my nephew!

MS: DNA tests of descendants show you almost certainly had kids with her.

TJ: DN-what?

MS: Let's just say science has come a long way since wooden dentures. Admit you fathered kids with Ms. Hemmings.

TJ: Sally was a wonderful mother. I freed her—our—children before I died.

MS: Seems you had quite a few extramarital affairs. Elizabeth Walker, wife of General John Walker.

TJ: He asked me to take care of her when he went off to fight in the Indian war.

MS: Nice. Next, Maria Cosway, wife of famous painter Richard Cosway.

TJ: Well he was a fop; that doesn't count!

MS: The list goes on, sir. Dolley Madison?

TJ: I did not . . . have . . . sexual relations with *that* woman.

MS: Sir?

TJ: Really. I'd been widowed for twenty years when I took office and asked her to play the role of presidential hostess. That is all.

MS: OK, but you weren't exactly a feminist.

TJ: Women have a great purpose in life: marriage, children, and pleasing their husbands.

MS: You should have your own show on right-wing radio. On the flip side, you are known for being the principal author of the Declaration of Independence.

TJ: It was really a joint effort with our whole committee [John Adams, Benjamin Franklin, Robert R. Livingston, and Roger Sherman].

MS: They didn't do squat. Modesty does not suit you.

TJ: Truth be told, I took a lot of the language from George Mason's Virginia Declaration of Rights [passed on June 12, 1776], and Thomas Paine, of course, as well as ideas from the incomparable John Locke.

MS: Such as?

TJ: His *Two Treatises of Government* [1690] was inspiring. Said that God's greatest gift to man was the ability to reason. So it stands to reason that humans should examine their lot in life, and their governments, and see if the situation is to their liking.

MS: Give us a behind-the-scenes look at what went on during deliberations for the Declaration.

TJ: I'll tell you what got left out—my criticism of the slave trade, thanks to our friends in South Carolina and Georgia.

MS: Here we go again.

[Jefferson takes out a crumpled piece of paper from his jacket pocket and reads.]

And I quote myself:

> *He has waged cruel war against human nature itself, violating its*
> *most sacred rights of life & liberty in the persons of a distant*
> *people who never offended him, captivating & carrying them into*
> *slavery in another hemisphere, or to incur miserable death in their*
> *transportation thither.*

MS: Wow. That woulda changed things.

TJ: The damn Second Continental Congress mutilated over five hundred words of my masterpiece, and I ain't happy about it. They also deleted a nice long section blasting the Brits and their tyrant king, which they thought was "too harsh." Pansies!

MS: What do you think was the key to gaining independence from the British?

TJ: The Atlantic Ocean, if truth be told. I mean, the colonies had already been bustling with economic and political activity for over one hundred years, while the monarchy was plodding along in the old world, fighting with France and Holland and Spain over resources and power. America was wide-open—and independent-minded. It was just a matter of time before we took a stand.

MS: Did you have conflicting thoughts on democracy?

TJ: I put it this way: A democracy is nothing more than mob rule, where 51 percent of the people may take away the rights of the other 49 percent. Still better than a dictatorship.

MS: So you didn't really trust democracy.

TJ: Experience hath shown that even under the best forms of government, those entrusted with power have, in time and by slow operations, perverted it into tyranny. The tree of liberty must be refreshed from time to time with the blood of patriots and tyrants.

MS: Please. I just ate.

TJ: Put another way: When the people fear their government, there is tyranny; when the government fears the people, there is liberty.

MS: For such an articulate guy, you were a lousy governor.

TJ: Agreed, and it was a lousy job. The Virginia Constitution gave all the power to the legislature, and I couldn't stand it.

MS: In fact, when the British attacked Richmond, you actually fled.

TJ: True, true. In my own defense, I was reelected in 1781 and refused to serve a second term.

MS: You spent five years in France. How did Frenchie treat you?

TJ: Ben Franklin was a tough act to follow, let me tell you. I was sent to Paris in 1784 to negotiate treaties. I took my daughters [Martha and Mary] with me, and we had a lovely time enjoying the French cuisine and wines. Oh, the *vin*!

MS: What'd you think about the revolution over there?

TJ: King Louis XVI was a good friend during the American Revolution, but when the French Revolution broke out in 1789, I must say I hoped it would succeed, simply on principle.

MS: Coming back to the United States, you served as the first secretary of state, under George Washington. You clashed quite a bit with Secretary of Treasury Alexander Hamilton.

TJ: I saw our great country as an agricultural nation living on the bounties and beauty of the land, while Alex saw nothing but heavy industry and cut-throat commerce. Our differences were fairly sizable.

MS: You formed the Republican Party.

TJ: Which would make me a Democrat today.

MS: OK, that's confusing.

TJ: Hamilton was backed by the Federalist Party, and they were big on creating monetary policies that favored the rich.

MS: I hear that!

TJ: My caucus was called the Democratic-Republican Party. We wanted more states' rights and sided with the revolution in France. That clear things up?

MS: Sort of. Thing is, in 1796 you were vice president under John Adams, and he was a Federalist.

TJ: Yes, well, in my day, the fellow who ran second in the presidential race got the job of vice president.

MS: Wow. If that were still the case, our vice president would be . . . Wow.

TJ: Makes you want to start your own party, hmm?

MS: Question: If you hated Hamilton so much, why'd you have a statue of him at your house?

TJ: I set up busts of him and me facing one another in the entryway. That way, we could be opposed in death as in life. Though my statue's bigger.

MS: Um, is that a globe in your pocket or are you just glad to see me?

TJ: Oh, yes, I enjoy recording measurements and have surveying compasses and the like with me at all times.

MS: What else is in there?

TJ: Let's see, we've got a thermometer, a small scale, a level, some drawing instruments. . . .

MS: People don't know this, but you invented a lot of stuff.

TJ: Practical tinkering, I'd call it: The portable copying press was my idea, great for record keeping and correspondence when I was on the road.

MS: You wrote over sixteen thousand letters.

TJ: No cell phones in my day, young man. Had to stay in touch! I also invented the swivel chair, the folding ladder, the calendar clock, the pedometer, and the lap desk to hold all kinds of things—pencils, files, and such.

MS: And didn't you invent the ring decoder?

TJ: I believe you're referring to the wheel cipher. We used it during the American Revolution to scramble and then decode messages we didn't want anyone to read. Ingenious, actually. Glad I thought of it.

MS: All I ever hear about is Monticello this, and Monticello that. What's the big deal?

TJ: It is quite the estate, let me tell you.

MS: I have a feeling I don't have a choice.

TJ: Over the years, I tricked it out with all kinds of doodads—automatic double doors, alcove beds, revolving bookstands, and a dozen skylights.

MS: So it was like the ultimate bachelor pad.

TJ: If you wish. I also had dumbwaiters in the dining room that went down into the wine cellar.

MS: How 'bout the yard? Got a barbecue out there?

TJ: My "yard" has more than 160 species of trees and a garden featuring over 250 varieties of herbs and vegetables. I hope you're taking notes.

MS: Tell me, what was your beef with the media?

TJ: There was no "media" at the time—just newspapers, and they took advantage of our freedom in order to publish scurrilous gossip and lies!

MS: So, not a big fan of the First Amendment, then?

TJ: I helped write it, you fool!

MS: You said, "The man who reads nothing at all is better educated than the man who reads nothing but newspapers."

TJ: I also said, "If I had to choose between government without newspapers, and newspapers without government, I wouldn't hesitate to choose the latter." Our liberty depends upon the freedom of the press, but that doesn't mean I have to like it. They beat up on me worse than they did on Clinton during Monicagate!

MS: Well, you'd love the *National Enquirer.*

TJ: I'm just saying that while a free press that investigates and criticizes our government is essential, it's equally as important that truth and reason is illuminated. What editors *should* do is divide papers into four sections: Truths, Probabilities, Possibilities, and Lies.

MS: Did you really think every citizen should be a soldier?

TJ: This was the case with the Greeks and Romans, and should be so with every free state. Remember that I also said I abhor war and view it as the greatest scourge of mankind.

MS: Please elaborate, like I had to ask. . . .

TJ: I believe in the principle that America should have nothing to do with conquest. I hope our wisdom will grow with our power and teach us that the less we use our power, the greater it will be.

MS: Yeah, that ain't happening. We're invading countries left and right.

TJ: I figured as much. I am an educated man, you know?

MS: In fact, your library had over nine thousand volumes.

TJ: Not to be a braggart, but I could read in seven languages. Never read translations where you can read the original.

MS: Who are your some of your favorites?

TF: Molière, Cervantes, John Locke. Voltaire and Thomas Paine are always on my reading list as well.

MS: Did you really make your own Bible?

TJ: I adapted one. I can say this now that I'm dead, but I didn't see Christ as a divine being, so I cut out the passages about miracles and Christ's divinity. Left the stuff on Jesus's moral philosophy, though.

MS: Why did people think you were an atheist?

TJ: Folks had trouble with my idea about creating a wall that separates church and state. Human rights are endowed by a God, but religious opinions are a personal matter. One of my proudest accomplishments was passing the Bill for Religious Freedom in 1786. Made Virginia the first state to disestablish religion. In my humble opinion, it does me no injury for my neighbor to say there are twenty gods, or no God.

MS: Living the Jefferson lifestyle was spendy. As chief executive, you ran up a wine bill alone of $10,800.

TJ: We all have our habits, son. Unfortunately, my debts grew as I got older, and I never did balance my own budget.

MS: No kidding: You were $107,000 in debt when you died. Your daughter had to sell Monticello and its contents. Including the slaves.

TJ: Any idea what became of my book collection?

MS: Yeah—they started the Library of Congress with it.

TJ: That's nice.

MS: You died on the Fourth of July, exactly fifty years after the signing of the Declaration of Independence. Was that on purpose?

TJ: No, but it goes well with the red, white, and blue underwear I was wearing on the day I passed.

MS: Please tell me you're kidding.

TJ: Had you going, didn't I? Listen, I was eighty-three, I'd been retired for seventeen years, and it was time to go.

MS: You requested that your grave be inscribed with three particular accomplishments: "Author of the Declaration of Independence [and] of the Statute for Virginia for religious toleration & Father of the University of Virginia."

TJ: And not a word more.

MS: But it's missing the fact you were governor, secretary of state, VP, and president!

TJ: That's what I've got you for. Besides, my legacy doesn't seem to be going anywhere.

END
of Interview

SHE STARTED OUT a normal little peasant girl; then, around age thirteen, she began to hear voices from above telling her to take up arms against the Brits and help coronate the crown prince.

Though she may have seemed nuts at the time, somehow Joan of Arc got the ear of the future King Charles VII and convinced him to let her lead his army and drive the English from their country.

A fearless and persistent soldier, Joan fought medieval battle after battle against the English (though never on Sunday), most notably at Orléans during the Hundred Years' War, helping Charles win the crown on July 17, 1429.

Joanie could have retired to the king's palace a noble, but couldn't keep herself away from the front lines. She directed one daring raid too many, was captured on May 23, 1430, and taken to the Duke of Burgundy.

Joan was tried for heresy by the pro-English clergy. Seems the church didn't like that she was communicating directly with God [that was *their* job], and, if they could prove her a witch, King Charles would look as though he'd been crowned by a demon—a PR problem, without a doubt.

Saint Joan's wondrous story, of course, ends when she's burned at the stake by the Duke of Bedford at age nineteen, increasing her fame and making her a figure of strength for the French in times of duress through the ages.

MICHAEL STUSSER: Sometimes I hear voices.

JOAN OF ARC: Is zis true? You as well? *Incroyable!*

MS: Yeah, but it's usually just my kids in the next room. What's your story?

JA: Mine are real, you see! Saint Michael, Saint Catherine, Saint Margaret. The angels of heaven all speak to me, and I can see their beautiful faces as we speak.

MS: Do they tell you to get them Popsicles?

JA: No, monsieur. Zee saints speak to me of goodness and strength. Zey give to me courage to fight evil in zis world and enemies of zee king.

MS: Evil, like the British?

JA: *Oui.* Invaders and sinners of any kind. It was my raison d'être.

MS: There seem to be a couple of kings of France during the time. Can you clear that up?

JA: Zee crown was split in my country between, eh, zee followers of Charles, zee crown prince, and zee English side, zee imbecile Henry VI. At zis time, Henry is, ah, just an infant. Enfant terrible!

MS: OK. Whose side were you on?

JA: I was loyal to the Dauphin [crown prince], of course! Charles of France! He was zee son of Charles VI and should have been crowned as king upon his father's death. Voices told me to seek him out and help him gain his true glory.

MS: Loud voices?

JA: Not so loud, you see, but persistent enough so that at zee tender age of sixteen, I go to zee captain of his forces and ask if I might join heem.

MS: How'd that work out?

JA: I was, how you say, sent packing. Zey sink I am crazy, yes? I try once more a year later, and am taken to Charles's castle.

MS: Persistent little bugger. What was your meeting with the Dauphin like?

JA: I think, perhaps, he believes I am out of zee control. He hides among many servants, but I am able to pick heem out immediately. It is my gift, you see. When I tell zis honorable man I wish to fight the British and have him crowned as king, I am brought into his fold.

MS: Just like that?

JA: Oh, no. Church elders question me for three weeks. Zey were quite concerned zat I was a witch, and, of course, I don't blame zem. Eventually I convince zis council zat I am pious and truthful. And zey let me join zee army to advance on zee city of Orléans. Do you hear?

MS: Not sure what you're talking about.

JA: He speaks to me in golden whispers!

MS: You're hearing the TV in the suite next to us, Ms. Arc. Now please focus. Your leadership on the battlefield is legendary.

JA: *Merci.* I am protected and inspired by God, yes? He encourages me to push on, and victory cannot be taken from us.

MS: What was with the cross-dressing?

JA: *Pardonnez-moi?*

MS: Oh, yes. The wearing of men's clothes, the short hair, the knickers.

JA: I wear men's clothes for—to keep my chastity. We are in zee field quite often, yes, with all zees men, and I am only woman. Better not to have a skirt, you see? Zis also works to fend off English guards when zey take me as prisoner later. [*She cups her hand to her ear.*] I hear you, Great Saint, and will obey.

MS: I just want you to know that I didn't hear anything, and this is getting a little weird.

JA: Glory to the true king!

MS: After the coronation of King Charles, you kept fighting the British at every turn. Why not chill at the castle and see if a truce could be worked out?

JA: Our victory was not complete!

MS: And you got captured. Did the voices tell you that was gonna happen?

JA: Zey told me to escape, and I tried valiantly, believe you me!

MS: The Duke of Burgundy handed you over to the counselor of the English occupation government [the Bishop of Beauvais] for 10,000 francs.

JA: If you ask me, monsieur, I am priceless.

MS: Obviously not, *mon amour.* You were accused of being a blood-thirsty killer. Is that true, the bloodthirsty part?

JA: Zee truth ees, I never killed a soul.

MS: But you fought all sorts of battles.

JA: Yes, and I prefer to carry zee banner in combat, bearing Christ's image and two angels. Indeed, I often show mercy to zee enemy soldiers, giving zem water with a little lavender on the side, lovely smell and—

MS: The court tried you not as a war criminal, but for heresy.

JA: Zey say I am opposed to zee church. Zis is not true! What I am, is opposed to this pro-English church you see. I appeal to the pope—but no.

MS: Let's review some of the seventy charges, and you say "yay" or "nay." You claim divine revelation.

JA: *Oui.*

MS: Yay or nay, please. Endorsed letters with the names of Jesus and Mary?

JA: *Oui.*

MS: Professed to be assured of salvation?

JA: *Oui. Pardon*—yay.

MS: The cross-dressing.

JA: I wore white armor in battle. So, *oui.*

MS: And here's the biggie: Believed to be taking orders directly from God himself.

JA: *Oui!* Why else would a sixteen-year-old girl do zees things? Of course, zee church had a beeg problem with me hearing directly from zee saints. Indeed, zey have the self-centered opinion zat it is only *zey* who can communicate directly with God.

MS: They threatened to torture you if you didn't submit to the church, but you refused. That's ballsy.

JA: *Merci.* I hold myself accountable only to zee saints, you see. Speaking of which, one is talking to me now. Yes, Margie? What is it you desire?

MS: When you got the death penalty, you decided to repent and sign a confession. Why the change of heart?

JA: I wish to live, you see. And zey had taken me to zee cemetery to read my pronouncement, and it was, how you say, very creepy, yes?

MS: So they take you back to prison, and a few days later, there you are again, in men's clothing, and talking about how Saint Marge has pardoned you. Not smart.

JA: But true, yes? And I thank you, Margie!

MS: Not to be indelicate, but what's it like being burned alive?

JA: Oh! Hot, yes? Not like warm, but when you are with zee hand in the oven and "Ouch!" But for much longer. Zen, not so bad.

MS: It may not help with your sunburn, there, but twenty years later, the pope revoked your sentence.

JA: I am innocent, you see! It might have been nice for my king to come to zee rescue while I am alive, but, no matter. I am with zee angels.

MS: Yeah, you were also canonized by Pope Benedict XV in 1920, so you got that goin' for you.

JA: How you say, too leetle, too late?

MS: Say, Saint Joanie, I'd love to continue our little chat, but voices in my stomach are telling me it's lunchtime.

JA: And my own voices tell me I will not see you on zee other side, monsieur. I bid you adieu. Au revoir.

Rᴏʙᴇʀᴛ Lᴇʀᴏʏ Jᴏʜɴsᴏɴ not only *had* the blues, he helped invent the blues, man. You may not know Mr. Johnson, but he was a killer guitarist and an emotional blues singer and surely inspired some rock 'n' rollers on your iPod.

Born in Hazlehurst, Mississippi, young Bob was an originator of the Delta blues—music from the Mississippi Delta region—though it stretched beyond those limits, all the way from Nashville to Chicago. It's dark stuff, often some drunk guy screaming about his lost loves while jamming on a slide guitar, then blowing on the harmonica. Johnson's originality improved the genre, making the blues more melodic and accessible.

To play the blues you gotta have the blues, and Johnson suffered plenty, including losing his wife, Virginia (she was only sixteen), in childbirth in 1930. Living during the Depression probably didn't help matters, but the music soared, and Johnson became known for playing on streetcorners and juke joints full of lumber laborers and WPA road gangs.

Artists influenced by Johnson's style are like a Who's Who: Jimmy Page (Led Zeppelin), R. L. Burnside, John Lee Hooker, Paul Pena, Muddy Waters, Eric Clapton, Bob Dylan, and even Elvis.

For a fella as influential as Johnson, you'd think he recorded thousands of songs, but in fact, the number was twenty-nine. Among them were, "Come on in My Kitchen," "Sweet Home Chicago," and "Cross Road Blues," since covered by dozens of artists.

Along with the notoriety came heavy drinking, partying, gambling, and groupies galore. (Nothing's changed in that regard.) Johnson's ultimate demise, at age twenty-seven, is still surrounded by rumor and innuendo.

Johnson's legacy and influence lives on. *Rolling Stone* magazine listed him at number five of the hundred greatest guitarists of all time, and in 1986 he was inducted into the Rock and Roll Hall of Fame. As modern bluesman Keb' Mo' put it, "All blues seem to revolve around Robert Johnson."

MICHAEL STUSSER: Legend has it that you sold your soul to the devil at the crossroads of two highways, U.S. 61 and U.S. 49. Any truth to the rumor?

ROBERT JOHNSON: Sold it for *what*? Didn't have great health. Didn't have no long life. Didn't have no house. Didn't have no Escalade, much less one with spinners!

MS: Sold it in exchange for playing the guitar like a man possessed, I guess.

RJ: Well, that's hogwash, now. I was a wicked guitar player 'n all, but that was God's gift, ya hear, not Beelzebub. Hell, rumor probably got started by some sad-assed jealous musician, ya know?

MS: Still, some said you had the evil eye.

RJ: Sheet. What I had was cataracts, man, messin' with my eyeball. It's the reason I smoked that weed, speakin' of the devil.

MS: Did the guitar come naturally to you?

RJ: Hail no. I played harp [harmonica] to start, and then would grab Son House's guitar during breaks. People'd get all pissed at the racket I was makin', tell Son, "Git that guitar from the boy, right quick! He's drivin' us nuts!" I had to work at it, man, no question.

MS: What's the key to playing the blues?

RJ: You ever had the blues?

MS: Well, sure.

RJ: Ever scream and holler about feelin' blue?

MS: I guess.

RJ: Well you strap on a slide [guitar] and howl 'bout how she left ya, and you can be a blues master, man. Passion and some moonshine helps some, too, now.

MS: That's it?

RJ: Aw, ya gotta have rhythm, here. Forgot to mention that.

MS: I'm out. What's the saddest tune you ever wrote?

RJ: "Love in Vain" is a damn depressin' ditty. I loved playin' it though, cuz the words meshed right with my style and all. Blues, baby, blues.

MS: You influenced musicians from Elmore James and Muddy Waters to Clapton, but who influenced *you*?

RJ: All sorts a folks. Willie Brown showed me all kinds of moves on the harp and guitar. And Charlie Patton played Robinsonville, where I was livin' as a teenager, and we'd go see him at juke houses fo' sure. And, have to say Son House, most definitely. Boy had the passion of a preacher, hollering with that rough voice on songs like "Death Letter Blues." Plus, he just went *at* the guitar, ya know? He attacked the damn thing, man.

MS: What about Ike Zinnerman?

RJ: Aw, *hail* yes! You think *I* got a reputation for bein' odd, that old man learned to play guitar in a graveyard at midnight while sittin' on top-a tombstones. I picked ol' Zinny's brain for all kinds a tips on playin' and singin'. Ike was the best ever was.

MS: Did you earn any money playing?

RJ: Took a while, but it came in. I started buskin' on the steps of the courthouse at lunchtime just to have an audience, man. Then I played house parties that'd give me a pint a beer or a shot of whiskey, maybe, and we'd try to meet dames and have fun out there. Later on, I made some serious coin cuz folks would come from all over when they heard I was playin' a joint. Mo ladies, baby, mo and mo ladies!

MS: What about records? Any money there?

RJ: I made some dough on "Terraplane Blues," which was my hit, I guess. We had 78s back then, and people called my tunes "race re- cords"—thought maybe that would get black folks wantin' to listen. They paid me ten bucks a track, is all, and no royalties, neither. Chump change, but the legend grew, man, cuz in case you didn't notice, I was *damn* good.

MS: You're often called the greatest blues singer of all time, but there are songs I've heard that make you sound like you just stepped on a cat. What's up with that?

RJ: You ain't got no ears, man! Dead cat my ass. What you're hearin' is perfect pitch, put together with howlin' raw emotion, baby!

MS: Sounds kinda like a cat.

RJ: Well then, I oughta book your cat for a damn tour, cuz she must be fine! Hell, maybe you're just used to your slick stereo and albums all mastered in studios and all. When we laid down tracks in my day, it was a tape recorder in a barn if we was lucky, ya hear? It's gonna sound thin compared to your uppity overproduced crap, come on!

MS: Keith Richards, of the Rolling Stones—

RJ: I *know* who the cat is! I may be dead, but I ain't deaf, now!

MS: Well, when his bandmate Brian Jones introduced him to your music, Richards said, "Great player, but who is the other guitarist?"

RJ: And I was playin' *solo*, as usual. I could stoke that thing, no question, made it sound like I had five boys in my band.

MS: You seemed a little paranoid about other players stealing your stuff.

RJ: Aw, they was always watchin' me, man, tryin' to take my songs, figure out how I tuned my guitar. That's my bidness, man. Can't have nobody takin' away my livin' or I'd have to go back pickin' cotton, and I ain't all right with that.

MS: Musicians were amazed by your ability to listen to a song once and be able to play it.

RJ: Just listenin' and repeatin', no thang. I had to play all kinds a music—hillbilly, square dance, pop, even polka, man. Folks wanna hear it, I'm gonna play it so they throw some coin in my case, ya know. Give the people what they *want.*

MS: And what did they want?

RL: Aw, hell, it was always "Yes, Sir, That's My Baby," and "Tumbling Tumbleweeds." Plus some sentimental "Happy Birthday" crap, ya know.

MS: Seems you had a particular method for finding a woman in every port.

RJ: *Ha!* You heard 'bout that, huh? Yeah, don't sound great, but I'd find the ugliest gal I could, and sweet-talk her and all. Thing with the homely ones is they ain't got a man, so they'll put you up in no time, and no one's gonna care that you is with her. I was nice to 'em all, though, made it worth their while.

MS: Let's talk about your death.

RJ: Yeah, that oughta be a good time.

[Johnson sings from his "Preachin' Blues (Up Jumped the Devil)."]

The blues is a low-down achin' heart disease.
Like consumption killing me by degrees.

MS: Story goes you were with another man's wife. . . .

RJ: Story of my life.

MS: And he slipped some poison into your whiskey—after Sonny Boy Williamson warned you about drinking out of open bottles.

RJ: Aw, what are you, my momma? Now the poison part's right as rain: The bastard put strychnine in ma whiskey, and I'm drinkin' free whiskey no matter *who* gives it to me or how *open* the damn bottle is or how many *lips* been on it. The dyin' part ain't right. . . . I kicked the bucket three days later on account a pneumonia. Stuff was goin' 'round, man, and it was nasty.

MS: You'll be happy to know the blues are alive and well.

RJ: Naw, that don't make me happy. That means there's some nasty, down-hearted bidness goin' on, or they'd be playin' happy love songs and leavin' the blues behind.

MS: So you're sad about the success of the blues?

RJ: Get me right now: That's the way it's always gonna be—lonely heartbreak and wars and strife ongoin'. What I'm sayin', bro, is I'm glad to be a part of the scene and all, though woulda been nice to be *paid* more and have the *blues* less, I tell ya. HA! Reminds me of a song I wanna write down. Still workin', I can tell you that. Come on!

END
of Interview

BORN ON THE outskirts of Mexico City, Frida Kahlo (Magdalena Carmen Frida Kahlo y Calderón) incorporated her pain-filled life into paintings in a format as revolutionary as her politics.

Though she suffered from polio as a child, the worst of Frida's grief came from a nasty accident on September 17, 1925. The bus Frida was riding on collided with a trolley car, breaking her spinal column, collar bone, ribs, pelvis, leg, and lunch box, no doubt. (A metal rod also pierced her womb, making her unable to have children—a fact she learned only after several miscarriages later in life.) Frida made a miraculous recovery, but the hurt, both physical and psychological, would stay with her throughout her days.

She completed 143 paintings in her brief life, 55 of which are self-portraits, often showing severed body parts and grotesque dreams in graphic detail.

Proud of her Mexican heritage, Kahlo also integrated aspects of her culture, folk art, and the history of Mexico into her work. Though she claimed not to be a surrealist, her paintings included bizarre fantasy images, along with the honesty about her miscarriages, intrusive surgeries, and an unbridled lust for life. In addition to painting the internal self (I am Woman, hear my intestines), Frida also laid her external thoughts on canvas, revealing her cultural and political ideas on revolution and race.

Her marriage to muralist Diego Rivera (whom she divorced, then remarried) was a rocky road filled with abuse and instability. (Sorry to be such a downer, but she had it bad.) Though she may have been overshadowed during her life by Rivera, today it is Frida who is considered one of the great artists of the twentieth century.

Kahlo was a proud Communist, and hobnobbed with Leon Trotsky, praised Stalin, and called China "the new Socialist hope." When Trotsky was exiled by Stalin in 1936, Rivera and Kahlo housed him for several years.

Kahlo's pain stopped at age forty-seven, after she succumbed to any one her dozens of ailments. Her work lives on in books, films, and, if you're lucky enough to see one, brilliantly colored canvases.

MICHAEL STUSSER: Gotta ask about the facial hair. Why not trim up the old mono-brow and wax the 'stache, you know?

FRIDA KAHLO: Yes, I now see this is going to be like sitting with a pig for an hour. Why don't you shave your back? I am beautiful the way I came from the womb. If you were my lover, which you would never be, I would let you pluck me anywhere you desired.

MS: You'll be happy to know that your family has launched Frida Kahlo Tequila, and I brought a little along, perhaps to warm things up a bit.

[Frida throws back a shot and lies back in her bed.]

MS: Maybe one more, for good health. *Salud.*

[Two more shots are tossed back; the interview continues.]

MS: A lot of your paintings show pain and suffering.

FK: Ever been in a bus when it flips over and crushes most the bones in your body? Not good, *comprende?*

MS: Still, there's an emphasis on anatomical references in your work. I feel like I'm in pre-med or something.

FK: The pig makes a point! Before my accident, I wanted to be a doctor, so I had an interest in anatomy. Then, after finding myself in constant frickin' traction with corsets and broken legs and plaster casts, pretty much the only thing I could do was lie there and paint.

MS: You had something like thirty operations.

FK: *Es verdad.* So you start to paint what you know—in my case, lots of X-rays and internal organs.

MS: Tough to do self-portraits when you're bedridden, huh?

FK: This is why I say God bless to my beautiful *madre y padre*, who not only paid my medical bills but made a special easel. It had a sort of canopy with a mirror so I could see myself and do self-portraits on this damn gurney.

MS: Don't take this the wrong way, but do you have a thing against men?

FK: No, I have a thing against abusive idiots, regardless of their sex, *chico.*

MS: Are we talking about your husband, Diego Rivera?

FK: Among others, you bet. He had what you now call "anger management problems," to put it nicely.

MS: He beat you.

FK: *Sí.* Often. And let us remember his size—the man was over six feet tall and three hundred pounds. I'm five foot three! It's not fun to be a punching bag, let me tell you.

[She grabs the tequila bottle and takes a swig.]

MS: He was twenty years older than you. Where'd you guys meet?

FK: The first time I saw him was at my high school, when he was being paid to paint a mural in the auditorium. Diego was already famous, and I suppose I was a little starstruck. . . .

MS: Is it true that he had an affair with your younger sister?

FK: *Sí,* Cristina. As I have said, I suffered two grave accidents in my life. One involved a bus, the other accident is Diego.

MS: But he was also a great admirer of your work.

FK: Push-pull, push-pull, all day and night! We took great pride in each other's work and also found time to torture each other. Still, I loved him as my child, my lover, my universe.

MS: My goodness.

[The interviewer takes a swig of tequila.]

FK: In the end, I guess I understood him. I let him play matrimony with other women, because Diego was never anybody's husband and would never be. But he was a great comrade.

MS: Tell us about the Blue House we are meeting in. [Today it is home to the Frida Kahlo Museum.]

FK: Casa Azul was my parents' home, but at that time it was pink. We repainted the outside and slowly added folklore and gardens and other Mexican influences. Diego and I both had studios here.

MS: Is that a monkey?

FK: There she is! She's one of my favorite pets. I also have deer and parrots and a few dogs—but hairless. For my allergies.

MS: You've got some interesting portraits on the wall there.

FK: Oh, I love that one. *[She points at a portrait of Karl Marx.]* Mao and Stalin look so serious in theirs—of course, they were fairly serious hombres. And the one on the end is my favorite. [Engels, in bright colors.]

MS: Is it true you had an affair with Leon Trotsky?

FK: Can't a woman be a good Communist without sleeping with the leader?

MS: Ya did, didn't you?

FK: When he was assassinated in his home, I was actually arrested for murder. After that, I always told people that the reason we invited him to Mexico was to have him killed. *Ha!* Can you imagine? *You*, I might kill. Leon was a sweetheart.

MS: At what point did you consider yourself a success?

FK: I think after André [Breton] organized an exhibition for me in Paris in 1938, I began to finally gain real confidence. The Louvre bought a picture, and I remember meeting Picasso and Kandinksy and Duchamp, and they made me feel a part of their group, you know? A lot of critics were still scared by some of my themes, but I finally felt popular.

MS: What did you think of all the surrealists?

FK: They thought that I was one of them—Breton, especially. But I never painted dreams; I painted my own reality. To be honest, I thought they were a bunch of cuckoo, lunatic sons of bitches.

MS: Today, you're a major feminist cult figure. I'm talking huge. Forget Steinem or Ellen DeGeneres. You're the "It Girl" when it comes to this stuff.

FK: Do not call me a girl, or "It," por favor.

MS: Right. Sorry. What I meant was that you're an inspiration to people who want to toss out the rules and expectations. You wore beautiful gowns but also men's suits. You slept with men, and, of course, women.

FK: I always thought it was ridiculous that Diego didn't have a problem with my affairs with other women, but when I slept with another man, he'd get insanely jealous.

MS: Men! Pigs, really. Not to obsess here, but just give me the *si* or *no* on whether you slept with the following: Actress Dolores del Rio.

FK: *Si.*

MS: Actress Paulette Goddard.

FK: Oh, *si.*

MS: Georgia O'Keeffe.

FK: *Si.*

MS: Really? How about Emmy Lou Packard? Maria Felix? Josephine Baker!

FK: *Si. Si. SI!*

MS: Today you're a huge celebrity. In fact, a one-named celeb, which is even cooler!

FK: I saw my face on a pair of underwear the other day.

MS: Oh, you don't know the half of it—shirts, keychains, mouse pads. You're even a popular Halloween mask.

FK: This is more sad than all my pain and suffering combined. I'm hoping my art is shown from time to time as well.

MS: Oh, yeah. That too. Your work is featured on over sixty-five thousand Web sites, and you even got a stamp in 2001!

FK: Mexican or American?

MS: Well, it was a U.S. postage stamp. But thirty-four cents! That's a lot. The first Hispanic woman ever featured on a stamp.

FK: How you say, whoop te doo. Pour us more tequila. Ahora!

[The Frida Kahlo brand is poured.]

MS: You only had one exhibition in Mexico [1953].

FK: And I was in such bad shape my *estupido* doctors told me not to attend.

MS: Did you?

FK: No way I'm missing that. I actually arrived in an ambulance, and they carried me in on a stretcher. I had my giant four-poster bed delivered to the gallery, and they put me right in the middle of the action.

MS: Quite an entrance!

FK: I lied there all night, drinking and singing and having a great time.

MS: Everyone speaks of how brave you were. How stoic, even though you were clearly suffering. How did you do it?

FK: The Demerol helped. Really, painkillers and some tequila would allow me to joke around and feel happy. And luckily, painting completed my life. Work, for me, was the best thing.

MS: You tried suicide a few times.

FK: Can you blame me? Thirty operations, endless infections, and complications. *Dios mio!*

MS: Did you finally commit suicide? No one did an autopsy, so we aren't sure.

FK: My last diary entry will shed some light: "I hope the leaving is joyful and I hope never to return."

MS: And yet here we are. Before I go, I'd like to apologize for the mono-brow comment I made earlier.

FK: *Sí.*

MS: I mean, Salma Hayek, one of the hottest women on the planet, played you in the movie of your life [*Frida*, 2002], and even with that thing, you—or she—looked to-die-for. My point is, not that it matters, but you're very attractive. Inside and out, of course.

FK: I would still not sleep with you if my life depends on it, *si*? But *gracias, y adios.*

GENGHIS KHAN

(ALSO SPELLED CHING-GIS, JENGHIZ, JINGHIS;
BIRTH NAME TEMUJIN)

BORN 1162
DIED 1227

GENGHIS KHAN WAS the main force behind the Mongolian Empire (1206–1368) and one of most aggressive and innovative military and political conquerors the world has ever encountered. And talk about back hair!

Genghis was hugely influential with his own people and widely respected for ending ten thousand years of Mongol infighting. By crushing opponents all over the Eurasian continent (from the Adriatic Sea to the Pacific coast of China), he finally brought economic and political stability to the Mongolian Empire. His cavalry was fierce, well organized, and tended to have a nasty reputation due to the plundering and killing.

Khan wasn't all about murder and mayhem (though the Russians, Chinese, Afghanis, Indians, and Persians might disagree); his life also had a spiritual element, combining shamanism with a nomadic lifestyle that embraced wide-open spaces and communal living (not to mention a harem that would fill the Superdome).

He created a written set of laws called *Yassa*, which the Mongols followed to the letter, creating order among his tribesmen. The Mongols tended to follow the strict code, mainly because violators would be put to death. The rules were pretty unusual for the time and included freedom of religion, tax breaks for artists and teachers, making animal-stealing and adultery punishable by death, teaching tribes how to read, and not allowing women to be sold into marriage (which got him a large percentage of the Mongol female vote).

In the end, Genghis was quite the double-edged sword: He and his armies may well have killed millions (the losers never had a chance to tally the dead), but the Mongols opened up new trade routes, and his philosophical agenda was pretty darn open-minded—for a madman.

MICHAEL STUSSER: First off, any relation to Chaka Khan?

GENGHIS KHAN: Khan is bestowed only upon Universal Emperor by Mongol chieftains [1206], you little runt!

MS: Genghis, aka Chingis: Why so angry?

GK: My father was killed when I was nine, and I lived in time of constant raids and murder.

MS: That's it?

GK: When I was young boy, I was kidnapped by rival tribe. They place wooden collar around my neck and treat me like animal.

MS: But you did get away.

GK: It left a mark!

MS: What do you want to be known for?

GK: I am Chingis Khan!

MS: Yes, I am aware of that, Mr. Khan, but what in particular would you like to be remembered for? Bringing stability to the Mongolian Empire, or—

GK: Chingis!

MS:—ending years of infighting—

GK: Khan! Khan!

MS: Is this . . . Do we need an interpreter?

GK: I wish to be known as greatest genius to walk the earth! I am instrument of the wrath of heaven!

MS: Don't be shy.

GK: In my time I controlled half of the world!

MS: Well, to be fair, half of the *known* world.

GK: Chingis!

MS: Not this again. Is it true you were born of divine origin?

GK: My ancestor was the gray wolf, and I was born with a destiny from heaven on high.

MS: That reminds me of a John Denver song.

GK: Chingis on high!

MS: Great. Yes. When your father was poisoned, you were made the clan's new chief before you could even go on the rides at Disneyland. How did that turn out?

GK: Tribes refuse to be led by mere boy, and we became nomads living on foraged berries and marmots.

MS: Wow. That is rough. What does a marmot taste like?

GK: Chicken.

MS: Your mother, Hoelun, taught you some valuable lessons in the wild.

GK: Yes, such as surviving in nature, making marmot soup, and need for allies. She also taught me etiquette, common sense, and how to wash loincloth.

MS: The Mongol way of life talks about the "Five Snouts." Whose snouts are we talking about?

GK: Horses are key to our nomadic life. Then there are sheep, goat, bovine, and my aunt Gertrude.

MS: Aunt?

GK: I make joke! Camels are final snout.

MS: You guys really are big on horses.

GK: Which reminds me: We must now drink wine from the mare's milk.

MS: Please, no.

GK: Chingis wishes you to drink!

MS: They make wine from *grapes* now. You should try it.

GK: Drunkenness is revered and honored in my culture.

MS: I'm going to fit in well, I think. Now, your written teachings, known as *Yassa*, are pretty insightful. I guess I'm surprised.

GK: We have proud, nomadic tradition. I tell Mongols not to focus on wealth and pleasure, but to stay close to land. We keep on the move with only what we need on our backs.

MS: So you aren't into settling down, having a nice white-picket fence, two-car garage?

GK: I give away goods from conquests to those in need. My home was a yurt—I need nothing more.

MS: One of the laws you created was about kidnapping.

GK: My wife was kidnapped when I was teenager and it make me sad. AND ANGRY! I make kidnapping illegal.

MS: You also outlawed torture, abolished the sale of women, promoted tolerance of other cultures. On the inside, you're a sensitive sap!

GK: Do not push me or you will feel the wrath of Khan.

MS: Great movie! *Star Trek*? Ricardo Montalban? Never saw it? [Genghis begins sharpening a blood-rusted sword.] Seriously, though, not forcing your own religion on all the folks you dominated—that was some wacky stuff for the time.

GK: To conquer a nation, you must conquer hearts of its people. My interest is not in separating a nation from their god, but in separating them from their goods, and sometimes from their wives. Worship Buddha or Jesus or Allah, but do it under my rule.

MS: I'm just saying, the Mongols were a bunch of, well, *Mongols* for the most part, before you came along. You guys fought among yourselves and tribes hated one another. How'd you clean that up?

GK: Khan have strong will! Mongol chiefs make me ruler of all between oceans! Chingis rules!

MS: Yeah, we heard that, Chiggie. My question is, how'd you get everyone to start behaving?

GK: Code of law is very serious. All follow same law.

MS: OK, let's say I commit an offense—like lying.

GK: Death will come to you!

MS: Adultery?

GK: Death!

MS: How about something minor, like peeing in a tent?

GK: Also death! Death for wasting food! Death for stepping on threshold of chief! Death!

MS: Let's talk about psychological warfare, which you pretty much invented.

GK: We give many villages simple choice: surrender or die. If they choose to fight, we kill almost all—send a few on to next village to tell them how cruel we are.

MS: I bet that was effective.

GK: Not as effective as taking enemy and using him as human shield in battle.

MS: Ruthless. The one where you poured molten steel into a guy's ears was impressive.

GK: Thank you.

MS: Watching the Mongol army come into town was a scary sight. What the hell were you guys wearing?

GK: We adorn ourselves in boiled leather as armor.

MS: Nice look.

GK: Under leather we wear silk undershirts.

MS: Now we're talking.

GK: This allow us to twist arrow out easily, and silk plug wound. We also carry sabers, spears, axes, ropes, rations. Each warrior also have bow and many types of arrows.

MS: Arrows are arrows.

GK: You know nothing! We have poison arrows, piercing arrows, blunt stun arrows, and even whistling arrow used as signal.

MS: Wow. I stand corrected.

GK: And helmet is key. Tell kids, when you ride—must wear helmet.

MS: Speaking of helmets, it's estimated that you may have fathered over 15,000 children from eastern Europe to China. How is that even possible?

GK: Conquer country. Form harem. Bring girl every other hour for four hours. Sleep. Repeat.

MS: Still, you make Wilt Chamberlain look like a virgin.

GK: I not know this Wilt man, but I can tell you that I am sleepy. Very sleepy.

MS: You were a bit of a collector.

GK: Khan not understand! Give me that strange object.

[He reaches across the table and grabs the tape recorder.]

MS: See, this is what I'm talking about. You took things from those you conquered, even if you had no idea of its purpose.

GK: Shiny. Chingis like.

MS: Give that back, please.

GK: Does this make music? Sing for Chingis!

MS: It's a tape recorder. It was recording our conversation.

GK: I take abacus and compass from enemy. I take explosives from Chinese. Look: Chinese firecrackers!

MS: Please don't light that in here.

GK: We conquer many lands and exchange goods. Merkits, Tatars, Persians. You need a rug? Good price!

MS: The Mongols had a reputation for stealing objects they thought were "new." Come to think of it, where's my cell phone? Genghis?

GK: I know not what cell you speak of.

[A distinct ringing sound comes from Genghis's loincloth.]

MS: Ah-HA!

GK: Great Chingis take what he needs for road!

MS: You can say that again.

GK: Great Chingis take what he needs for road!

MS: Germans taught you how to mine, Indians showed you astronomy, Muslims taught you math, Italians showed you how to be silversmiths. It's time you learned something for yourself.

GK: Are you calling me a *mongoloid*?

MS: No. That's a derogatory term for retard. You're obviously not a retard.

GK: All right. Here is kill phone. Now we drink more mare wine.

MS: Before I forget: What's the key to conquering the world?

GK: My success has more to do with enemies' weakness than my army's power. Moderation is key. While others wallow in luxury, we stay lean—live close to land.

MS: Bet your habit of building giant columns with human skulls didn't hurt.

GK: It had an effect. Now we drink mare wine.

MS: Hoo boy.

END
of Interview

ABE LINCOLN WAS born in a one-room Kentucky log cabin and wound up the sixteenth president of the United States of America—which goes to show you that square footage (or lack thereof) is quite the motivating factor. Best known for his Gettysburg Address (not to mention the neck-beard and stovepipe hat), Abraham's résumé includes putting an end to slavery, which is impressive enough to get your mug on Mount Rushmore.

Honest Abe got by with less than a year of formal schooling and eventually taught himself law to pass the bar, setting up a practice in Springfield, Illinois, in 1836. He was a state legislator and member of the House of Representatives until being nominated by the newly established Republican Party for a spot in the Senate in 1858.

In 1860 Lincoln ran for president, and though gaining only two-fifths of the popular vote (let's just say the South didn't love his positions on slavery—he took only 2 of 996 counties there), he still won by a huge margin in the electoral college.

By the time Lincoln was inaugurated, seven states had seceded from the Union (four more would follow), which led to the American Civil War. Lincoln never backed down from his opposition to slavery, and in 1864 he was reelected with a platform of emancipation. Slavery was outlawed a year later with the passage of the Thirteenth Amendment.

Though the war dominated his legacy, Lincoln had a number of impressive political successes: He signed the Homestead Act (1862) and encouraged the development of the American West, centralized the powers of the federal government, revived national banks, established the U.S. Department of Agriculture, and—to the horror of millions of turkeys—declared Thanksgiving a national holiday.

Lincoln was shot and mortally wounded on April 14, 1865, only five days after the Union forces (commanded by Ulysses S. Grant) defeated Jefferson Davis's Confederacy, which ended the Civil War.

MICHAEL STUSSER: People think of Honest Abe and your desire to abolish slavery, but many don't know you had an excellent sense of humor.

ABRAHAM LINCOLN: Well, I kept it under my hat. *Ha!* Hat! I wore a big-ass hat!

MS: Your stump speeches often made fun of your gangly looks. What's up with that?

AL: I'm six foot four, with an odd face, and the first prez with a beard. If I could make fun, say, of my crooked nose, I could get folks to look beyond my appearance.

MS: Did anyone have the nerve to actually comment about how you looked?

AL: I remember someone calling me two-faced during a disagreement, and my reply was, "If I had two faces, do you think I'd be wearing *this* one?"

MS: Tell us how you met your wife, Mary.

AL: We were at a ball in Springfield, and I told her I wanted to dance with her in the worst way. As she later said, that's exactly what I did—danced with her in the worst way.

MS: Your two left feet seemed to have worked.

AL: Yeah, though it wasn't easy. Mare's sister hated me, and we had to date in secret for a while. Eventually we got hitched.

MS: Why did people dislike Mrs. Lincoln so much?

AL: Well, she was loony as a jaybird, for one. And at the time, an ambitious, opinionated First Lady didn't sit well. Now it's expected. The séances she held didn't help.

MS: She also knew how to spend, huh?

AL: Oh, my. Mary had expensive taste, that's for sure. She turned the White House from something that looked like a dirtbag motel to what it is today. Bought some great china, too.

MS: What made you a great president?

AL: I'm a patient man, always willing to forgive on the Christian terms of repentance.

MS: Easier said than done in your case. A lot of people wanted your head on a platter.

AL: Yeah, and that's when I gave 'em a big bear hug to break the tension. In 1860, I picked the three gentlemen whom I had beaten for the Republican presidential nomination to be in my cabinet. I had no right to deprive the country of their services, and it was a stroke of managerial genius, if I do say so myself.

MS: Is it true your secretary of war, Edwin Stanton, made your youngest son, Tad, a lieutenant?

AL: Hah! Taddy was big on make-believe, and so when the little guy was eight or so, we gave him a uniform and fake sword—before you know it, he's firing guards at the White House.

MS: Did he really sentence a doll to death by execution?

AL: Ten times. I've got the presidential pardon to prove it.

MS: Switching gears, Mr. President, there are rumors about your homosexuality.

AL: I'm not familiar with the term.

MS: Sorry to be blunt, sir, but did you have sex with men?

AL: I did a little snuggling with my best friend, Joshua Speed, during my late twenties and early thirties. In my day, plenty of men shared beds. Winters were brutal and the heating units sucked.

MS: Let's talk about depression.

AL: You're just a bundle of joy.

MS: Your first love, Ann Rutledge, died before you had a chance to marry her, your mom passed away when you were nine, and you struggled with a nation at war with itself.

AL: Thank you for those lovely milestones—it's a good thing I'm already dead, or you would have sent me over the edge.

MS: Did you think about killing yourself?

AL: It is true that I pondered suicide several times in my twenties, and was pretty darned sad a lot of the time. Melancholy, I think I'd describe it—and for good reason. Wasn't like I was governing in the best of times.

MS: Were there any positives to having depression?

AL: I had a lot of empathy, which I brought to the presidency, and I think at the time that was real important, with all our internal conflicts.

MS: Did you hate the South?

AL: No sireee. I always said southern people were no more responsible for the origin of slavery than the North. If slavery did not exist among them, they would not have introduced it.

MS: People differ as to your true thoughts on slavery. Care to clear the record?

AL: My paramount object was to save the Union and was not either to save or to destroy slavery. If I could save the Union without freeing any slave, I would do it; if I could save it by freeing all the slaves, I would do it; and if I could save it by freeing some and leaving others alone, I would also do that.

MS: Your views on slaves changed over time.

AL: No, it did not. For the record, I said, "If slavery is not wrong, nothing is wrong."

MS: At one time you suggested that freed slaves colonize in Central America or Africa, but changed your mind on that around 1863. How come?

AL: Tens of thousands of African Americans were enlisting in the Union army, and—while I may be many things—I'm no dummy.

MS: Bottom line?

AL: You ever hear the phrase "A house divided against itself cannot stand"? That's mine—with a little help from Jesus. I wanted to do two things: Preserve the union, and make sure our government allowed freedom to all mankind. You can't talk about equality and have slavery hangin' over half the households. Then you're a hypocrite.

MS: The Reverend Martin Luther King Jr. started his famous "I have a dream" speech with a nod to your Gettysburg Address: "Five-score years ago, a great American, in whose symbolic shadow we stand, signed the Emancipation Proclamation." How does that make you feel?

AL: I'm proud of our nation. My respected acquaintance Frederick Douglass [former slave, brilliant writer, and abolitionist] gave me the ultimate compliment in his autobiography. He said, "In his company I was never in any way reminded of my humble origin, or of my unpopular color."

MS: Changing to a tough subject: Did you know that John Wilkes Booth was the gunman?

AL: Gunman? I just thought it was a long intermission.

MS: You might not have been killed if your bodyguard wasn't in the audience watching the play at the time.

AL: *Our American Cousin* is a good show, so I don't blame him. If it hadn't been him, woulda been somebody else.

MS: Can you forgive Booth?

AL: That's a complicated question, son. I can't forgive him for shooting me in front of my wife, who was already a nervous wreck. But for the act against me, I truly can forgive Mr. Booth. Over a half million Americans willingly paid the ultimate price for liberty and the sake of a strong union. I was a big part of the war, and I had to be willing to do the same, or it would've disgraced the honor of their own sacrifice.

MS: Sometimes I forget how damn articulate you are, Mr. President.

AL: It's because I look like a homeless person.

MS: Can I just tell you about some weird similarities to JFK?

AL: Who?

MS: Both of your last names have seven letters, both of you lost kids while living in the White House, and both of you were shot on a Friday.

AL: That's a little weird.

MS: Your secretary was named Kennedy, and Kennedy's secretary was named Lincoln. Both successors were named Johnson.

AL: Common name.

MS: Booth ran from the theater and was caught in a warehouse. Oswald ran from a warehouse and was caught in a theater.

AL: Weirder.

MS: You were shot in a theater named Ford. Kennedy was shot in a car called Lincoln, which was made by Ford. Both killers were assassinated before their trials.

AL: Freakin' me out.

MS: And here's the weirdest: A week before Lincoln was shot he was in Monroe, Maryland. A week before Kennedy was shot, he was in Marilyn Monroe. *Ha!*

AL: Looks like this JFK character got the better deal. . . .

MS: It's been a real pleasure, sir. You're the best.

END
of Interview

THOUGH NOT A member of the Marx Brothers, Karl was an innovative German revolutionary, Communist, and founder of Marxism. His aim: to overthrow capitalist society and emancipate the workingman. He was also a writing machine, churning out intellectual theories on class struggles as fast as the sweatshops he opposed made tennis shoes.

Karl's main claim to fame was *The Communist Manifesto* (1848), which he wrote with lifelong collaborator Friedrich Engels (who also funded him throughout his entire life). The *Manifesto*'s main elements include the abolition of privately held property; a progressive income tax; and centralization of credit, factories, means of transportation, and communication. Oh, and the equal liability of all to labor—and yes, that means you.

Witnessing the harsh realities of the Industrial Revolution, he was inspired to write his masterpiece, *Das Kapital*, known as "the Bible of the Working Class." And he oughta know—the Marx family lived in extreme poverty throughout their lives, even selling each and every piece of furniture they owned in order to survive.

During the last few decades of his life, Marx spent all his time in the British Library, writing *Das Kapital*. Though chronically depressed in his final years, he continued to influence leaders of working-class and social movements. He died in London, not long after the death of his wife and eldest daughter. His theories lived on in the hearts and minds of many, most notably sparking the Communist Revolution in Russia in 1917.

MICHAEL STUSSER: Ya know, if you'd been a capitalist, you would have gotten rich from royalties on your books. [An estimated five hundred million copies have been sold.] Does that make you want to switch teams?

KARL MARX: Vat is zis, teams? I am zee pillar of Communist thought! I vish nothing of profits and riches!

MS: Well, I do, and I'm telling you, we could have made a killing. *The Communist Manifesto* alone would have brought you eight figures.

KM: I tell you about figures: It figures your small bourgeois mind vould only think of turning me into zis moneymaking machine, unt not an ounce of thought to zee ideas within zee books zemselves!

MS: Let's discuss some of your theories.

KM: Now vee are getting to zee richness of thought. Reason has always existed, but not always in reasonable form.

MS: Can you describe the theory of Communism in a single sentence?

KM: Abolition of private property.

MS: What about the condo I have in Laguna Beach?

KM: Communism deprives no man of zee ability to appropriate zee fruits of his labor. Zee only sing it deprives him of is the ability to enslave *others* by means of such appropriations.

MS: As much as I like having my own bank account, you did have some good ideas: abolition of inheritances, free education for kids, the progressive income tax, abolition of child factory labor—not bad for a Commie pinko.

KM: Zee proletarians have nothing to lose but zere chains!

MS: Well, I don't . . .

KM: Zey have a vorld to vin! Vorkingmen of all countries, unite!

MS: OK, please sit down. Surprisingly, you were a bit shy for a revolutionary.

KM: I am both rebel unt intellectual. I vas never much into zee rah-rah rallies unt demonstrations. Unt public speaking is simply not a strong point. I prefer zee pen.

MS: You were supposedly an avid intellectual. Does that mean you read a lot?

KM: I spent most my life in zee reading room of zee British Museum. Novels, manifestos, poetry, epics, I loved zem all. Especially Sir Walter Scott, Balzac, unt Dante. And I vas a Shakespeare fanatic! Zee whole family vas.

MS: Religion, you said, is "the opium of the people." How would you know? Did you ever smoke opium?

KM: It is metaphor! Of zis you understand?

MS: Of this you smoke opium?

KM: Blind fool! Religion is zee sigh of zee oppressed creature, zee heart of a heartless world, and zee soul of soulless conditions!

MS: Let's take it down a notch, hmm? You had horrible health: boils, hemorrhoids, back and liver problems, bronchitis, and head infections.

KM: You try to live on potatoes and rock soup!

MS: Smoking, stress, poor eating habits, heavy drinking, and poor personal hygiene, my friend. That's what brought ya down.

KM: Bourgeois pig!

MS: You got expelled from a lot of places—France, Prussia, Belgium—did that hurt your feelings?

KM: I used zeez petty hacks to my advantage. When zey tossed me from Paris in 1849, I published zee final issue of my Communist newspaper in *red* ink—like zee blood zat would flow from zere elitist veins!

MS: Again, if you'd sit, please. You wrote *The Communist Manifesto.*

KM: Vith my collaborator, Friedrich.

MS: Well, there's a new book out by Ray Bennett called *The Underachiever's Manifesto.*

KM: I assume zis takes our brilliant vurk of class struggle unt illustrates how capitalism has turned your citzens into zee couch potato, no?

MS: Actually talks about joining hands and doing less—like taking a nap.

KM: So many oppressed still to educate!

MS: You had perhaps the best last words I've ever read.

KM: "Go on, get out," I said. "Last words are for fools who haven't said enough."

MS: At your funeral, Engels said this about you: "He was the best-hated and most calumniated man of his time."

KM: About sums it up, yah. He also said I died "beloved, revered, and mourned by millions of revolutionary fellow vorkers." I liked zat part. And the vodka at my vake, of course. *Provost!*

MS: In *Das Kapital* you describe how, under capitalism, the misery of the working class would increase—until finally, and I'll quote you here, "the knell of capitalist private property sounds."

KM: "And the expropriators are expropriated."

MS: Didn't happen.

KM: No?

MS: 'Fraid not.

KM: But all is not vell in your society, yah? Zee more zee division of labor and zee application of machinery extend, zee more does competition extend among vorkers, zee more do their vages shrink together.

MS: I can't afford health insurance, if that's what you're getting at.

KM: Thus, it's not over until zee fat lady sings, my comrade. Zee struggle continues!

END
of Interview

MONTEZUMA

BORN 1466
DIED 1520

IN 1502 MONTEZUMA became the ninth emperor of the Aztec Empire. Ruling the city of Tenochtitlán (now Mexico City), Montezuma was revered as an intellectual, warrior, and chief priest . . . and had a nasty habit of sacrificing folks on pretty much an hourly basis. Though he may not have invented the technique, he mastered the practice of tearing a victim's heart out and tossing the body down the pyramid steps. (Sorry if you were eating dinner during that. . . .)

These ritual killings actually became a full-time job for good old Montezuma: increased sacrifices (around thirty thousand per year by the time the Spaniards arrived) meant more bodies required. (In case the sacrifices and cannibalism didn't scare the crap out of the enemy, Montezuma had a theater made out of 135,000 skulls and mortar.)

A great general, Montezuma ruled with a stern hand. He conquered many area tribes and was despised for his looting, taxation, and murder in the name of religious zeal. His empire stretched from the Atlantic to the Pacific—what is now Honduras, Nicaragua, and parts of Guatemala.

Montezuma's end came with the arrival of Spanish explorer Hernán Cortés in 1519. Mistaken by many Aztecs as a god (Aztec legend had a bearded white deity showing up to bring on the apocalypse), Cortés convinced many tribes to aid in his effort to oust Montezuma.

After winning some small battles along the coast of the Yucatán, Cortés rolled into Tenochtitlán and stormed the palace. Believing that Cortés was, indeed, a god, Montezuma welcomed him with open arms. Bad idea—the Spanish took Montezuma hostage and threatened to kill the emperor if the Aztecs resisted.

After a massacre of almost one thousand Aztecs in the main temple, Montezuma appeared on the balcony of the palace on July 1, 1520, and told his angry followers to back off. The crowds became furious at their meek ruler, stoning him with rocks and hucking spears. Injured and no longer in charge, Montezuma was held captive until his death a few days later.

Subsequent clashes with the Spanish and previously subdued tribes took over 250,000 lives, thus ending the Aztec empire and giving birth to Mexico.

MICHAEL STUSSER: "From the halls of Mont-e-zuma . . ."

MONTEZUMA: Why do you sing?

MS: Montezuma, aka Moctezuma, Motecuhzoma Xocoyotzin, the "archer of heaven," "ruler by his rage." Can I just call you Monty?

M: Can I use your head as a soccer ball?

MS: Point taken. Speaking of soccer, you pretty much executed people for the sport of it. Young people, old people, virgins, maidens . . . Heck, sometimes you went to battle just so you could capture warriors for sacrifice. What was your beef?

M: The great god Huitzilopochtli demands precious water for strength.

MS: That would be blood, right?

M: Food for the gods!

MS: Seems one of your main food groups was *xocolatl*: chocolate syrup. Historians say you slammed fifty goblets a day? You should have put a Starbucks in one of your palaces.

M: Our potion is quite different than your caffeine fixation. We mix roasted cocoa beans with red chiles, spices, and vanilla—and drink out of golden chalices.

MS: Like hot chocolate?

M: More like Viagra. It is aphrodisiac, and gets me ready for my harem. Wa-hooo!

MS: Too much information, Oh-Frisky-One. Can we change the subject? Is it true you used astrologers to make decisions, kinda like Nancy Reagan?

M: The stars tell messages mere mortals cannot understand in our brief, pathetic lives.

MS: Did the stars tell you to enforce the death penalty for robbery and drunkenness?

M: Perhaps you have been drinking.

MS: Perhaps I'll get Montezuma's revenge.

[No reaction.]

MS: It's a term that implies you got ahold of some gnarly food and, you know, have to sit? On the toilet?

[No reaction.]

MS: Moving on: I hear your coronation was one *big* party. Legend has it that guests were given mescaline [a powerful psychedelic drug] to make the bash seem even more spectacular.

M: I know nothing of this. [*He looks around suspiciously.*] But I told everyone: "If you must experiment, only take half a tab."

MS: Is it true that you particularly feared a god named Quetzalcoatl?

M: The white-bearded deity was to return from the Orient and exact terror and fear on my people!

MS: Yeah, but it actually turned out to be Spanish explorer Hernán Cortés, cruising the coast of Mexico.

M: What are the chances? He arrives the exact year the god-king is supposed to show up. He also has white beard! To me, they all look the same!

MS: You tried to head him off with gifts of gold, jeweled necklaces, and even a wizard.

M: That is not all. I also honor him with flowers from my own garden [the highest tribute of all]. But White Godhead has insatiable thirst for gold. *Gold!* Like hungry pigs they continue inland on trail to find us.

MS: Didn't you at one point send a decoy—a fake look-alike—to test the waters?

M: Moctezuma is unsure of this new alien invader. I dispatch one of my ambassadors dressed as me in case they attempt to murder the great Montezuma!

MS: The Aztecs outnumbered the Spaniards by almost one thousand to one, but somehow you lost your empire to this guy.

M: They have guns. And horses.

MS: And?

M: [*Whispering, head hanging*.] We thought they were gods.

MS: See, this is part of the problem. You Aztecs prayed to more than fifteen hundred gods—one for nature, one for shelter, one for gambling, one for crops, one for . . . well, anyway, it's a lot. And not everything is a sign from above. Sometimes you just get a cold.

M: Is this interview a sign?

MS: Yeah, a sign that you're dead. Part of your demise came when Cortés recruited thousands of Indian warriors who, no offense, hated your guts. [The Tlaxcalan tribe and many others.]

M: Yes, there was that, too. It also helps that the Bearded Batwano is completely insane! He sinks his own boats so that his men have no choice but to march with him or starve.

MS: The Spaniards arrived at Tenochtitlán on November 8, 1591. Tell us what happened.

M: I am in good mood. After a little gift exchange, I invite Cortés to stay at my palace for some wine, women, and song.

MS: You were planning on killing him.

M: Never got chance. Before I know it, his henchmen overpower my guards and put me under arrest. Bad enough they try and covert us proud Aztecs to Christianity.

MS: They thought the human sacrifices, cannibalism, and false idols were a bit much.

M: Turns out HE is a false idol! I am hostage in my own land! Oh, how I wish we had given the usual greeting and lopped off his head and served him for dinner!

MS: Um, there's some confusion about your death. . . .

M: I was murdered by the evil Spanish lizard king! [Aztec writers suggest this is true.]

MS: *Riiiiiiiiight.* But it's also been suggested that after surrendering to Cortés and helping him keep the peace, your own people lost respect and stoned you to death.

M: We play soccer now!

END
of Interview

WOLFGANG AMADEUS MOZART

BORN JANUARY 27, 1756
DIED DECEMBER 5, 1791

CHILD PRODIGY, MUSICAL genius, supernatural composer, and pompous tyke, Mozart's likeness won't come around any time soon. The Austrian began banging away on the keys at age three, composed a concerto at four (lazy little rugrat!), a symphony at eight, and mastered the violin soon thereafter.

Father Leopold, a leading music instructor in Europe, knew a cash cow when he sired one and took little Mozart on a concert tour through the courts of Munich, Paris, and London, visiting two hundred cities in the next ten years. By age sixteen, Mozzie had picked up musical ideas the world over and had written twenty-five symphonies.

Even with a less-than-stellar work ethic, Mozart was a melody machine, spinning off operas, string quartets, and sonatas far ahead of their time. A musical innovator, Mozart created syncopations, mock counterpoint, and compositions in dozens of genres. It wasn't all chamber music and religious concertos—Wolfgang also created music for dances and other light ditties and entertainment.

Mozart married Constanze Weber in 1782. From a musical family, Connie was sophisticated and sang like a bird; Mozart wrote several solos for her over the years.

As talented as Mozart was, most courts and patrons wouldn't touch the immature egomaniac with a fifty-foot cello bow. To supplement his income (lessened by gambling and womanizing), Mozart began teaching, as well as performing in his concertos as conductor and soloist. While his opera *The Abduction from the Seraglio* was a huge success, he blew most the dough living a little too large, a habit he'd have till the end.

Mozart spent his last years in Vienna, crafting some of his most brilliant masterpieces and worrying nonstop about his finances and declining health. He died in 1791 at age thirty-five (most likely of chronic kidney disease), leaving behind the twenty-nine-year-old Constanze, two small children, and a body of work that will live on forever.

MICHAEL STUSSER: Much is made of you being a genius at a very early age. Did that put a lot of pressure on you?

WOLFGANG AMADEUS MOZART: I'd rather be a genius than a dolt, like you!

MS: Well, you're a nasty little chimp.

WM: Try mastermind. *Am-a-Deus:* "loved by God." It runs in the family. My sister Nannerl (Maria Anna) was a prodigy on piano, almost my equal—but no! We played all over Europe, and kings and queens came to see us! We were like an early version of the Partridge Family— except a lot better.

[Mozart grabs a long stick and uses it as a hobbyhorse to hop around the room.]

MS: When you were age eight, noted London lawyer Daines Barrington came to interview you. Apparently, you made quite an impression.

WM: I was just monkeying around. I messed with the harpsichord, I think, and sang some stupid love song for the buttoned-up old bugger.

MS: You also played a complex opera on piano, wrote a mini-symphony, and chased the cat around the room.

WM: I was a child. A very bright child.

MS: In his final report, Barrington said your ability was tantamount to quoting from Shakespeare while simultaneously giving running commentaries in Hebrew and Greek.

WM: OK. You've stroked my ego. What is it you want?

MS: It's just a chat, Mozart.

WM: Well pick up the pace, fart-face, I'm late for a nap.

MS: Tell us about Leopold, your father.

WM: Hmmm. Made good pancakes.

MS: I was thinking about in regard to your development as a musician.

WM: Can we try some better questions? Wanna play patty-cake? We could do it in time with one of my concertos! And try rhyming filthy verse along side!

MS: Maybe a little later. Can we talk about your dad for a second?

WM: Well, he taught me piano and violin, *duh*! He was also a task-master—said Salzburg was too small for us, and that the world should hear us play.

MS: So he was like your manager.

WM: If that makes it easier for you to understand, doofus. He'd set up tours and exhibitions, pay for the whole lot. Three years, eighty-eight cities . . . Makes me tired just thinking about it. In fact, I almost died of smallpox, strep throat, and scarlet fever along the way. And all I got was this lousy T-shirt!

MS: In 1782 your father wrote that his son was "far too patient, or rather easygoing, too indolent, perhaps even too proud, in short, that he is the sum total of all those traits which render a man inactive."

WM: He also called me a "God-given miracle," in case ya don't see that in your little notes, there. Give me a lollipop or I'll clam up.

MS: He went on to say you were actually quite lazy.

WM: Lazy! If he'd lived long enough he'd be able to review six hundred works, twenty-one stage and opera compositions, fifteen masses, forty-one symphonies, twelve violin concertos—

MS: OK, that's impressive.

WM:—seventeen piano sonatas, twenty-seven piano concertos, twenty-six string quartets, should I go on, Mr. McFarty?

MS: Speaking of which, your letters show a man obsessed with breaking wind and using filthy verse—sometimes set to beautiful music.

WM: No, I didn't. Maybe *you* did.

MS: To your mother, you wrote, "Yesterday, though, we heard the king of farts, it smelled as sweet as honey tarts." You may have even had Tourette's syndrome.

WM: Gasbag! Stick to the musical line of questioning or I'll bolt, you mental midget.

MS: You really are quite a pisser.

WM: You really are quite a pisser.

MS: What'd you think of Beethoven?

WM: What? I can't hear you! *Ha*-hee! Naw, Beetlejuice was a talented fellow, no doubt. I only met him once, and I remember saying he'd give the world something to talk about.

MS: Any favorite composers?

WM: Well, Joseph [Haydn], of course, was fantastic. I picked stuff up from Bach, Handel, all sorts of people.

MS: Anyone impress you today?

WM: That Yo-Yo Ma has a unique sound, as do Les Nubians. I like them. They're smokin'. Still, I'm better. Much. No more talking! Now we're mimes!

[Mozart begins pantomiming letters and symbols in the air.]

MS: You used to spend money like it was going out of style.

WM: Oh, I like that turn of phrase. Brilliant! Sorry you're not!

MS: Point is, you spent more than you brought in.

WM: I had some items I enjoyed and would not live without. And yes, some of that was extravagant. But I'm Mozart, dickweed.

MS: Lucky for Mozart you had a fiscally sound wife.

WM: Constanze was quite smart when it came to money. Heck, she probably kept us from starving.

MS: How so?

WM: When I was on the road with my brother-in-law around 1790, she moved us into a smaller house, got some loans, and negotiated a royalty deal for publications. Loved that woman! Squeezed her bum!

[Mozart jumps on the couch and begins a strange little dance jig.]

MS: Just so you know, after you died, she got you out of serious debt by organizing a series of memorial concerts with your music. She and her sister sang, and Beethoven even played in one.

WM: Wish we'd thought of that while I was still standing. I'd have bought more lollipops! And gals to go with them! *Hee!*

MS: Let's talk about Antonio Salieri (1750–1825), court composer to the Holy Roman Emperor.

WM: Let's not.

MS: Let's. *Amadeus*, the movie version of your life, made your feud quite dramatic.

WM: Salieri was jealous of my effortless talents and on several occasions tried to ruin me. End of story.

MS: Really?

WM: *Exactamundo.*

MS: Because didn't he teach Franz Xaver [Mozart's younger son] at one point?

WM: Lookie-loo—Salieroo was a super teacher. That doesn't mean he didn't want me dead.

MS: Puh-leeze.

WM: In fact, *he alone* made the public despise my opera *Le nozze di Figaro.*

MS: In *fact*, no one liked it at the time. Emperor Joseph II hated the piece.

WM: Whose side are you on! Bully-boo!

MS: In 1788, when Salieri was appointed Kapellmeister, he submitted your *Figaro* instead of one of his own operas.

WM: That's true.

MS: And you guys composed a song together, "Per la ricuperata salute di Ofelia."

WM: A lot of people hate the Germans! I'm not the only one, ya know?

MS: In your last known letter, you wrote your wife about Salieri coming to your opera and bellowing "Bravo!"

WM: I guess our feud may have been a little overblown on my end. *'Kay?* Feel better?

MS: And your claim that he poisoned you?

WM: When you're in the throes of death, you say things, all right? What did I know? I was thirty-five! I'm not a flippin' doctor. I thought I'd been poisoned, dude!

MS: We'll change the subject.

WM: Let's talk porn!

MS: There's been research that shows that listening to your music can help people perform certain types of mental tasks known as "spatial-temporal reasoning." They call it "the Mozart Effect."

WM: I've heard about that—some idiot plays my music to his newborn and thinks it will make the brat smarter.

MS: Is there anything to it?

WM: I'm gonna say yes, especially if I get a royalty check out of the deal.

MS: All right, let's say I don't know anything about music.

WM: OK, you don't know anything about music.

MS: Where would you suggest I start listening to your music?

WM: Are you serious?

MS: Yes.

WM: Begin with my String Quintets in C major and G minor [1787]. Then *Le nozze di Figaro* [1786].

MS: "The Nose . . ."

WM: "The *Marriage* of Figaro."

MS: Sure! Sure, I've heard of that.

WM: *Don Giovanni* [1787]? Heard of that one? Then move on to the serenade *Eine kleine Nachtmusik* [1787].

MS: Will do!

WM: Better yet, play the music for the nursery rhyme "Twinkle Twinkle Little Star," which I also wrote. If you're still interested, give me a call. And I'll hang up on your fat face.

MS: Is it true you died penniless and forgotten?

WM: Well, isn't that a nice thought? YOU WISH! In fact, though perhaps not a millionaire like Eddie Vedder, I got commissions from various courts till the end. Can't keep a great man down. People in Prague loved me!

MS: Sort of like how they love David Hasselhoff in Germany?

WM: What are you, like, five-thousand years old? If you'll excuse me—and you will—I have to go finish this.

MS: What is it?

WM: A composition called *Requiem*. Some mysterious Count Chocula type wanted it for his wife's funeral, and I needed the commission. Then I got sick, and realized I was basically writing my own requiem.

MS: That's creepy.

WM: A fitting end to a life of music. Too bad a bunch of hacks had to piece the last few movements together and butcher the whole composition after I bit the dust. Do me a favor and just listen to the first seven bars.

MS: One last thing: In *Amadeus*, Tom Hulce played you as an immature, drunken, nutty sex fiend. How'd that sit with you?

WM: I'd say "Sticks and stones can break my bones," but the truth hurts. I have feelings. . . . *Not!* Now go buy some of my albums. I need the cash, Bugger. Toodle-*ew*!

End
of Interview

BENITO AMILCARE ANDREA Mussolini ruled Italy as prime minister from 1922 to 1943. The poster child for egomaniacal dictators, Mussolini was a charismatic fellow who used the triple threat of terror, propaganda, and flat-out murder to turn a perfectly lovely country into a Fascist state.

Mussolini got his start in politics in 1904 as a union organizer and showed a brutish side early on by proposing violence as a political solution. The young socialist wrote for a variety of papers, then fought briefly in World War I before being injured in a training exercise (likely excuse), and returned home in 1917.

The chaos of war and failure of Socialism to grab hold of the populace convinced Mussolini that extreme political measures were needed—like perhaps a dictator. Fascist militia groups called "the Blackshirt squads" helped him keep order, burning down left-wing opposition offices and killing Communist leaders. By 1921, Fascists controlled most of Italy.

When a trade union called for a general strike in the summer of 1922, Mussolini and the Fascists declared that they would end the strike themselves—by taking over the government. After a march on Rome by the Blackshirts, Victor Emmanuel III decided to avoid bloodshed; on October 31, 1922, Mussolini became prime minister.

Using a theatrical style of oratory (often with his pet lion, Italia Bella, by his side), Il Duce played fast and loose with the facts, wowing audiences with awesome rhetoric and economic reforms from the balcony of Piazza Venezia.

Mussolini's first Fascist step: tearing up the Republican Constitution that had made him prime minister. Step two: outlawing opposition parties, trade unions, and free press. Step three: crushing and arresting the opposition. (Repeat as necessary.) Result: By 1929, Italy had become a totalitarian state.

Mussolini woke up on the wrong side of the World War II bed, cozying up to Nazi Germany and Japan, and making Italy Public Enemy Number Two for Allied forces.

The Allies invaded Sicily in July 1943, and Mussolini knew he'd soon see his last *panini*. Arrested and exiled to a remote hotel in the mountains, Mussolini was freed by German commandos and placed at the head of a puppet government in northern Italy. As the Allied armies reached Milan, Mussolini tried to escape to Switzerland. Disguised as a German soldier, he was recognized (tough to hide that mug), and, along with mistress Claretta Petacci, executed on April 28, 1945. Two days later, Hitler comitted suicide, leading to Germany's unconditional surrender. VE-day could finally be celebrated.

MICHAEL STUSSER: *Signore*, Il Duce—"The Leader." So much terror in your leadership style, and not so much joy. That's not very Italian.

BENITO MUSSOLINI: We Italians are always, "Wine, women, and a song." It is-a hard to conquer the world with this attitude, eh?

MS: If I may be so bold, how does a guy go from being a populist Socialist to a brutal dictator?

BM: I come-a back from a fighting in the war a man of—how you say—destiny, eh? I ree-uh-lize, that a man is-a needed who is-a ruthless and energetic enough-uh to make a clean sweep. Too much-a corruption and economic-ah mess. *Basta!* Enough—we need-a tough love, *capisce?*

MS: So you got a bunch of thugs together to put you in power.

BM: If I were alive-a right now, you would-a not be.

MS: Go on.

BM: I form-a what I call *fasci di combattimento*—fighting bands.

MS: Music?

BM: Not-a musica. We are-uh groups of fighters who want new government: anarchists and radicals and-a discharged soldiers, as well as-a people-a who are-a hungry. We are-a, how you say, pissed off, yes?

MS: Is that why you wore black shirts?

BM: *Non capisco.*

MS: I mean, why not red shirts, or mauve? Mauve is nice.

BM: *Idiota! Camicie nere!* Black-a shirts! We adopta the colors of the Elite Italian Army from-a the first-a World-a War. Helps-a recruit-a war veterans into our-a cause, eh?

MS: Let's step back a second and talk about your childhood.

BM: *Necessito un espresso!*

MS: Basically, you were a fat little bully from the get-go. In fact, you were described as an obnoxious, aggressive, and unruly little tyke.

BM: My family was-a poor, eh?

MS: Not really.

BM: We-a fought over the linguini—very small portions, *si*? I needed to be forceful to eventually lead-a my people.

MS: Your family would have had-a more money if your father didn't blow it on mistresses.

BM: He's an Italian, eh?

MS: Your dad sent you to boarding school and, even there, you were out of control.

BM: I stabba few people, eh? Just a penknife, no-a harm done. *Va bene.*

MS: Two more schools kicked you out—more stabbings—yet somehow you passed final exams without a problem.

BM: I gotta big brain here! Just a little impatient, *capisce?* I read-a everything I canna get-a my hands on: Marx, Kant, Nietzsche, Hegel. Pick and-a choose what I like, make it a my own *filosofia.*

MS: You became Italy's youngest prime minister, and somehow you turned it into a dictatorship.

BM: Benito is always in the lead, eh? First-a the parliament gives me-a dictatorial powers for a year, then-a we write a new law that makes-a mi Fascists the majority. When-a we had elections in 1924, I had-a all the power. *Bellissimo!*

MS: How did Johnny on the street like you at the beginning?

BM: You mean-a Giusseppe. I was-a popular because-a the Italiani were-a sicka the strikes and the riots and the lousy economia. Not to mention our-a shame from a World-a War One-a. I was-a the man they thought could bring Italy from-a chaos into a *bel futuro*, eh?

MS: Bet they didn't think their bell-future included outlawing free speech and a network of secret police to watch their every move.

BM: You're-a makin' me sound so *bad*! The middle-a class in-a my country, we need-a new way. They don't-a want a Communist revolution, they don't-a want the weak-a liberal-ism, they want-a *strength*, they want-a capital-ism—so we canna buy our shoes and our *vino rosso* and our-a Giorgio Armani. We wanna power in the world lika we had during the Roman Empire!

MS: Bet you had a catchy slogan.

BM: "Italy wishes to be treated by the great nations of the world like a sister, and not like a waitress."

MS: One of your cockamamy ideas was "the Battle for Births" [1927].

BM: Not-a cockamamy! Italy have-a such a small population, you know? We want to getta young girls to-a marry, and-a have bambini— children. It's a good idea!

MS: Yeah, but you thought the *only* role for women in the Fascist State was to bear children.

BM: We give 'em a tax-a break. The more-a little ones, the less-a taxes. In 1933, I have-a special meeting with ninety-three mothers who had-a produced thirteen hundred kids. That's an average of thirteen each. *Molto bene!*

MS: Part of your plan was to take prostitutes off the street and into state-run brothels.

BM: Yessa, to be-a less tempting for the men. So they'd-a go home and-a be with their wives.

MS: You once missed a press conference so you could stay in your hotel with a prostitute.

BM: I'm-a Il Duce, huh! Mistresses are-a part of the package.

MS: Too bad your pro-family message made it hard to obtain contraception and made abortion illegal.

BM: I'm-a almost done with-a *you*. *Ascolti*—I needed to work-a with the Vatican, eh? The pope, he's-a popular *guy*! I'm-a workin' with *Italian* people. The Roman-a Catholics liked the [Lateran] Treaty [1929] that-a created the independent Vatican state. I'm a politician—and I'm a tough guy. *Capisce?*

MS: And for a while, you were darn popular. In fact, if you'd just stayed in Italy, people might have actually said great things about you. But then ya got greedy and started invading *other* people. Ethiopia was first.

BM: It's a Roman tradition to-a go out and-a expand-a the empire.

MS: Caesar never gas-bombed innocent people.

BM: He had-a only chariots! It is humiliating to remain with our hands folded while others write *historia*. It matters little who wins, eh?

To make a people great, it's-a necessary to send them to battle even if you have to kick them in the pants. That's-a what I did.

MS: Whether you like it or not, you're always mentioned in the same breath with Hitler. How's that suit you?

BM: By the time that nut-a-case became the Führer, I had-a been Il Duce for more than-a ten years!

MS: Joining World War II on the side of Nazi Germany. That just wasn't a good call.

BM: Lissen-a. I-a understand that peace is-a key to Italia's well-being, eh? But Hitler was rolling along and I-a felt-a it woulda be good for the country. He was-a crushing France, and probably comin' for us, *capisce?* So we declare a little-a war on France, and I figure it's-a over.

MS: What was he like?

BM: Adolpho? *Strano*, eh? Strange. First time we meet in-a Venice, and I wear-a my nice military uniform, try and impress-a the guy, you know? He not talk-a much. "*Ach-tung-a*" this and-a "*Ach-vee-terzein-a*" that. . . .

MS: Would you say you were friends? *Amici?*

BM: No. I think of him as a muddleheaded *idiota*. Most-a the time he is incoherent—*pazzo!* And he has so many-a secrets, eh? In 1937 I'm-a the last one to know he's-a invading Austria. . . .

MS: And Czechoslovakia in-a '39.

BM: He forgets to-a mention he's going to occupy Romania or invade-a the Soviet Union!

MS: Let's face it, you were second banana.

BM: So I-a decide to invade Albania without-a telling *him!*

MS: They'd been under your thumb for years. . . .

BM: And then-a we attack *Greece!*

MS: Hitler had to bail you out of that debacle.

BM: May I have some-a *vino rosso, per piacere?*

MS: First, give me one redeeming quality that you may actually have.

BM: I like-a the artists. I know-a their importance. In-a fact, I begin each-a day by reading a canto of Dante. I even-a lika black-a jazz *musica*, and you can-a tell-a that to a Hitler. I'm not-a brute, but a man who knows how to be sophisticated, eh?

MS: You said it best: You thought Italy needed a man with the delicate touch of an artist and the heavy hand of a warrior.

BM: And I make-a the trains run on time.

MS: No, ya didn't. Not only did the trains *not* run on time, you couldn't even manufacture the trains in the first place!

BM: We agree to disagree-a.

MS: What epitaph did you want on your tombstone?

BM: "Here lies one of the most intelligent animals who ever appeared on the face of the earth."

MS: Well, it didn't turn out that way, Bennie. Instead, ya got buried in an unmarked grave and were even dug up and stolen for a while. [In the 1950s he was returned and moved to his hometown.]

BM: *Allora*, may I have-a my *vino rosso* now?

MS: Sorry. We're all out. Got some German beer you might like, though. . . .

BM: Madonna!

End
of Interview

NOSTRADAMUS
(BORN MICHEL DE NOTREDAME)

BORN DECEMBER 14, 1503
DIED JULY 1, 1566

BEFORE BECOMING KNOWN as a man who could predict the future, Nostradamus started out as a sixteenth-century physician and astrologer in France. Helping patients during the plague, he cured the sick with innovative ideas like clean water and bedding (go figure!) and invented the "Rose Pill" (basically a megadose of vitamin C).

Nostradamus got into the psychic game in 1547, publishing almanacs that made predictions based on astrology and various occult sciences. In 1555, he produced the first editions of his *Centuries*, writing in rhymed quatrains (four-line poems).

Though he never claimed to be a prophet, nobility came from far and wide for advice and horoscopes. In fact, the king and queen of France eventually appointed him as their own physician and "special consultant."

His book of prophecies, *Les Prophecies*, contained almost one thousand quatrains, many of which are credited with predicting such incidents as the atom bomb, JFK's assassination, and even 9/11. Full of vague allegory and ambiguity, readers have interpreted them over the centuries for their own purposes and often see what they want to see.

MICHAEL STUSSER: Ya know, I shouldn't even have to ask any questions, you should just *know* what I'm thinking.

NOSTRADAMUS: You'll be dead in three months.

MS: *Hey!*

N: Kidding. My gift doesn't work like that.

MS: Does that mean you can't give me the winning Lotto numbers?

N: 23 5 42 11 32.

MS: What year?

N: I envision the pattern—you figure out the rest.

MS: See, that's just the thing—you spew all this general stuff, but, I mean, even a broken clock's right twice a day.

N: The reason I wrote in anagrams and mythological allusions was to disguise the meanings of my vision. This was the time of the Inquisition—my writings weren't exactly sanctioned by the church—and I'm not real into bonfires, if you know what I mean.

MS: What did people think when you first published your book of prophecies?

N: Some thought it was evil, and others came running for advice. Most villagers looked at them as fortune cookies: You eat 'em up, and ten minutes later you're hungry again.

MS: If you're so good, why didn't you predict your king [Henry II of France] getting killed while jousting?

N: I did:

> *The young lion will overcome the older one,*
> *on the field of combat in single battle,*
> *He will pierce his eyes through a golden cage,*
> *Two wounds made one, then he dies a cruel death.*

MS: And that relates . . . how, exactly?

N: Both had lions embossed on their shields, the king demanded a second bout after the first ended in a draw, and his younger opponent's lance pierced his visor and stabbed him in the temple.

MS: Wow.

N: To top it off, he endured ten days of horrible pain before he met his maker.

MS: Oh. Well, that *is* impressive.

N: Made me fairly famous in my time. The queen wouldn't even get her hair done without checking with me first.

MS: People claim you predicted all sorts of things: The French Revolution, the Elephant Man, the O. J. verdict.

N: Nailed 'em!

MS: Here's what you supposedly said about Hitler:

> *Beast ferocious with hunger will cross the rivers,*
> *Most of the army will be against Hister,*

The great one shall be dragged in an iron cage
When the child of Germany observes nothing.

I don't get it.

N: Hister? *Hitler?* Anyone?

MS: It's a stretch.

N: It's deep—perhaps you're not. The Danube crosses Hitler's native Austria. And I have lines about indoctrinated German youth that you may not understand.

MS: How'd you get into making predictions in the first place?

N: I was a doctor during the plague, and we were desperately seeking answers. Traveling around France, I met all kinds of underground doctors, alchemists, and mystics.

MS: You into Kabbalah? That's still hot.

N: Among other things. I dabbled in cosmetics, magic, even wrote an almanac.

MS: Predict the weather?

N: Not well. In fact, I ruined so many crops that I gave up on short-term predictions.

MS: How'd you do with horoscopes?

N: Again, not my real forte—turns out I was prone to putting the planets in the wrong signs. Predictions, though, darn accurate. The Big Picture! That was the ticket!

MS: When did you know you had the gift?

N: After my wife and children died [from the plague], I wandered for years. One day in Italy I came across a group of Franciscan monks, and I felt the urge to throw myself at the feet of one of them. Felice Peretti was his name, a pig herder. I remember saying, "I must bow before His Holiness."

MS: That's odd.

N: Yeah. Turns out, twenty years after I died, he became Pope Sixtus V.

MS: OK, so what was your technique? Did ya use a Ouija board or something?

N: I entered a sort of trance state by gazing at a candle flame or at a bowl of water. Stills the mind.

MS: What's the key to predicting the future?

N: I made predictions with fairly long cutoff dates, so they could apply to contemporary events no matter what century you're in.

MS: Good one.

N: And it's always smart to use ambiguous language that allows people to conjure up their own meaning. One guy thought I predicted the coming of Barney [the dinosaur] because I'd mentioned a purple plague. Barney!

MS: Anything else?

N: Well, I always tried to emphasize the hits, and not so much the misses, you know? Makes one seem a bit more accurate.

MS: You wrote,

> *In the City of York there will be a great thunder,*
> *Two twin brothers torn apart by Chaos,*
> *while the fortress falls, the great leader will succumb,*
> *The third big war will begin when the big city is burning.*

Was that about 9/11?

N: I have no idea. I didn't write that garbage—it was a hoax about me on the Internet.

MS: Oh. Sorry. Gotta get a better fact-checker here. You did write:

> *The blood of the just will be demanded of London,*
> *Burnt by the fire in the year 66.*

N: The Great Fire ruined London in 1666.

MS: So you *do* have the gift.

N: You should check out what I said about Harry Potter.

MS: You paraphrased tons of stuff from the Bible, Plutarch, and a bunch of other astrologers. Plagiarism's not so cool, Nasty.

N: It's how educated men did it in our day—toss in some Latin and French vernacular, and you've got yourself a best seller.

MS: You wrote of three Antichrists—we think maybe Napoléon and Hitler were two of them. Who's the third?

N: Look no further than your television.

MS: Jerry Springer! I knew it! Or is it Oprah?

N: I get paid for this kind of thing.

MS: You had some odd last wishes.

N: Not so odd—I wanted to be entombed upright in a wall of my church so that no one would be able to put their filthy feet on my throat.

MS: Legend has it that you made one last prediction from the grave.

N: Oh, yeah, I knew they'd come after me.

MS: In 1700, city officials decided to move you.

N: And I had a medallion around my neck inscribed with the year 1700. They ran like babies from the tomb! Served them right for awakening the great Nostradamus's sleep!

MS: You probably already know this—

N: I do.

MS: But you're as popular as ever!

N: I have heard of this wide web of world that many gaze into. For some reason the masses seek me there.

MS: Yeah, along with Pamela Anderson. After the terrorist attacks on 9/11, Google rated *Nostradamus* as the most searched term.

N: Who is this Google? And what does he know of me!

MS: Is it true you predicted the end of the world?

N: Oh, yes—cataclysmic events are my specialty.

MS: So? When?

N: Sometime between 1999 and 3797.

MS: Guess I'll keep the life insurance policy, after all. . . .

N: Our interview is over.

MS: How *did* you know that?

END
of Interview

BEST KNOWN FOR his macabre poem "The Raven," Poe was an odd, eloquent, freak of a man who ironically spent most of his forty years trying to find his true voice in a world of surreal dreams.

Orphaned at age three, Poe was taken in by John Allan, a successful businessman in Richmond, Virginia, and his wife, Frances. They provided for the boy, albeit at a distance, sending the oft lonely lad packing to various boarding schools.

At seventeen, Poe attended the University of Virginia for a year but dropped out after too much drinking. Falling out of favor with foster father Allan (who wouldn't pay off his bar tab), Poe ran off to Boston, writing short stories to stave off the depression and earn a buck (literally).

Poe published his first volume of poetry at age eighteen and his second two years later. Edgar's first real recognition came in New York, where he whipped out a collection called *Poems* (ooh, that's deep).

Poe married his thirteen-year-old cousin, Virginia Clemm, on May 16, 1836; after brief stints in Richmond and New York City, he moved to Philly, where he published a book right up his alley: *Tales of the Grotesque and Arabesque* (1839). His innovative story "The Murders in the Rue Morgue" (1842) basically created the genres of detective fiction and murder mystery that we know today.

Fame (but not fortune) found him in 1845, after "The Raven" was published in the *Evening Mirror*, followed by *The Raven and Other Poems* and the classic story "The Tell-Tale Heart." Though he often worked fifteen hours a day, Poe could never make ends meet, sometimes drinking profits, other times simply being underpaid for his magnificent stories.

Virginia died of tuberculosis in 1847 at age twenty-four, the same age Poe's mother had succumbed, and he was never the same. He tried to kill himself the following year, then became engaged to various women, only to ruin each relationship with his drunken antics. Things went from bad to worse, and Poe died after being found in a crazed condition in Baltimore.

MICHAEL STUSSER: Haunted houses, ghosts, red plagues, tales of decay: You're a weird one.

EDGAR ALLAN POE: Don't push me. I'm liable to kill myself.

MS: Lest you forget, you're already as dead as a doorknob. What happened between you and John Allan?

EAP: Let's see how you'd feel if your foster dad intercepted letters from a girl you really liked [Elmira Royster], and by the time you found out, she was engaged to another man. Baaa!

MS: Yeah. That's bad.

EAP: Then he sent me to West Point to instill some discipline, had a son with his new wife, and forgot all about me. Good times.

MS: Grist for the revenge writing mill, eh?

[Poe carves a stick figure into the arm of his chair and proceeds to stab the eyes out repeatedly.]

MS: After you were dismissed from West Point—

EAP: The generals were less than impressed with my naked drill exercises.

MS: Not a good look for you. Next you moved to Baltimore with your widowed aunt.

EAP: Sweet Auntie Maria [Clemm] let me stay rent-free, thank God, as I had no moolah at the time.

MS: You also lived with your aunt's daughter, Virginia.

[Poe stares, eyes black like a raven.]

EAP: Let's hear it.

MS: Well, she was nine when you moved in, and in 1836, when she was thirteen, you married her.

EAP: Lest you forget, I loved her. It was the beginning of the end, however.

MS: How so?

EAP: I didn't start the really heavy drinking until Ginny got sick. January, I think, in 1842, she had a lung hemorrhage, and that was the first sign she was ill. I didn't handle it too well. Down. Hill.

MS: But you actually had a job—at the *Southern Literary Messenger*. What happened there?

EAP: I didn't see eye-to-eye with the publisher.

MS: He said you were drunk on the job.

EAP: That, too.

MS: Editors at *Graham's Magazine* thought you looked so bad they actually took up a collection up for ya.

EAP: [*Hiccup*.] They raised about $15, God bless 'em, which was more than I got for my poems.

MS: On a brighter note: In 1845 your poem "The Raven" appeared in the *Evening Mirror*, making you a literary lion.

EAP: Yeah, and I got chump change for it.

MS: Really?

EAP: Story of my life—freelancing doesn't pay the bills, my friend. Hell, "The Raven" was reprinted all over the world, but we didn't have copyright protection back then. Chump change!

MS: The ladies loved you, though.

EAP: It's true that some women in the literary circles sat at my feet during my peak, courting me with their love poems. But it is also true that none of these literati of New York could replace my long-lost beloved mother or wife. I need a drink.

MS: Don't you mean, *another* drink?

[Poe rummages through cabinets until he finds some rubbing alcohol.]

MS: What was your favorite story?

EAP: Probably my prose poem *Eureka* (1848). It's scientific and spiritual all at once.

MS: One hundred pages of explaining the future of the universe. Who's got the time?

EAP: Are you aware that I anticipated the big bang theory about one hundred years before anyone else even thought of it?

MS: Do you really think that souls from other parts of the universe travel the same paths as our own?

EAP: Sure as I'm sittin' here.

MS: I just got a chill. You were into cryptography.

EAP: I liked breaking secret codes—actually had a column [in the Philadelphia paper *Alexander's Weekly Messenger*] where readers would submit stuff and I'd solve anything tossed my way. Apparently there *were* methods to my madness.

MS: No kidding—some of your systems were used to decipher the German codes during World War I.

[Poe pulls a flask from his torn, inside-out jacket and lets the last drops fall onto his black tongue.]

MS: Why do you think young people are so turned on by your writing?

EAP: Kids like a good yarn about life and death, especially if it's a mystery that has a terrific scare in it. Plus, all my poems are around one hundred lines, so they can be read in a single sitting.

[Poe removes several pills from a tin and begins to grind them on the table.]

EAP: And to be honest—and I say this after over one hundred years of analysis—I think after my mother died at such an early age that perhaps my emotional development was stunted. How's that for psychobabble?

MS: Still, no one has quite captured the dark, bizarre world you wrote about. How'd you do it?

EAP: I was never really comfortable in this world, so my imagination could create a new one with fewer pitfalls than reality. I escaped in these abnormal places.

MS: You'd be more accepted now.

EAP: Truly?

MS: Well, yeah. The Mystery Writers of America named their awards for excellence the Edgars, in honor of you; Vincent Price played you in the movie version; and the Baltimore Ravens football team is named for ya.

[Poe begins to weep.]

MS: I'm serious. Now you're an icon. Hell, you're featured in *The Simpsons* Halloween episode, and even made the cover of the Beatles' *Sgt. Pepper* album!

EAP: Too little, too late. If I had made a penny for every refrigerator magnet or goth T-shirt I was placed on, I'd have lived a healthier, happier life. But it was not to be.

MS: Why do you think you were more popular overseas than in the States?

EAP: They get the macabre over there. It helped that I had Charles Baudelaire translating my stories into French. Took him fourteen years to do it. Paul Valéry and Marcel Proust loved me as well—so did the Swedes and the Russians. Nabokov even mentions me in *Lolita*.

MS: Eventually you had famous fans all over the world: Arthur Conan Doyle, Ray Bradbury, Jules Verne, Alfred Hitchcock, even Lou Reed!

EAP: "Take a walk on the wild side"—*that* I can relate to.

MS: Gotta ask about "The Raven." Is the bird some supernatural creature from beyond, or just a lost pet trained to say a word that happens to fit the narrator's depressed condition?

EAP: Like I'm going to answer that.

MS: Come on!

EAP: Nevermore! Poems are puzzles. You need to provide the answers for yourself, bend your mind, get to the bottom of your own soul.

MS: Well, is your stuff autobiographical?

EAP: Do you think I was threatened at knifepoint by an orangutan ["The Murders in the Rue Morgue"]?

MS: No.

EAP: Tortured during the Inquisition ["The Pit and the Pendulum"]?

MS: No.

EAP: How 'bout sealing a guy up in a wall ["The Black Cat"]? Did I do that?

MS: No.

EAP: But I did kill an old man and buried him under the floor you're standing on ["The Tell-Tale Heart"].

MS: Oh, God.

EAP: Kidding! Still, we write from our own experiences—that's why my poems are full of insufferable anxiety and the untimely death of a beautiful woman. Mommy!

[Edgar begins eating the lead in his pencil.]

MS: Mr. Poe, after Virginia died in 1847, you dated another poet, Sarah Helen Whitman. How'd you meet her?

EAP: She sent me a poem called "To Edgar Allan Poe."

MS: Any good?

EAP: Good enough that I asked her to marry me. We were quite the match. She was a mystic, you know, a medium? Wore a tiny wooden coffin around her neck.

MS: A match made in weirdo heaven.

EAP: Think I scared her off a bit. She said we couldn't wed due to her frail health—she was quite a bit older—but I doubt that was the real reason. It was her mother who hated me. Ruined our courtship. *Ruined!*

MS: All right. Settle down, now.

EAP: Pills! Where are my damn opium pills?

MS: Seems that's what got you in trouble in the first place.

EAP: I tried to OD, if that's what you're implying, yes.

MS: Somehow you got it together enough—after your suicide attempt and broken engagement—to finally go out with your childhood sweetheart.

EAP: Elmira Royster and I were to be married in Richmond upon my return from New York, but, again, I met up with some friends—one round led to another. I sort of forgot to get back to her.

MS: There's quite a mystery surrounding your death. How'd you finally bite it?

EAP: Drinkie-drinkie. Some pills.

MS: Pick one and go with it.

EAP: Nervous breakdown. Broken heart. I may have also been mugged at some point.

MS: Not only were you found delirious, but you were wearing someone else's clothes and a palm-leaf hat. Care to elaborate?

EAP: It's all over now; write "Eddy is no more."

MS: You may not be aware, but your grave site in Baltimore is a huge tourist attraction.

EAP: They like me?

MS: Not only are you popular, young Edgar, but every year since 1949, your grave has been visited on your birthday by a mystery man known as "the Poe Toaster."

EAP: You're just saying this to torture me.

MS: Really. He comes in the early hours, draped in black with a silver-tipped cane, and toasts your grave with fine cognac.

EAP: Hope he leaves some. I'm dyin' of thirst here.

MS: Funny you should mention it. The Poe Toaster always leaves the bottle half-full, along with three red roses.

EAP: I'll be damned.

MS: You can sleep now, Edgar.

END
of Interview

TO BE, OR not to be, the greatest. That is the question. Too often we hear about "the greatest of all time"—and the reference is for some soon-to-be forgotten pop star with a reality show and good teeth. In William Shakespeare's case, it's unanimous: Greatest Playwright in History.

Writing during the English Renaissance, the playwright excelled in sonnets, tragedy as well as comedy, verbal gymnastics, and even a few songs along the way.

A lot is unknown about Shakespeare—the schools he attended, how he got such wonderful grammar (Latin, for God's sake!), his exact birth date, if he was a soldier or lawyer, even the spelling of his name (also spelled Shakspere). What *is* known is that he was an unparalleled word-smith, and, at age eighteen, had a shotgun wedding with Anne Hatha-way. The couple was married until his death in 1616 and together had eight children (though only two daughters survived him).

The Swan of Avon worked at a fever pitch between 1588 and 1616, cranking out 154 brilliant sonnets and at least 36 plays, most of which you've been forced to sit through at one point or another. Comedies such as *The Tempest, Measure for Measure,* and *A Midsummer Night's Dream;* historical works such as *Henry IV, King John,* and *Richard III;* and un-forgettable tragedies including *Macbeth, Hamlet,* and *Romeo and Juliet.*

In over twenty years, Billy the Bard penned over a million words of now famous prose. *The Tempest* (1611) was Shakespeare's true swan song, a comedic and dramatic tale of the life and influence of an artist in his world. The Bard's words reflect on his own genius: "Your tale, sir, would cure deafness." All's well that ends well. . . .

MICHAEL STUSSER: Good fortnight, honey-tongued scribe, what a pleasure to meet thou!

WILLIAM SHAKESPEARE: Hey. How ya doin'?

MS: Whoa! I was expecting a more flowery quip: "How art thou, strange, stony-hearted bed-fellow," or something.

WS: Look, I'm not working, all right? It's not like you're paying me ships of gold. . . .

MS: Could you punch it up just a little?

WS: I am not bound to please thee with my retort.

MS: *That's* what I'm talkin' about! Some have said that the William Shakespeare they knew couldn't have written all your plays. You hadn't traveled the world, attended university, or roamed in aristocratic circles.

WS: Uh, books, anyone? You read: Homer's *Iliad*! Ovid's *Metamorphoses*. Christopher Marlowe. Samuel Harsnett. The Bible!

MS: I can do that.

WS: And you talk to people—nobles, peasants, couriers, madams. You learn. You acquire manners. Ya take notes. Ya fake it.

MS: So you're not really Edward de Vere, Seventeenth Earl of Oxford?

WS: No. He died in 1604.

MS: How 'bout Francis Bacon?

WS: No, and no.

MS: Well, why do you think so many people have trouble believing you wrote these gems?

WS: It's much ado about nothing. Aristocratic snobbery, no doubt, miscreants unable to conceive that brilliant words could flow from a man of humble origin, I suppose. And some others simply wished to take credit themselves, and for this, I cannot blame them.

MS: You coined a lot of phrases: "The better part of valor is discretion," "eaten out of house and home," "snail-paced," "a sorry sight." Do you have a favorite?

WS: In *Othello*, I describe the nasty as "the beast with two backs." I like that one.

MS: A lot of the time, when I see one of your plays, I just wish you'd have used plain English. It hurts my brain.

WS: Love looks not with the eyes, but with the mind. Theater is not for the faint-hearted.

MS: Anyhoo, saw *Shakespeare in Love*, and it was so romantic!

WS: And completely without merit. There was no love affair of that sort; I was eighteen at the time of my betrothal and thirty-one years of age by the time I wrote *Romeo and Juliet*.

MS: But I thought it was based on a true story.

WS: *Romeo and Juliet* was based, in fact, on the life of two families—the Capulets and the Montagues—who lived in Verona in 1303, if that makes you feel any better.

MS: I kinda feel gypped, actually.

WS: Never fret, fair scribe, for you'll see better days. Alas, every dog will have his day.

MS: What's the key to being such an amazing playwright?

WS: Vocabulary. Mine? Around thirty thousand words. And yours? Closer to two thousand.

MS: Huh.

WS: Well put, dismal-dreaming gudgeon. Conversation, in my mind, should be pleasant without scurrility, witty without affection, free without indecency, learned without conceitedness, novel without falsehood.

MS: I'm tryin' here. Did you act in your theater company?

WS: From time to time I took a secondary role—the Ghost in *Hamlet*, Adam in *As You Like It*. My talent's not on the stage, but elsewhere.

MS: Something's rotten in Denmark: Women kinda got the short end of the stick when it came to plum parts.

WS: Aw, there's method to the madness: In my day, female parts were written for young boys. Rather than have them flub their lines, I simply gave them small roles so they could make their bedtime. It was nothing against the ladies, but a practical matter. There's the rub.

MS: The play's the thing, and some great actors have done them on film—Douglas Fairbanks in *The Taming of the Shrew*, Judi Dench in *The Comedy of Errors*, Orson Welles in *Macbeth*, Richard Burton in *Hamlet*.

WS: And that idiot Ethan Hawke is a sorry sight [*Hamlet*, 2000].

MS: The fault, dear Brutus, was his lack of star power. Do you have a favorite performance?

WS: Laurence Olivier in *Richard III* [1955]. And *Looking for Richard* [1996], because I simply adore Al Pacino. Hoo aw!

MS: How's the interview going thus far?

WS: I did never know so full a voice issue from so empty a heart, but the saying is true: "The empty vessel makes the greatest sound."

MS: Um, ouch? Tell me, what was the Globe Theatre like?

WS: Lovely venue, almost like one of your so-called open-air stadiums today.

MS: Like a football stadium?

WS: If you must make fool-hearted analogies. We had seating in the round, and VIP boxes up high. Sadly, the acoustics sucked.

MS: Did you just say "sucked?"

WS: We practically had to shout our lines to be heard. Additionally, our plays had to be finished by four in the afternoon—after all, there wasn't any lighting in our bygone era. I suppose that's what you get for a penny. Two if you wanted a balcony seat.

MS: So there wasn't a lot of money in the theater game?

WS: All the world may be a stage, but few wish to pay to see it. Sadly, writers are most often paupers.

MS: Tell me about it.

WS: Skill helps, lad. I did, however, gain favor as a member of the theater troupe and shared in the profits therein.

MS: So you were kind of a rock star of the age, then?

WS: No, child mind, the magnitude of my words weren't realized until long after my passing. In fact, plenty of poets were better known at the time, including Edmund Spenser and Philip Sidney.

MS: Who?

WS: Tell *me* about it! Plays simply weren't taken seriously in my era—in fact, many thought they were bawdy or disreputable. Luckily, I did gangbusters in real estate over the years, buying property, and a house the size of a small castle in Stratford.

MS: Still, the royalties musta been nice.

WS: I never published any of my plays.

MS: Say what?

WS: The only reason you read my plays now is because John Hemminge and Henry Condell [fellow actors] wrote thirty-six of them down— seven years after I was in the grave. [*The First Folio*, published in 1623.]

MS: Pray tell, why wouldn't you sell your works to a publisher?

WS: No one cared for them as literary works. Scripts existed to be performed!

MS: But surely other theaters would have wanted to perform them.

WS: Why give my masterworks to some other group of thespianic dolts if we were planning on doing one of the plays the following annum? To thine own self be true—in this case, it was about coin, cashola, competition, and currency!

MS: It seems you wanted to be a poet as much as you wanted to be a playwright.

WS: "My words fly up, my thoughts remain below: Words without thoughts never to heaven go."

MS: *Hamlet.*

WS: Bingo. My plays are poems, and vice versa.

MS: Some have suggested that you were gay. Care to comment?

WS: At times I was quite gay—ebullient, even; and of course there were darker times where the misery poured like a winter's gloom.

MS: I think people are referring to all the cross-dressing and gender-bending in your plays, and that your love poems were addressed mostly to a "Fair Lord."

WS: For goodness' sake, you play fast and loose with these lies! The sonnets you speak of are a conversation from one to another about a young man who wished not to marry. I also wrote many to a "Dark Lady." Does this mean I'm into witchcraft and sorcery? Pomp and circumstance!

MS: Poems were dedicated to Henry Wriothesley, Earl of Southampton.

WS: Thou brazen-faced pigeon egg, the earl was not only a friend, but sponsor, allowing me to buy my stake in our acting company. So give me a break, eh?

WS: Did you really lose a play?

WS: I wrote *Cardenio,* a play that was performed in my time and yet somehow lost after my sleep of death, never again to appear on our fair shores. Damn shame, really.

MS: Why do you think your work survives?

WS: Well, I'm witty, perhaps, and understand the human condition, which lends itself to translation in any language. And I think people simply like my name.

MS: You're buried in the chapel of the Holy Trinity Church in Stratford-upon-Avon. Quite the honor!

WS: Yes, well, it would be a delight if it had been due to my fame or theatrical prowess, but alas, I was set in thy hallowed ground because I purchased a share of the tithe of the church for a ton of money at the time. All that glitters *was* gold—and they had no trouble pocketing it.

MS: There's a spooky epitaph on your grave.

WS:

> *Good friend, for Jesus' sake forbear,*
> *To dig the dust enclosed here.*

> *Blest be the man that spares these stones,*
> *But cursed be he that moves my bones.*

MS: Yeah, like I said, spooky.

WS: I wrote it so no one would dig up my grave—as was tradition in those years.

MS: Is it true you were buried with unpublished plays in your tomb?

WS: Why don't you get a shovel and find out?

MS: So what have you written lately?

WS: I wish you well and humbly take my leave of you, I pray you know me when we meet again.

MS: Oh! I know this— *The Merchant of Venice*! Um, "Dear sir, of force I must attempt you further: Take some remembrance of—"

WS: No, I'm serious.

MS: Parting is such sweet . . .

WS: I'm outta here.

END
of Interview

SUN TZU WAS a great and mysterious Chinese general and military theorist who wrote *The Art of War* over two thousand years ago. His cunning tactics and subtle strategies have been studied and replicated by warriors as diverse as Napoléon, Mao Zedong, Ho Chi Minh, and the generals of Operation Desert Storm. A guide to outsmarting your opponent, *The Art of War* (literally "Sun Tzu's Military Strategy") is also useful in board games like Risk and Stratego: "You sank my battleship!" indeed.

In addition to aiding those in military circles, Sun's concepts are useful tools for business sharks, modern politicians, and anyone looking to succeed in a field where you may be stabbed in the back.

The Art of War was written in the Taoist tradition and contains spiritual and psychological elements that are less about going to war than avoiding it, while still getting what you want. The ultimate goal is to attain invincibility: By knowing your opponents, understanding conflict, and disrupting alliances, you may attain victory without battle. As Sun Tzu put it, "To win without fighting is best." Especially if the other guy's bigger.

It is thought Sun Tzu wrote *The Art of War* between 400 B.C. and 320 B.C., but it may have been later. The man was elusive, to say the least. The rich martial culture of China gave Sun Tzu a unique environment to ponder philosophy, put his strategies to use on the battlefield, and create an influential work of genius for all time.

MICHAEL STUSSER: Sun Tzu, not much is know of your personal life. Can you enlighten us about your childhood?

SUN TZU: No.

MS: Some say you didn't even exist—that your texts are a "Best of" compilation from many philosophers.

ST: Do I sit here before you?

MS: That's a complicated question, since we're re-creating. . . .

ST: I am an enigma because I chose to be. The glory goes to my words. Unlike my grandiose mentor [Wu Tzu-hsu], I lived below radar, as you modern militarists might say. I vanished into mist, leaving my work behind.

MS: Retired?

ST: My next book? *The Art of Golf!*

MS: Not to belabor the point, but you don't appear in the primary records of the period. You are never mentioned.

ST: Nor is Confucius, but do you doubt his existence? I was not famous figure at the time. Just a brilliant one.

MS: Why did you write *The Art of War*?

ST: Effort made to compile lessons of commanders. Avoid errors of the past.

MS: Understood! I have four ex-wives.

ST: Four ex-wives! We draw on three thousand years of prolonged civil war!

MS: That's a lot of fighting. Still, if you'd met any of my—

ST: Thousands of years ago, Chinese villages constantly in armed struggle with brutal tribes. Aggressive clans. Barbarians with war on minds. Only way to defeat these nomads and keep them from imposing their will over common man is through skilled commanders. Chop, chop!

MS: Many consider your strategies unorthodox.

ST: Yes, if orthodox means obvious frontal assault that blind man can see coming, then I am unorthodox strategist.

MS: You liked sneaking up on people?

ST: Indirect routes. Behind-the-lines forays. Spies! To expect the unexpected!

MS: What about shock 'n' awe?

ST: All warfare is based on deception. When we are near, make enemy believe we are far away; when far away, we must make him believe we are near. Hold out baits to entice enemy. Feign disorder— and crush him.

MS: OK. Speed round: If you outnumber your enemy?

ST: Surround him.

MS: If you're five times his strength?

ST: Attack.

MS: If double his strength?

ST: Divide him.

MS: If weaker in numbers?

ST: Be capable of withdrawal.

MS: And if totally outnumbered?

ST: Be capable of eluding him.

MS: To be honest, some of this seems obvious. Were you the first to write any of this stuff down?

ST: Most teachings were passed over generations by word of mouth and in secret. One had to be careful what is scribed. In my day, possession of military strategy in private hands was evidence of conspiracy. Death to conspirators!

MS: OK. But you *did* write them down.

ST: Generals like myself could write and store items in imperial library—restricted to emperors and scholars.

MS: Hypothetical question: Let's say I'm in a battle with a fierce enemy—OK, it's my neighbor. What's the surest way to victory?

ST: To win without fighting is best.

MS: Say what?

ST: My treatise is about war—and peace. Understand conflict in order to find ways to resolution.

MS: I was told you could help me kick ass.

ST: Taoist tradition states: "Have no hard feelings toward anyone who has not shown you enmity, do not fight with anyone who does not oppose you."

MS: Let's say I *do* oppose you. Let's say you've got weapons of mass destruction pointed my way—or a dog that keeps knocking over my garbage can.

ST: He who excels at resolving difficulties does so before they arise. He who excels in conquering his enemies triumphs before threats materialize.

MS: Well, I could try that, I guess. While you're here, I gotta ask you about the war in Iraq.

ST: Now when the army marches abroad, the treasury will be emptied at home. Victory is main object of war. If this is long delayed, weapons are blunted and morale depressed.

MS: Yeah, that's depressing, all right. Is that all, or should I curl up in the fetal position?

ST: When your weapons are dull and your ardor dampened, your strength exhausted and your treasure spent, other chieftains will spring up to take advantage of your extremity.

MS: Here's a quote that seems a little less sane: "Regard your soldiers as your children, and they will follow you into the deepest valleys. Look on them as your own beloved sons and they will stand by you even unto death." That's just sick.

ST: I went on to say if you are kindhearted, but unable to enforce your commands and incapable of quelling disorder, then your soldiers must be likened to spoiled children; they are useless for any practical purpose.

MS: I want my blanky. Can you simplify any of this? It's complex stuff, Sun-man.

ST: I understand comic book version of *The Art of War* now exists. Avail yourself of it . . . and march onward.

END
of Interview

THOUGH MOST FOLKS don't know it, Serbian-born Nikola Tesla was probably the greatest inventor of all time. He leaves behind the legacy of alternating current (AC), the electrical flow that today is the heart of electric power for most of the world. Throw in the induction motor, the spark plug, the bladeless turbine, the loudspeaker, radar, transformers, fluorescent lighting, and principles that enable wireless technology to function, and you've got a damn fine résumé.

Tesla's parents worked young Nikola's brain overtime. His father, an Orthodox Christian priest, quizzed him with constant flash cards and memory tests, while his mother had Nikki help around the house by creating inventions for household tasks. Incredibly, Tesla had the ability to solve complicated equations without the need to write them down. (He spoke of building—and testing—machines in his mind, examining them for wear and tear, then making detailed corrections.)

Tesla had a serious work ethic—too serious, in fact: He worked twenty-hour days and was hospitalized several times for exhaustion. The brainiac had some unhealthy ticks (OCD, perhaps), often feeling the need to succeed on a problem, or believing he'd die without the solution.

At age twenty-five, Tesla devised the polyphase system of AC that would run motors of all kinds and change the world forever. Funny thing, though: No one wanted anything to do with it. It took years for Tesla to get anyone's attention, and this only after he built, proved, then patented his inventions. When Tesla was thirty-three, George Westinghouse finally gave him an offer he couldn't refuse—a million bucks plus royalties.

Though Tesla's discovery of AC for electrical power is one of the most important findings of the modern era, already famous super-inventor Thomas Edison had his own version of electricity (the inferior DC), thus starting the "War of Currents" in the late 1880s. (In an effort to discredit Tesla, the Edison gang not only invented the electric chair using their competitor's juice but went on to create an ad campaign with the slogan, "Would you like your wife to be cooking with AC?") In the end, Tesla won out—his system could transmit electricity economically for hundreds of miles over transmission lines, while Edison's went a mile at most, underground, and was more expensive to boot.

With creditors breathing down his neck and profits from his numerous patents the last thing on this brilliant mind, Tesla shuttered his lab and tinkered alone for the last years of his life. When manufacturers used his Tesla coils without compensating him, Nikola couldn't be bothered to sue, for he had too many new innovations knocking around his noggin.

Though he made billions for other businessmen the world over, Tesla died impoverished and alone with his pigeons in 1943, still working on various ideas that included a dynamic theory of gravity and a death ray. He had no family, probably due to his belief that celibacy was the key to creativity.

MICHAEL STUSSER: First off, enough with the constant power outages. We know you're out there.

NIKOLA TESLA: Yes, OK, but you don't see Edison with such power, eh?

MS: Speaking of Edison, you're best known for inventing the first practical use of electricity. Why is it no one has any idea who the hell you are?

NT: Because of your love for this Edison! When we work together, it was always, "DC current this, DC current that." But Edison knew full well that my AC current system could transmit electrical power much farther. I mean, *hello*, there is reason mine became the GOLD STANDARD!

MS: Sounds like a sore subject. Let's move on.

NT: You know, one time that jerk bet me $50,000 that I couldn't make his generation plants more efficient. After working for months, I redesign dynamo systems and add automatic controls, saving time and money! Edison says to me, "Tesla, I was only kidding about this bet. You really don't understand American humor." He is right! I quit on spot! Finished with this bad man!

MS: Easy, tiger.

NT: Sorry. I get very charged with this subject. Charged! You understand. It is pun! I am also poet.

MS: You came to the United States with four cents to your name.

NT: That is not all! I also have book of poetry, very nice, and a letter of recommendation.

MS: From whom?

NT: Charles Batchelor was boss man from previous job and friend of Edison. I show this letter to him and it reads, "I know two great men, and you are one of them. The other is this young man." I get job.

MS: I hear you had a great party trick. Can you show us?

NT: Yah. It's a little something I came up with at the Chicago World's Fair in 1893. Most people at the time were afraid of electricity. I want to show them it is harmless. Look.

[At this point in the interview, Tesla lights a lamp without any cords by sending two hundred thousand volts of electricity through his body. It's a lot like watching Mr. Electro at the freak show.]

MS: Amazing! Your hair's kinda on fire, there. . . . Any more tricks up your sleeve?

NT: Are you kidding? At Madison Square Garden I demonstrate the world's first remote control by playing with boat in giant pond! I invent early radar, neon, shadowgraphs [X-rays], flying machines, wireless broadcasting, and a death ray. A DEATH RAY! For defensive purposes only.

MS: That's it?

NT: I also had an idea for Internet, "which I called World Wireless System," and would distribute information and entertainment all over the world.

MS: You gotta be kidding.

NT: There is no kidding. I predicted that, and I quote myself here: "The household's daily newspaper will be printed 'wirelessly' in the home during the night."

MS: Wow. So much for Al Gore, huh?

NT: Who is this Al Gore?

MS: I'm just suggesting that maybe you should get partial credit for the World Wide Web.

NT: Much credit is due to me. In 1944, Supreme Court invalidate patents held by Macaroni [Italian inventor Guglielmo Marconi] for radio equipment and give them to *me*! Macaroni is already rich—won a Nobel for his work. I have nothing! In fact, I am dead one year before!

MS: How does the man who invents electricity not become the richest guy in the world?

NT: Money is not my motivator, you see? I wish to show the world my ideas and free human kind from hard labor.

MS: But you hooked up with George Westinghouse, right? He had tons of money.

NT: Mr. Westinghouse offered one million dollars for my patents, and a royalty—one dollar per horsepower. This would have made me billions. BILLIONS, I tell you!

MS: You deserve it. How else am I going to power up my fridge or, more importantly, my flat screen TV, baby! Five feet o' plasma magic!

NT: Yes, tell me about this, I know! But times get hard with Depression, and George comes to me and says if I might be good man and drop this royalty provision because it means end of Westinghouse company. This man take chance on me four years earlier, give me million on spot, show world my electrical power system.

MS: It would have netted you billions of dollars, man. Every time a guy turns on a lightbulb, kah-CHING!

NT: This I understand.

MS: Kah-CHING!

NT: I am man of my word. But yes, it is mistake.

MS: I'll say.

NT: I just say!

MS: Kah—

NT: Kah-ching, yes, I get it! George was my friend—one of the true, noble pioneers in America. He asks me to tear up royalty contract to save his company, I say OK.

MS: Let's switch gears. Switch. Light switch. It's a pun, get it?

[Tesla has rewired the table lamp and is getting a holographic image where the bulb used to be.]

MS: How'd you work in the lab? What was the method to the madness?

NT: My method is different. I do not rush into actual work. When I get new idea, I start at once building it up in my imagination and operate device in my mind. When I have gone so far as to embody everything in my invention, every possible improvement I can think of, and when I see no fault anywhere, I can give the measurements of all parts to workmen. When completed, all these parts will fit, just as certainly as though I had made the actual drawings.

MS: At the time of your death you were working on a device that would actually photograph thoughts.

NT: Yes, and you, maybe, are happy I do not have these thought-photos right now, yes?

MS: Of all your inventions, how do you want to be remembered?

NT: For my Tesla coil, which everyone still uses to transmit radio and television waves.

MS: You often signed the initials GI after your name. What did that stand for?

NT: It's short for "great inventor." OK, I have ego. So sue me.

MS: How come you never married, Nick?

NT: I do not think there is any thrill that can go through the human heart like that felt by the inventor as he sees some creation of the brain unfolding to success. . . . Such emotions make a man forget food, sleep, friends, love, everything.

MS: How about a little time off for some fun with the ladies, huh, Nick?

NT: Celibacy is key to creativity! I do not think you can name many great inventions that have been made by the married man. My body was a tool to feed the mind and elevate the human race with my inventions!

MS: So, got any favorite movies?

NT: I have no time for this. You know I have over one hundred patents? By age of five, I had invented the waterwheel and forced myself to read the complete one hundred-volume set of Voltaire. I sleep only three hours per night!

MS: You also claim to have received signals from outer space in your Colorado lab.

NT: I have recorded evidence of existence of life on Mars! They sent repetitive radio signals in clicks: one, two, three, four. I am telling you! I have been contacted!

MS: You also said in your autobiography that you were an alien avatar born to Earth parents.

NT: How would you like an electroshock sandwich?

MS: Near the end, you showed symptoms of obsessive-compulsive disorder.

NT: Three windows in this room.

MS: I'm sorry?

NT: Three doors. Three couches. Three windows. I must walk. Must walk around block three times.

MS: We've got medicine for this problem now.

NT: Yeah. Three missing buttons.

MS: Did ya know that two rock bands are named after you?

NT: This is true?

MS: AC/DC and Tesla.

[Tesla tears up.]

MS: Tell us, what was with the pigeons? You loved pigeons.

NT: Interview is over.

MS: Thanks for your time. Now, let's take that walk, huh?

END
of Interview

VINCENT VAN GOGH is known for his wild moods swings and lopping an ear off, not to mention paintings now auctioned for hundreds of millions of dollars. If he'd only known. . . .

Born in southern Holland to a Protestant pastor, Vincent was an intense, quiet kid who spent long periods of time wandering the countryside alone. At age sixteen, Vinnie started working at his uncle's art dealership, where he got an appreciation for great art. Van Gogh was too honest for the gallery game; he berated customers who liked works that were poorly composed and sent clients fleeing in terror.

Van Gogh also had odd jobs in a bookstore, as a language instructor, then took up theology. Luckily for the rest of us, he gave up the idea of the priesthood and got to drawing.

Van Gogh worked his ass off to acquire his skills—he studied methodically and met with as many painters as possible to absorb their styles and technical expertise. He absorbed Japanese prints, impressionist elements, and social commentary, tossing it all into his own brand of brilliance.

Van Gogh's talent was famously aided by madness: He was frequently hospitalized for panic attacks and suicidal tendencies.

Vincent's final days were spent in a village community in France, where he laid down some of his most expressive work. Unable to make a living as a painter (oh, to only have had twenty spare dollars in 1870), he became despondent about draining the finances of his brother, Theo. Lonely and depressed, he shot himself in the chest. A few days later, at age thirty-seven, he died in the arms of his ever-present sibling.

MICHAEL STUSSER: Thanks for meeting with me. I know you're extremely anti-social.

VINCENT VAN GOGH: Please leave.

MS: I don't know if you're aware of this, but you got incredibly popular after your death.

VVG: I heard that. Then again, I hear lots of things. Did you hear *that*?

MS: No.

VVG: Doorbells. Or swordsmen!

MS: When I say you became popular, I'm not talking about popular, like, "Gee, she's the most popular girl in class." I'm talking, "Gee, I think I'll pay $85 million for *Portrait of Dr. Gachet.*"

VVG: Makes me want my ear back.

MS: We've got reconstructive surgery now.

VVG: I painted over eight hundred oil paintings and did over seven hundred drawings in my lifetime. Know how many I sold?

MS: Three hundred?

VVG: One! *The Red Vineyard* [1888]. *One!*

MS: Well, they've sold plenty now, my one-eared wonder.

VVG: It's getting dark in here. Any chance of you pushing on?

MS: You've become the poster child for the tortured, starving artist. Is that a fair assessment?

VVG: I'd say yay. Poor, struggling, unappreciated, isolated, self-mutilating, wacko! Does that fit the bill? Happy now?

MS: What was the impetus for your depression, Vincent? When did the gloomy artisan first get his parade rained on?

VVG: My London love dumped me in 1874, and that was the flippin' end, I tell you. It was all downhill from there. Girls! I was never good enough . . . they didn't like the paint under my nails . . . my undies were too dirty. Always somethin'.

MS: Most people are sad for a while, then move on. You may have been bipolar, suffered from epilepsy, or even schizophrenia.

VVG: Are you a doctor?

MS: No, but—

VVG: Then *save* it! Everything is in God's plan.

MS: Was it God's plan to give you the clap from the prostitutes you frequented?

VVG: You! YOU! The best way to know God is to love many things.

MS: Was it God's plan to kick you out of the ministry?

VVG: I would have been a great pastor, just a bit antiauthoritarian by nature. A good Christian, you know, but I don't like to be told what to do. *Stop pointing fingers!*

MS: So, after you got dismissed as a minister, is that when you went bonkers?

VVG: I went into solitude. I'm shy! OK? There's a difference. I need my medication. I NEED MY MEDICATION!

MS: Can someone get him his meds, please?

VVG: My goal was always to aid humanity, console people— *whom I had difficulty dealing with*—through my paintings. A good painting can heal the soul; it's like a good deed.

MS: So you helped yourself get out of your little funk, then?

VVG: I had a damn productive run, that's for sure. Ten great years [1880–90].

MS: Took you four to learn how to draw.

VVG: Ya know what? My stick figures are better than anything you could ever *dream* of!

[Van Gogh scratches a line drawing of his shoes into the chair with his nails.]

MS: I'm gonna want that when you're done.

VVG: I started doing charcoal sketches while working in a mining town.

MS: Good idea.

VVG: It was, but I realized early on that self-training would not do— *as you mentioned*—so I sought some guidance. I went to museums for inspiration and studied technique. And worked with Anton, of course.

MS: Dutch painter Anton Mauve.

VVG: Who told you *that*?

MS: You just did.

VVG: Yes. Anton taught me landscapes and encouraged me to focus on my craft. To focus! Gotta focus. Does anyone have any paint? Or how about some rubbing alcohol? Could use a drink.

MS: You were talking about focus.

VVG: Huh? Oh, yes, I took Anton's advice and went to Drenthe [a remote part of the northern Netherlands] to be alone with nature.

MS: That couldn't have been good for a guy with, well, issues.

VVG: It was quite isolated. *Not a whisper!* I moved back to be with people after about three months.

MS: You were incredibly close with your younger brother, Theo.

VVG: He always believed in me. . . . What happened to him after I passed?

MS: He went insane and died a year later. Oh! Maybe I shouldn't have—

[Van Gogh runs out of the room and returns an hour later clutching a Stress Ball.]

MS: We'll come back to your brother, huh?

VVG: Are you trying to get inside my brain?

MS: Well, sort of. It's an interview. Why so many peasants in your work?

VVG: My paintings reflect the struggle, the hardships of daily life, the countryside these workers cultivate, and the small villages they inhabit. Do you think that coffee just appeared by itself?

MS: No, I got it at a Starbucks. Vincent, let's talk about Theo now. Your loving brother, Theo.

VVG: Yes, let's. After I left the Antwerp Art Academy, I joined Theo in Paris. He tried to sell some of my paintings.

MS: Obviously not a lot of luck there, huh?

VVG: I was ahead of my time. . . . What time? Time to go!

MS: Is that where you met Gauguin? In Paris?

VVG: Yes, and Henri [de Toulouse-Lautrec] and Camille [Pissarro], Émile [Bernard], and Georges [Seurat]. So many friends.

MS: Well, that must have been nice.

VVG: Oh, yes. They opened my eyes to so many forms, so many impressions.

MS: And ya got your groove on!

VVG: My style gelled, if that's what you mean, yes. I started really *stroking* the brush and *slamming* some gorgeous colors in there! Blues and orange! They complement each other like a man and a woman! It was wonderful.

MS: But you left in 1888 for the south of France.

VVG: Yeah. Got tired of city life. Real tired. Wanted to get back to nature. *Breathe!* You see, there are better colors out in the fields. I realized that flowers and landscapes are my thing. Blossoming fruit trees, portraits of the postman—ya can't get those in the big city.

MS: Didn't you start up a commune, at one point?

VVG: "The Studio of the South," in Arles. I decorated a yellow house with sunflower paintings. I invited some artists to join me in our movement.

MS: How'd that go?

VVG: Not so good. Paul [Gauguin] was the only one to show, and he was there only a few months before we started to get on each other's nerves. The guy never did the dishes. He could *eat*, but didn't know how to clean up!

MS: Your arguments were about more than the dishes.

[Van Gogh begins to pace nervously.]

VVG: We agreed on so much. We both wanted to create art that was sacred, you know? A brotherhood of artists! For me, the highest form of prayer is my painting; attention to one's gifts—one's craft. But when you're dealing with Catholics . . .

MS: Too much guilt?

VVG: The guy just beat himself up constantly. He was obsessed about suffering—sexual suffering, misery of the age. . . . I was depressed enough already, thank you.

MS: Christmas Eve 1888. You blew a fuse.

VVG: I was exhausted.

MS: Not so exhausted that you couldn't chase Gauguin around with a razor.

VVG: *WHY?* Why do you torture me so?

MS: And then, maybe after a few too many rounds of absinthe—

VVG: Heresy! It was turpentine.

MS: You wound up lopping your own ear off somehow.

VVG: It was just the lobe, the lower half of my left ear. . . . No big deal.

MS: O-Kay. It's just not very normal behavior.

VVG: Normal never made anyone a legend!

MS: What'd you do with your ear, anyway?

VVG: I went to a brothel and gave it to a prostitute I was in love with—Rachel was her name. I remember asking her to "guard this object carefully."

MS: Ya know, if she'd had any idea how famous you'd be, she could have saved the lobe, and her family could have sold that thing on eBay for, like, a billion dollars.

VVG: I don't wanna talk anymore.

[We take a break, and the interview continues the next afternoon.]

MS: Feeling better?

VVG: I get homesick sometimes. When I paint, I don't like to work from memory. My best pieces come from direct observation.

MS: Speaking of direct observation, you asked to be placed under medical watch at an insane asylum [1889–90]. What happened?

VVG: I began to lose touch with reality. And I was sad. Real sad.

MS: Did the asylum help?

VVG: They tried to have me do "calm" painting. Muted colors, mellow subjects like gardens and wheat fields. Plus some portraits of doctors. Whatever I could see from my cell.

MS: Sounds soothing.

VVG: Made me even more depressed. My style was about vivid, sun-drenched colors— *wild brush strokes*! It's how I do it, man.

MS: Still, ya did some great stuff there.

VVG: Oh, you can't repress a brain like mine. Not without some electroshock or serious meds. No, the more I tried to make my paintings calm, the more my imagination got involved in the still life: My lines became *bolder* and the forms more dynamic. I started in on the SWIRLS. The swirls!

MS: *The Starry Night.*

VVG: I had to get the hell out of there. As soon as I started to draw souvenirs of Holland, I knew it was time to bail.

MS: In hindsight, do you think maybe you should have stayed?

VVG: Why? 'Cuz I shot myself? What do *you* know?

MS: It would have been nice to have you live a long, happy life, that's all.

VVG: Sorry. I've misjudged you. It's just that you struck a chord there. . . .

MS: In your last seventy days, you cranked out almost seventy paintings.

[He breaks down crying.]

vvg: I put my heart and soul into my work, and lost my mind in the process. I just messed everything up. I even botched shooting myself. Did you know it took me *two days to die*! [*Muttering*] I would have liked to see Theo's son grow up.

ms: You'll be happy to know that you and your brother are side by side in the cemetery, with identical tombstones.

vvg: I should paint that.

ms: Wish you could.

vvg: Happiness, I always said, lies in the joy of achievement, in the thrill of creative effort. I may have been nuts, but while at work, I was ecstatic.

End
of Interview

GEORGE IS OUR first and most famous president, as well as our toothless poster boy; he adorns the one-dollar bill, Mount Rushmore, postage stamps, the quarter; a state is named after him, and he is the subject of about one thousand biographies. He's also America's first true hero.

Young Georgie was raised in Virginia, and, strangely enough, wanted nothing more than to be an officer in the British army when he grew up. (He liked their crisp red suits and tight formations and fought on the side of the British in the French and Indian War, 1754–1758.) Instead, his experience and reputation as a levelheaded soldier made him the perfect choice to lead the Colonial army; General George thus wound up fighting *against* the Brits in the Revolutionary War. Over eight long years, Washington led a ragtag crew to victory and independence. (GW actually lost more battles than he won, but was a helluva inspiration to his men and, most importantly, victorious in the end.)

Though a fierce commander on the battlefield, he really was Gentle George off it: Once the war was over, he showed a more sensitive side, even pardoning some opponents with whom he had direct clashes.

Washington's early work surveying land in Virginia gave him what he later needed as president: Common sense, resourcefulness, a firm handshake, and the understanding that he didn't know everything. Surrounding himself with great minds (Jefferson, Adams, et al.), he was our nation's first team builder.

On April 30, 1789, G-Dub was unanimously elected by Congress as our first commander in chief. Being first is never easy, and George had to figure out everything from how taxes would be collected to where the nation's capital should be located (Washington, D.C., of course). As it turned out, he could have stayed for as many terms as he could handle, but bowed out after eight great years.

He retired in 1797 to Mount Vernon, where he walked daily with his wife, Martha, tended to his eight thousand acres, and passed away after lousy medical treatment for a cold on December 14, 1799.

MICHAEL STUSSER: Gotta ask about the whole cherry-tree episode.

GEORGE WASHINGTON: Never happened.

MS: *What?* So you lied about cutting down your father's cherry tree! You *can* tell a lie!

GW: No, you see, the story you're referring to was written after I was gone.

MS: How do I know you're not lying about this?

GW: Listen, Mason Locke Weems made the story up in a biography about me the year after I died. [*The Life and Memorable Actions of George Washington*.] But let's not be too hard on him, here—Mr. Weems was simply spinning a little yarn to give the youngsters some moral guidance. No harm done.

MS: At least *you* didn't lie about not lying about it. Now, tell us about the ol' wooden dentures.

GW: They weren't actually wooden.

MS: Here we go *again*.

GW: I had a bunch of sets made to fit around the only tooth left in my head, see? One was fashioned out of iron, we tried cow teeth, another from hippo tusks—

MS: Whoa!

GW: Yeah, they smelled to high heaven, though, so I moved on to a set made from human teeth.

MS: How'd Martha like those?

GW: She was happy I didn't gum her to death.

MS: Is it true, Mr. President, that you often turned down dinner invitations so you wouldn't have to eat in public?

GW: True enough. Was a little embarrassed about my teeth falling out in front of folks. Blasted dentures were actually the reason I was a man of so few words—I just couldn't talk with the darn things in my mouth.

MS: Martha was loaded. Bet marrying the thirteen colonies' wealthiest widow had its advantages, huh?

GW: Young man, if you're implying . . .

MS: Well, she wasn't exactly a beauty.

GW: At ease, soldier! I loved Martha. She was a good housewife, we were married for forty wonderful years, and I will not hear of this!

MS: On a related subject, sir, much has been made about your love letter to Sally Fairfax—your best friend's wife—while you were engaged to Martha. Did you have an affair, Mr. President?

GW: Along with the advice about never telling a lie, I'd suggest never kissing and telling. What I will admit to is being a bit of a flirt. I will also say that, from what I've read about our recent presidents, I would be considered a saint, and let's leave it at that, hmm?

MS: As a kid, you wanted to join the British army. By the time you were in the Virginia legislature you were their toughest critic. What happened?

GW: Tell you the truth—

MS: You cannot tell a lie!

GW: I applied for a commission in the British army in 1754—and got rejected. Then I started paying attention to what the Brits were doing in the 1760s—taking away our rights and taxing everything from tools to playing cards.

MS: At what point did you realize you'd have to fight them?

GW: I think it was 1768 or thereabouts when I told George Mason I'd take my musket on my shoulder whenever my country called. Once Parliament passed the Tea Act [1773] and our boys dressed like Indians and dumped tea into Boston Harbor, I knew it was going to get ugly.

MS: Still, you didn't support colonial independence till 1776.

GW: That's correct. Took Thomas Paine's *Common Sense* to knock some sense into me.

MS: The British forces were better trained, better funded, better organized. What was your strategy for beating 'em?

GW: Stall tactics, really. We felt like the longer the war went, the sicker the Brits would be of the whole bloody mess.

MS: Anything else?

GW: Well, we took a page from the Indians' handbook and fought them from behind rocks and trees—stayed out of the cities whenever we could so the redcoats couldn't thump us too bad. I also paid our troops with my own money. Kept 'em from mass desertions and mutiny.

MS: One of the lasting images of you is a painting of your Christmas crossing of the Delaware.

GW: Never saw it. Was dead fifty years on.

MS: Oh. Right. Well, here's a copy.

[Washington is shown a copy of artist Emanuel Leutze's 1851 painting, Washington Crossing the Delaware.*]*

GW: Goodness. That boat looks like a sardine can.

MS: So, it wasn't exactly like that?

GW: What am I doing standing up in this painting? Makes me look like an idiot. And, though I love the sentiment, we weren't flying a flag: We were on an undercover mission—in the pitch dark! In fact—let me see that again—that looks like James Monroe holding the flag; he wasn't even in my boat. And is that a *woman* rowing at the stern? Pretty sure all aboard were male soldiers.

MS: But you did cross the Delaware in a blizzard in the dead of night, right?

GW: Sure, sure. Surprising 'em at Trenton was the turning point of the war, no doubt. Owe a lot to the fishermen from Marblehead [Massachusetts]. Without those boys I'd have been fish food, for sure.

MS: Most people think of you as a great soldier, but you bungled plenty of missions.

GW: And I thank you for pointing that out, son. You ever served?

MS: No, sir.

GW: OK, then. It's damn hard, let me tell you. Remember, we were greatly outnumbered, and our gents didn't want to fight if they didn't have to. My job was to keep the crew together, then pick and choose the right battles. And lest you forget, we won the thing.

MS: The United States and Great Britain signed a peace treaty in 1783 that recognized America's independence, and you "retired."

GW: Yep, that was the idea—head back to Mount Vernon, do a little fox hunting, put my feet up.

MS: Good plan. What happened?

GW: The States started going in different directions, see, and the Articles [of Confederation] didn't seem like they'd keep everybody together. So James [Madison] and Alexander [Hamilton] decided to put together a meeting in Philly to tweak 'em a bit.

MS: You're talking about the Constitutional Convention [1787].

GW: What? Yeah. So the delegates there picked me to chair the little powwow and we wrote up the document.

MS: The Constitution of the United States.

GW: Huh? Oh, yeah. Long story short, I was going to retire—once more—but the darn delegates picked me again.

MS: The electoral college. For president.

GW: Huh? Yeah, right, and so I did that for a while. . . . Then I, uh, retired again.

MS: No offense, sir, but you seem disinterested in our little chat.

GW: Huh? Oh, you still talking?

MS: Yes, sir, I was saying you seem a bit bored with our interview.

GW: Oh, no. No, see, I'm a bit hard of hearing. Blasted influenza hit me during my second term, plus my vision was shot to hell. I'm sorry. I'll pay more attention. Where were we?

MS: Retirement. If you wanted, you could have gone home after your first term.

GW: Yeah, guess that's true, it's just that in 1792 we were still a real young country. It was dicey—hit-or-miss if we'd pull the experiment off.

MS: Democracy.

GW: Mmm-hmm. The other reason I stayed was that they didn't run anybody against me, see, so I didn't have to campaign. I was OK with the business, though to be honest I preferred agriculture.

MS: You cannot tell a lie!

GW: Yeah. We get it.

MS: What did Martha think about being First Lady?

GW: You know, she took it like a champ. Fact is, Martha would have preferred staying in Mount Vernon as well, but she got to love Philadelphia and was a helluva hostess.

MS: Philly?

GW: What? Oh, yeah—ya didn't hear? The first capital was in New York, and then we lived in Philadelphia while we waited for the new one to be finished.

MS: But Philadelphia?

GW: Great cheesesteak.

MS: Being the first president must have been a bit weird, huh?

GW: You could say that. Martha and I didn't really know how to do it, you know? I wasn't a king, but at the same time, I was trying to be official. At first I didn't shake hands—did the powdered wig bit, and stood on this raised platform when people showed up for state visits. There was some trial 'n error, then I just got the hang of it.

MS: The phrase "Washington slept here." How'd that come to pass?

GW: I felt like, as the first president, I should go to as many inns and houses as possible. Meet n' greet, press the flesh. I hauled all up and down the Union, and people just started using that phrase, I guess.

MS: So it wasn't because of your rumored promiscuity?

GW: No.

MS: Remember, you cannot tell a—

GW: I said *no*!

MS: You owned slaves. That's not so PC these days.

GW: Guilty as charged on that account, and I'm not proud. I will say that I had good intentions. In 1786 I wrote that I hoped we could adopt some plan, by which slavery would be abolished by slow, sure, and imperceptible degrees.

MS: Yeah, like that was gonna happen. What changed your mind on the issue?

GW: After commanding multiracial troops in the Revolutionary War, I got to know the men, and realized slavery was a massive American anomaly. I also felt bad breaking up families when I purchased slaves in a lottery. You know, I did free half my slaves in my will. [Though George ordered his slaves freed upon Martha's death, she freed them all in 1800.]

MS: I'm sure the other half were thrilled. Here's what I don't get: At the end of the Revolutionary War, you were so popular that your generals wanted to make you king. Three terms, ten terms—you had no limits! Heck, you coulda been *Caesar*! Did ya think about it?

GW: Lord no! The thought of a one-headed government was painful. Truth be told—

MS: You cannot tell a lie!

GW: I almost resigned halfway through my first term. I remember telling John Adams when he was being inaugurated and I was finally retiring, "Well, I am fairly out, and you are fairly in. Now we shall see who enjoys it the most."

MS: At your funeral, Henry Lee said you were "first in war, first in peace, and first in the hearts of his countrymen."

GW: Aw, Light Horse Harry said that? The man had a way with words. Wish others had been that kind when I was alive.

MS: Well, it was a divided country.

GW: The anti-Federalist paper said I was "the scourge and misfortune of our country."

MS: Ouch. What do you think was the key to your success?

GW: The way I saw it, I was an ordinary man in an extraordinary situation. Kings and commoners could relate to me.

MS: How would you describe your leadership style?

GW: Surround yourself with people smarter than you. It was my idea to create the presidential cabinet—more heads in the room. I had Tommy Jefferson as my secretary of state and Alexander Hamilton running the treasury—pretty good crew.

MS: Wish those guys were running the show now, actually. You had an early warning about political parties.

GW: Factions, I called 'em. Point was that we needed as much cooperation as we could get just to survive. Too many selfish parties divide the country along partisan lines and that's just no good. But I'm sure democracy has solved those problems in the last two-hundred plus years.

MS: You have no idea, sir. Could I ask a personal question?

GW: Shoot. I am dead. What's it gonna hurt me?

MS: Did you grow marijuana?

GW: Oh, we grew plenty of cannabis on Mount Vernon. Farmed it for over thirty years.

MS: And did you . . . ?

GW: Remember the question you asked me about my false teeth? Well, with falsies come chronic toothaches, and nothing soothed the pain better than a little smoke now and then. 'Nuff said.

MS: What do you think about your image on the one-dollar bill?

GW: Let me see that.

[Washington inspects the image of him from Gilbert Stuart's 1796 painting.]

GW: Couldn't they have used a younger portrait? I'm damn near sixty-five in this thing, that's a flippin' wig, and I don't think I've got my dentures in, so it looks like my face's cavin' in. As a young man I was, how you youngsters say, hot.

MS: Now, sir. . . .

GW: I'm serious. In my younger days I was a hunk. Not to be a braggart, but I was six foot three—the average fellow was only about five foot six in my time. You know, I was a durn fine dancer, too. Aw, I don't know why I'm going on about it. Anyway, in answer to your question about the dollar bill, I don't care for it.

MS: Have you seen the Washington Monument?

GW: Yes, it's . . . well . . .

MS: Phallic! Five hundred and fifty-five feet of manliness!

GW: That's a bit much. I'm humbled.

MS: Well then, you gotta see Mount Rushmore, sir. Your head is sixty feet tall. Then go visit Washington State, and after that—

GW: You know, son, I think I'll pass for the time being.

MS: Bet you didn't know that we all get to take your birthday off from work!

GW: Speaking of time off, young man, I'd like to spend some time in Mount Vernon with Martha. Maybe take a nap.

MS: Oh, one of my favorite quotes from you is, "Far better to be alone, than to be in bad company!" So profound, sir!

GW: No lie. So, if you'll excuse me. . . .

END
of Interview

BORN MARY JANE West in Brooklyn, the future sex symbol began performing a vaudeville act at the tender age of five, billed as "The Baby Vamp."

A grown-up Mae knew that sex sells, and she used her feminine wiles (and voluptuous curves) to great effect, gaining fame and fortune, and finally getting the country to talk about (*ssshhh*) S-E-X! Her first play on Broadway (under the pen name Jane Mast) was called, yes, *Sex* (1925), and starred West as a prostitute. Critics panned it, audiences loved it, and city officials couldn't stand it any longer; they sent police to raid the theater and arrest West and the entire cast on "morals charges" in 1927.

The hourglass icon continued to write and perform in plays with controversial topics, including *Pleasure Man*, and *The Constant Sinner*. It was *Diamond Lil*, about a tough, racy, and sexually promiscuous bar madam, that made her a star. Mae moved to Hollywood in 1930, and took the character of Lil to the silver screen in 1933. She handpicked Cary Grant as the male lead in *She Done Him Wrong*; the film made Grant a household name, and earned an Academy Award nomination for Best Picture.

Because of West's overtly promiscuous messages (women can enjoy sex—go figure!) and growing influence, Hollywood censors began editing her scripts in the 1930s and making U.S. movies intercourse-free for almost forty years. Audiences, it turned out, wanted her risqué wit more than ever, and she was the highest-paid woman in flicks in the 1930s and '40s.

West took a break from the movies after 1943, and moved back to Broadway, then on to Vegas. In her later years she appeared as a guest on television shows including *The Red Skelton Show* and *Mister Ed*. When West starred (and she still looked mah-vel-ous, *dahling*), ratings soared.

Mae died in Hollywood at age eighty-seven. Smart as any business tycoon, her estate was worth over forty million dollars—not only from her films, but sharp investments in real estate and oil wells. Her star on the Hollywood Walk of Fame is at 1560 Vine Street. Why don't you come up and see it sometime?

MICHAEL STUSSER: No offense, ma'am, but for a dead woman, you look amazing!

MAE WEST: None taken, handsome. I always said it's better to be looked over, than overlooked.

MS: Miss West, I've heard so much about you. . . .

MW: Yeah, honey, but you can't prove a thing.

MS: For some reason, rumors run rampant that you are actually a drag queen. Care to clear the air?

MW: I'll do you one better.

[West pulls up her skirt and proves that she is, indeed, a woman.]

MW: So is that a gun in your pocket, or are you just happy to see me?

MS: Bad girl!

MW: When I'm good, I'm very good; but when I'm bad, I'm better. Hell, I've been on more laps than a table napkin.

MS: You changed your name from Mary to Mae. How come?

MW: I always hated seeing that *y* droop below the line, doll-face. I don't like anything downbeat.

MS: You made quite a splash on Broadway with your show *Sex.*

MW: We had a showstopper there, didn't we? I may be the only person ever arrested during a Broadway performance. They sentenced me to ten days for obscenity, and I got out in eight—the only time I ever got anything for *good* behavior.

MS: You didn't exactly shy away from controversial subjects in your next play.

MW: *The Drag* was about homosexuality, but I had to do it in Jersey because the prudes banned me from Broadway.

MS: You were constantly being censored. How'd that make you feel?

MW: Just fine—I made a fortune out of it! Of course, it's hard to be funny when you have to be clean, so I'd just add the double entendres and sex up the script that way. "If you don't like my peaches, why do you shake my tree?" Nothing to censor there. . . . There's more than one way to skin a pussy, hmmm?

MS: What was it like working with W. C. Fields?

MW: It would have been a lot better if I'd been as drunk as he was. Like I said, his mother should have thrown him away and kept the stork.

MS: And yet *My Little Chickadee* [1940] was a huge hit and outgrossed all of Fields's other movies.

MW: Well, I'm a *star*, sweetheart. Put me on the silver screen with a mouse and we'll bring in the big bucks.

MS: They wanted you to do two more movies with him.

MW: Once was enough, doll. Believe me.

MS: Is it true you worked with a dummy?

MW: Well, I already told you about W. C.

MS: No, a real dummy—a ventriloquist's dummy.

MW: Oh, right! I did Edgar Bergen's radio show, and we had a sketch about Adam and Eve that left people shocked for sure!

MS: How come?

MW: Well, I suppose people weren't used to sex in the Garden of Eden. What else are they gonna do there, hmm? Plus I couldn't keep my hands off that Charlie McCarthy. All that wood . . . *mmmmm*. They kept me off the radio for thirty-one years after that.

MS: Is it true that Marlene Dietrich kept offering to wash your hair on the Paramount lot?

MW: She did, love, but the hair she wanted to lather wasn't all on my head! Naughty girl.

MS: You were married briefly. What happened?

MW: Marriage is a great institution, but I wasn't ready for an institution. You know me—not a one fella kinda gal. Save a boyfriend for a rainy day—and another, in case it doesn't rain.

MS: How much of your stage persona was really your personality?

MW: It's all Mae, hon. I'm a girl who lost her reputation and never missed it. I mean, I loved men, sweetheart, no question about it, and in particular, tough guys. Gotta have meat on the bones, babe. Boxers, bodybuilders, six-footers, bring 'em on!

MS: A lot of people don't realize that, while you had a devilish side, you also had a spiritual side.

MW: I think I really was a lot like my character Diamond Lil, who wanted to weigh her good and evil sides, and wound up working with the Salvation Army. Folks need to realize there's goodness and evil embedded in all of us.

MS: Is it true you also wanted to communicate with the dead?

MW: After my folks died, I searched for all sort of answers. Mainly worked with Reverend Taylor of the Spiritualis Science Church of Hollywood.

MS: Any success?

MW: My goodness, I had so many spirits talking to me from the other side—mostly men, of course—that I finally told them I needed my beauty sleep and could we cut down on the visits!

MS: You came back after twenty-six years and did the movie *Myra Breckinridge*. Crowds adored you.

MW: Don't act so surprised, beefcake. At the premiere in New York, the cops had to hold audiences back like I was Elvis or something. All those screaming people—I loved it. Too bad the movie tanked.

MS: Actually, it's become a cult classic.

MW: People love a story with a sex change.

MS: Some have called you a leader in women's liberation, others have said you were a sexual degenerate. Which is it?

MW: Can I be both, babe? Let's face it, when I came along, women needed to get their groove on, and some men were glad it happened, too. Bold, confident women are a beautiful, sexy thing to behold. Ya know what message really shook up the Bible-thumpers? That a woman could be religious *and* sexual. Oooh! Spun their heads around. If you don't like it, crawl back in the cave you crawled out of.

MS: How'd you know so much about the opposite sex?

MW: First, I went to night school! And I'm no angel, but I've spread my wings a bit. Like I always said, "I feel like a million tonight, but one at a time, please!"

MS: You really do look fantastic. What's the secret?

MW: Surround yourself with virile men, and take up belly dancing. They both keep your hips moving, if ya know what I mean, darling. It's not the men in your life that count, it's the life in your men.

MS: I see.

MW: And I never smoked, never drank, and made sure to give myself a daily coffee enema.

MS: Did you just say "coffee enema"?

MW: Oh, and being busty helps. Keeps a man's eyes off the wrinkles, and right where we want 'em.

MS: Yes, ma'am, whatever you say. Do me one last favor.

MW: Anything, sweets.

MS: Say your famous line for me.

MW: I'll do you one better: "Come up and see me sometime. In fact, come up Wednesday—that's amateur night."

END
of Interview

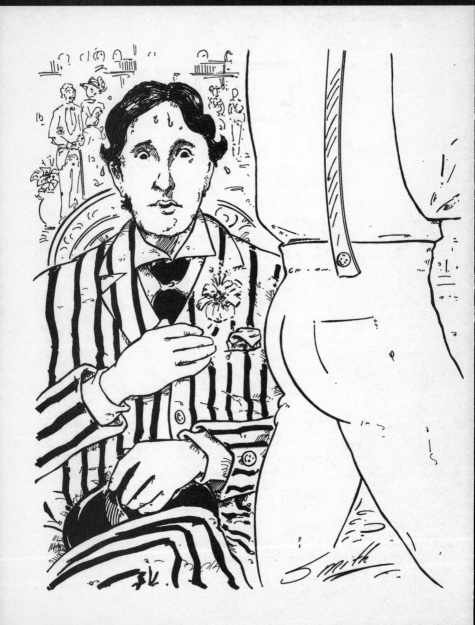

IF OSCAR WILDE were alive today, he'd be considered one of our most sassy, brilliant, and eccentric playwrights. Unfortunately, living the lavish lifestyle in Victorian London in the late ninteenth century, Ozzie was singled out for his public homosexuality, tossed into prison for "gross indecency" (1895–97), and wandered Europe after his release, living as a pauper until his death.

Wilde (Born Oscar Fingal O'Flahertie Wills Wilde) was best known for his Irish wit—unmistakable in theatrical gems such as *Lady Windermere's Fan* (1892) and *The Importance of Being Earnest* (1895). He was a diverse, sophisticated writer, penning reviews for the *Pall Mall Gazette*, editing *Woman's World*, and even publishing fab fairy tales for youngsters.

Fame came from his wonderful, dialogue-driven plays that turned French dramas on their head by combining farce, amoral indiscretions, and social commentary to wow audiences (and alarm uptight citizens).

Apparently AC/DC, Wilde married Constance Lloyd in 1884 and quickly cranked out two children. His "close friendship" with Lord Alfred Douglas was the one that got him in trouble: first with the Marquess of Queensberry (Douglas's father), and then with the law. After being accused of sodomy, Wilde sued the marquess for libel, but his case went south when the evidence showed he was, indeed, a sodomite. Arrested by British authorities, Wilde was eventually found guilty after a second sensational trial and sentenced to two years of hard labor. Constance changed her name and took the kids to Switzerland (talk about looking the other way).

Wilde died in Paris, three years after his incarceration, from acute meningitis brought on by a recurring ear infection. His humor was with him to the end; during the worst of his sickness he was quoted as saying, "My wallpaper and I are fighting a duel to the death. One or other of us has got to go."

MICHAEL STUSSER: Is it true that on your deathbed you converted to Roman Catholicism?

OSCAR WILDE: I was delirious.

MS: Still, you said you always intended to die a Catholic.

OW: So long as I didn't need to *live* as one!

MS: How'd you get the writing bug?

OW: My mother was quite the poet. A revolutionary, in fact, who wrote under the name of Speranza. Celtic myths and the like—I actually drew on her work when I needed some dark inspiration.

MS: Weren't you also a poet?

OW: Award-winning, my dear boy. [Wilde won the well-respected Newdigate Prize in 1878.]

MS: Any favorite authors?

OW: None you've heard of.

MS: Try me.

OW: John Ruskin, Walter Pater, Dante Gabriel Rossetti . . . ?

MS: You're right.

OW: Also, Oscar Wilde. That's why I never travel without my journal. One should always have something sensational to read on the train.

MS: You said, "Bigamy is having one wife too many. Monogamy is the same." Didn't like the girls, eh?

OW: I was an equal opportunity romancer. I would have stayed in Dublin, actually, if not for a lass who broke my heart: Florence Balcome. She got engaged to Bram Stoker, of all people. Sucked the life out of *me*, I can tell you that much. After that, I left Ireland for good.

MS: You were a big part of the aesthetic movement. Posing in velvet jackets with silk stockings and the long hair. Seems a bit . . . much, you know?

OW: I do *not* know. Art for art's sake is the movement's principle: Burn with a gemlike flame, live amongst objets d'art.

MS: Sounds a bit gay. I mean, scorning "manly" sports and decorating with peacock feathers?

OW: Oh, would that I could live up to my blue china! And you're not the first—or brightest—to criticize.

MS: Well, who does your wardrobe, anyway?

OW: Truth be told, I use theater costume designers. It's not easy to find silk robes edged with fox fur, you know.

MS: When you came to the United State in 1882 to give lectures on aesthetics, you supposedly told a customs agent you had nothing to declare but your genius. Think maybe your ego brought on some of your troubles?

OW: That is a stupid question, Quillie-boy. America is the only country that went from barbarism to decadence without civilization in between. And yet, Yankees loved me! I was like a bloody car accident they couldn't take their eyes off of.

MS: How'd the tour go?

OW: Brilliant! We extended from four months to a year, and I'm happy to say I met Walt Whitman, Oliver Wendell Holmes, and Henry Longfellow along the way.

MS: You said "long fellow."

OW: Good bloody gracious, could I stay on point? You're as bad as the marquess. Point was, Americans loved the flamboyance, they just didn't know it at the time, eh? Now decadence is all the rage! Have you seen P. Diddy's furs? Gwen Stefani's bling? I mean, J-Lo's got a clothing line that looks like she stole right from my own wardrobe! Timing is everything. I simply lived in the wrong era.

MS: Your writing changed over the years from good-conquers-all poetry and fairy tales to darker themes of lost innocence and decay.

OW: Should I lie on the couch for the remainder of our little chat?

MS: I'm just wondering if the guilt of being married while carrying on with young boys made you write more productively about pain and suffering.

OW: This interview is painful. Does that mean we're being productive?

MS: Does life imitate art?

OW: Does this scarf go fabulously with my knee breeches?

MS: Um, yes?

OW: Look, my plays always included a main character who's disgraced by some hidden sin that later bites him in the ass. Lo and behold, in real life, I'm busted for being a sodomite! Life—art. Voilà!

MS: Your novel *The Picture of Dorian Gray* [1891] had homoerotic themes; some even called it immoral.

OW: There's no such thing as a moral or immoral book. Books are well written or badly written. That's all.

MS: In reviewing your 1895 play, *An Ideal Husband*, George Bernard Shaw said you "play with everything: with wit, with philosophy . . . with actors, with the audience."

OW: Well, life—and certainly the theater—is much too important a thing ever to talk seriously about. Too bad the marquess never understood that.

MS: Ah, yes, the marquess. Gotta ask about the sodomy trial.

OW: Don't you all.

MS: If you'd have simply ignored Lord John Douglas, none of this would have happened.

OW: The cantankerous oaf was stalking me!

MS: Funny that *he* was called Queensberry.

OW: Yeah, funny. The man threatened to throw vegetables at one of my openings and left insults at clubs his son and I frequented.

MS: It's just strange that *you* sued *him* for criminal libel, then investigators found out you did, in fact, have relations with other men, and ya got arrested and tossed in the clink.

OW: Thanks for the recap, Judge Judy.

MS: At the trial, you described for the court "the love that dares not speak its name."

OW: It is that deep spiritual affection that is as pure as it is perfect. There is nothing unnatural about it. It is in this century misunderstood, and on that account of it I am placed where I am now.

MS: Sounds like the plot of *Brokeback Mountain*.

OW: I'll have to see it. That and *Cabin Boy*.

MS: What'd you do in jail?

OW: I wrote a letter to Bosie [John Douglas's nickname]. A looooong letter. Little brat said he never got it. . . .

MS: From what I understand, you basically flamed him for fifty-thousand words.

OW: Remember, *he's* the one who urged me to go to trial in the first place, and look who winds up doing time. Not to mention it was quite the distraction from work—I went bloody bankrupt.

MS: But you did get back with him after prison for a bit. . . .

OW: Well, I must not have been that upset, hmm? Too bad we ended in misery. As I've said, "In this world there are only two tragedies. One is not getting what one wants, and the other is getting it."

MS: Anything positive come of your prison time?

OW: I learned to short-sheet a bed, which I found amusing. And afterward, though I did so anonymously, I was proud to raise the issue of inhumane prison conditions in my long poem *The Ballad of Reading Gaol* [1898].

MS: You'll be happy to know that homosexuality is no longer a crime. In fact, many countries are legalizing same-sex marriages.

OW: I never said anything about marrying. If you ask me, to love oneself is the beginning of a lifelong romance. Besides, nowadays, all the married men live like bachelors, and all the bachelors live like married men. If that's the case, I should have stayed with my wife. . . .

End
of Interview

WITH MORE TITLES than Muhammad Ali, Chairman Mao was head honcho of the Communist Party of China from 1945 until his last breath over thirty years later.

While working at the University of Beijing (Peking) library, Mao studied Karl Marx and became a revolutionary bookworm. The Chinese Communist Party was founded in 1921, and Mao quickly gained popularity by bringing peasants as well as students into the Marxist mix.

Mao and his followers had to repeatedly fight off the attacks of Chiang Kai-shek's Nationalist forces, and eventually fled thousands of miles in what was known as the Long March (1934). In part because he was a fast walker, and in part due to his charisma, Mao emerged from the journey as the top Commie leader in the land.

Finally victorious over both the Japanese and Chiang Kai-shek, the Communists officially formed The People's Republic of China at Tiananmen Square on October 1, 1949.

Blending Marxism and Leninism into his own econo-brew (Maoism), his ideology was part Stalinism (hard labor or death to those who criticize), part Confucianism, and part his own wicked bag of tricks designed to speed up development, "reeducate" the masses, and keep power at all costs.

Mao the man is controversial. Many admire the first half of his run (the self-sacrifice, revolutionary idealism, and restoration of China's independence), and hate the second half (the murders, economic disasters, and cult of personality). One thing's for sure: China has never been the same.

MICHAEL STUSSER: You know, our famous artist Andy Warhol did a painting of you.

MAO ZEDONG: It is great honor.

MS: Yeah, well, he also painted a tomato soup can, so don't get too choked up. Tell me, Chairman, how'd you get the nickname Four Greats?

MZ: Followers consider me Great Teacher, Great Leader, Great Supreme Commander, Great Helmsman.

MS: Great PR. When did you start being a Communist?

MZ: At age of twenty-seven I attend first Party Congress in Shanghai. Two years later I am elected to Central Committee.

MS: Tell me about the Long March.

MZ: Chiang [Kai-shek] wanted to kill every one of us. This not so appealing—so, to avoid his forces, we walk eight thousand miles for one year from southeast to northwest. Make marathon look like baby steps.

MS: Word is you didn't walk the whole thing: in fact, they carried you for a lot of the journey.

MZ: Bad thong on left foot. Plus, I need reading and nappy time.

MS: Did you know that Chiang Kai-shek was being aided by the United States?

MZ: I know if pin drop in China. United States want to stop what they see as world Communism. We use this to get help from Soviet Union, who want to stop crazy capitalists. You ask me—all crazy.

MS: Speaking of crazy, one of your first orders after taking over was to build a swimming pool in your villa next to the Forbidden City.

MZ: Much great work done poolside and in bed.

MS: In fact, you jumped in pretty much any body of water you could find.

MZ: Strong symbol. Nothing to fear if one plunges in headfirst.

MS: Ever take the marriage plunge?

MZ: Four times, many belly flop. I escape arranged tying knot in youth, then marry and divorce, marry and divorce. Last wife Jiang Qing.

MS: The famous film actress?

MZ: One in same. Last role: power-hungry politico dragon lady.

MS: Your personal physician, Dr. Li Zhisui, wrote a memoir, *The Private Life of Chairman Mao*, that made you sound like a sex machine.

MZ: I thank you for directness. Long happy man.

MS: He also said you were constantly with a harem of much younger women.

MZ: I am sexual being. Taoist practice encourage much sex for longevity. Good for you!

MS: You often made passes at members of *both* sexes, demanding massages, if you know what I mean.

MZ: Large man. Large appetite.

MS: You're also an idea guy. What was the idea for Maoism?

MZ: Marxism-Leninism is like sleepy time for most Chinese. Good theory, but not make sense in our situation. Only way for peasants to take on revolution is if they see something in it for them.

MS: It's like that bumper sticker, THINK GLOBAL, ACT LOCAL.

MZ: Not see bumber stick. *Mass Line*, we call in China—Communist members make sure peasant's concerns are met. Real world.

MS: Such as?

MZ: We redistribute land from rich to poor. Set prices to stop inflation. Create farm collectives.

MS: Didn't you also mess with the alphabet?

MZ: We simplify Chinese characters in attempt to increase literacy.

MS: And what about the "Hundred Flowers" campaign in 1956?

MZ: We open freedom to express feelings about government. One hundred flowers bloom, and one hundred schools of thought contend.

MS: And how'd that work out?

MZ: Not so good. Many oppose party. Constructive comments from intellectual types go overboard, so we round up poisonous weeds who criticize and destroy one by one.

MS: So much for free speech.

MZ: Communism is not love. Communism is a hammer which we use to crush the enemy.

MS: Then there was the Great Leap Forward in 1958. Kind of leaping backward, huh?

MZ: Many suffered in our efforts to make people's communes.

MS: Between 1958 and 1962, up to 30 million people starved to death.

MZ: Not help we have drought midleap.

MS: Not help that one of your harebrained ideas was to have every citizen melt down industrial pots and smelt their own iron from scratch. Not to mention that while your people suffered the worst famine in history, you sold food for arms to the USSR.

MZ: Leap was unfortunate.

MS: No, unfortunate is when you break a teacup.

MZ: There is positive that must be discussed!

MS: I'm waiting.

MZ: Maoism created a unified China, free of foreign domination. World power! Illiteracy down. Life expectancy double!

MS: So'd the population.

MZ: This mean more beautiful Chinese people. I also improve women's rights. Believe women hold up half the sky.

MS: Why do you think *Quotations from Chairman Mao Zedong*, aka *The Little Red Book*, is so popular?

MZ: Every citizen must own and carry copy at all times or be imprisoned at once.

MS: So *that's* why it's the second-most printed book of all time! [One billion copies.]

MZ: What is first? *Men from Mars?* I love this book!

MS: The Bible, big guy. Tell us about your falling-out with fellow pinko Khrushchev in the '60s.

MZ: Before death of Stalin, everything A-OK. Then Khrushchev show up, not understand Marxism, try to de-Stalinize. Final straw when Soviet leader lose face with Cuban Missile Crisis.

MS: I was thinking of the time he supplied fighter jets to India during the Sino-Indian War.

MZ: This not help relations.

MS: Your relationship with Chinese leaders like Liu Shaoqi and Deng Xiaoping wasn't so great, either.

MZ: They want run shop. They want Mao only ceremonial head. I respond with [the Cultural] Revolution!

MS: All hell broke loose.

MZ: Yeah, OK. Idea *good*: Give power to Red Guards. Eliminate corrupt party officials. Implementation *bad*: Imprison intellectuals and destroy much of cultural heritage.

MS: Yeah, that "bad" part kinda outweighed the "good" stuff— another seven hundred thousand lives lost. But on the positive side, they started plastering your chubby face all over the place.

MZ: I have them put quote on poster: "Mao: A Red Sun in the Center of Our Hearts."

MS: Yeah, and I like: "Wishing the Chairman a Life of 10,000 Years." Subtle.

MZ: Tell me, please, what happen after my death?

MS: They embalmed you with enough formaldehyde to make an elephant stiff.

MZ: No! Who ruled? Who followed Great Chairman?

MS: Oh, Deng Xiaoping at first.

MZ: Oy! I have him dismissed. Twice!

MS: He kept the People's Republic going, I can tell ya that much. Good little Communist. But so much has happened.

MZ: Centralized Communism makes us strong.

MS: Yeah, they're kinda moving away from all that and selling Coca-Cola and stuff. And they have a nice way of describing your legacy now: "Seven parts right and three parts wrong."

MZ: I feel same about this interview.